# Builders
# of Emerging
# Nations

*Europe in Retreat*
*Four Cornerstones of Peace*
*The United States and Russia*
*Europe and the United States*
*Foreign Policy Without Fear*
*The Nature of the Non-Western World (with others)*
*The American Student and the Non-Western World*
*New Patterns of Democracy in India*
*Builders of Emerging Nations*

# Builders
# of Emerging
# Nations

BY VERA MICHELES DEAN

*Drawings by George Wilson*

Holt, Rinehart and Winston
New York - Chicago - San Francisco

Published, May, 1961
Second Printing, October, 1961
Third Printing, December, 1961
Fourth Printing, October, 1962

Published simultaneously in Canada by Holt, Rinehart
and Winston of Canada, Ltd.

Library of Congress Catalog Card Number: 61-8068

81783-0111

Designer: Ernst Reichl

Printed in the United States of America

# ACKNOWLEDGMENTS

Grateful acknowledgment is given to the following for permission to use copyrighted material:

Abelard-Schuman Limited, New York, N. Y., for material from *Mao Tse-tung* by Robert Payne, copyright 1950 by Robert Payne.

African-American Institute, New York, N. Y., for material from *Africa Special Report*, December, 1959, Vol. 4, No. 12, "We Cannot Afford to Fail," by Julius Nyerere.

The Africa League, New York, N. Y., for material from "A New American Policy Toward Africa," February, 1960.

American Universities Field Staff Reports Service, New York, N. Y., for material from "An Invitation to Manipulation" by K. H. Silvert, May 16, 1960; *Bung Karno's Indonesia* by William A. Hanna, 1959; "Study on the Military Regime in Pakistan" by Louis Dupree, August, 1959; "The Basic Democracies Programme: The Quiet Revolution Keeps Rolling Along" by Louis Dupree, January 18, 1960; "West Pakistan Revisited: First Impression After Eight-Year Absence" by Louis Dupree, August 27, 1959.

The Bobbs-Merrill Company Inc., Indianapolis, Indiana, for material from *Fidel Castro* by Jules Dubois, copyright © 1959 by Jules Dubois.

The John Day Company Inc., New York, N. Y., for material from *Glimpses of World History* by Jawaharlal Nehru, and from *The Magsaysay Story* by Carlos P. Romulo and Marvin M. Gray, copyright 1956 by Carlos P. Romulo and Marvin M. Gray.

*The Economist*, London, for material from an article on the United Nations, August 27, 1960.

*Foreign Affairs*, New York, N. Y., for material from "Pakistan Perspective" by President Ayub Khan, July, 1960, copyright © 1960 by Council on Foreign Relations.

Foreign Policy Association, New York, N. Y., for material from "Has Russia Changed?" by T. P. Whitney, *Headline Series*; and from "The Cuba Dilemma" by Vera Micheles Dean, *Foreign Policy Bulletin*, February 1, 1961.

Harper & Brothers, New York, N. Y., and Jonathan Cape Ltd., London, for material from *The Heretic* by Fitzroy Maclean, copyright © 1957 by Fitzroy Maclean, and from *The Soul of China* by Amaury de Riencourt.

Harper & Brothers, New York, N. Y., for material from *The Story of Indonesia*, by Louis Fischer.

22297

Harvard University Press, Cambridge, Mass., for material from *The United States and Turkey and Iran* by Lewis Thomas and Richard L. Frye.

Thomas Nelson & Sons, New York, N. Y., for material from *Ghana: The Autobiography of Kwame Nkrumah.*

*New Statesman,* London, for material from an article on the United Nations, August 13, 1960.

*The New York Times* for material from *The New York Times Magazine,* April 20, 1958; November 22, 1959; April 26, 1960; and June 5, 1960; and from *The New York Times,* December 31, 1959; March 14, 1960; and June 5, 1960.

Oxford University Press, London, for material from *Nehru: A Political Biography* by Michael Brecher.

*Pacific Affairs,* New York, N. Y., for material from "Nu, The Serene Statesman" by Hugh Tinker, June, 1957, and from "Sukarno, the Nationalist" by Leslie H. Palmier, June, 1957.

Smith, Keynes & Marshall, Buffalo, N. Y., for material from *The Philosophy of the Revolution* by Gamal Abdel Nasser.

Stanford University Press, Stanford, Cal., for material from *Moscow and Chinese Communists* by Robert C. North, copyright 1953 by The Board of Trustees of Leland Stanford Junior University.

*To Bill*
*delightful travel companion*
*and perceptive critic*

# Contents

# Builders
# of Emerging
# Nations

"The past is of use to me as the eve of tomorrow;
My soul wrestles with the future."

Maeterlinck

"Our slow world spends its time catching up with the ideas of its best minds. It would seem that in almost every generation men are born who embody the projected consciousness of their time and people.

"Their thought runs forward apace into the regions whither the race is advancing, but where it will not for many a weary day arrive . . . the new thoughts of one age are the commonplaces of the next. . . .

"The men who act stand nearer to the mass than the men who write; and it is in their hands that new thought gets its translation into the crude language of deeds. . . ."

Woodrow Wilson, 1890

"Since to exist is to change, nothing can hope to remain always the same, but I cannot believe that such changes destroy the once formed personality of a people or civilization, or alter their basic character."

Nirad C. Chaudhuri,<br>
A Passage to England.

"To understand a person who lived long ago, you will have to understand his environment, the conditions under which he lived, the ideas that filled his mind. It is absurd to judge of past people as if they lived now and thought as we do. . . . We cannot judge the past from the standards of the present. Every one will willingly admit this. But every one will not admit the equally absurd habit of judging the present by the standards of the past."

Nehru on World History<br>
(Condensed by Saul K. Padover<br>
from Glimpses of World History<br>
by Jawaharlal Nehru)

# Preface

One of the most fascinating questions in history is: What makes a leader? Does the man of the hour take the center of the stage because he has the qualities necessary to dominate events? Do events determine the kind of man required by the times and touch his brow with the charisma—the quality of extraordinary spiritual power—which makes evident to all that he is destined for leadership? Or is there a kind of mystic union of man with events which makes future chroniclers assert that he who became a leader was the one and only capable of assuming the task for which he was designated by destiny, or the gods, or the will of the people?

This question is all the more tantalizing when we study the upsurge of events not in the long-established nations of the West, but in the emerging nations of Asia, the Middle East, and Africa, reborn or newly born after years of Western colonial rule, and in the countries of Latin America which, although independent for over a century, are still in a state of turmoil. There, just as active volcanoes spew out of the entrails of the earth hot lava which may flow along unpredictable channels, societies where old and new elements are being churned into fiery mixtures throw up leaders whose ideas may blast out paths where none had been traced before. Of the many new men who emerge, who will be chosen—and who, if chosen, will stay the course in an age of kaleidoscopic change?

In the period since World War II, measured as fifteen years by the Western states but as centuries in many of the emerging nations where events, to quote President Nkrumah of Ghana, move at hurricane pace, dozens of leaders, either actual or potential, have already fallen by the wayside. Some have been assassinated, like Mahatma Gandhi in India and Aung San in Burma, or have died prematurely, like Barthélemy Boganda, premier of the Central African Republic, killed in an airplane accident in 1959. Others, whose star as national heroes once shone brightly, have either vanished without a trace—notably Subas Chandra Bose of India, who collaborated with the Japanese and, while presumed dead, is still thought by some adherents to be living outside the country; and pro-Communist Phanomyong Pridi of Thai-

3

land, now somewhere in China—or have had to go into exile, like pro-Japanese Pibul Songgram of Thailand in Japan, the playboy-Emperor Bao Dai of Indochina in France, Dr. Syngman Rhee of Korea in Hawaii, and the anthropologist-politician, Dr. K. A. Busia of Ghana, who is teaching in the Netherlands. George M. Malenkov, chosen by Stalin as his successor, is living in obscurity as director of an atomic power plant, while Nikita S. Khrushchev rules the USSR. Others, who seemed full of vigor and promise, have been removed from the scene through imprisonment, like Jomo Kenyatta of Kenya, or have withdrawn from politics, like Soetan Sjahrir of Indonesia and, most dramatically, the Socialist leader Jayaprakash Narayan of India, once regarded as the number one choice to succeed Nehru, who has decided that political struggle is ill-suited for the conditions of underdeveloped countries and has chosen to follow Gandhi's disciple, Vinoba Bhave, in his drive to obtain gifts of land for the landless. These and others have flashed like meteors across the sky, and like meteors have fallen to the ground, often forgotten except by a few.

What brought about their downfall or withdrawal? Some may have been ahead of their times; some may have come too late to make a significant contribution. Events in newly emerging countries are moving at such a pace that men who in less turbulent days might have had a long and honorable span of public service proved too moderate, like Naguib of Egypt or Kerensky of Russia, or too revolutionary in a period of consolidation, like Trotsky. Events got ahead of men, or else men lagged behind events. Napoleon, who might have passed unnoticed amid the furore of the French Revolution, appeared to be the man of destiny when France, having run its revolutionary course, turned to expansion in Europe; and was discarded when the French settled down to building the bourgeois society of the Second Empire and the Third Republic.

But what, then, are the qualities which have kept leaders now alive, on top, or those dead, alive in the memory and current development of their countries? Four qualities seem essential for survival—besides the factor of sheer luck in escaping assassination by malcontents. The men who now dominate the newly emerging countries, in reality or in popular recollection, or are being groomed for leadership, must have courage; they must have a deep and constantly renewed understanding of and communication with their people; they must have determination;

and they must have a comprehension of the world situation within which they must work.

It is important that they have physical courage, since many of them live in danger of assassination and, like Nehru and U Nu, have seen comrades fall at their side. They must also have the intellectual courage to assert and implement their ideas even when under fire—not only from foes but also, far more difficult, from friends; and the still greater courage to change their minds when circumstances seem to make this necessary, to be flexible when flexibility might be decried by critics as weakness, or even treason. They must have the determination, no matter what the obstacles, to reach the goals they have set for themselves, even if they change their means to meet changed conditions. Their understanding of their people must be profound so that they can reflect the aspirations of those they rule as the poet reflects the thinking of his times, and so that they can clearly and convincingly make these aspirations known to other nations; and it must be constantly renewed through personal contacts so that they do not become alienated from their fellow citizens by success and succumb to the arrogance which success often engenders. And they must have a comprehension of the world—past, present, and future—so that they can chart the course of their countries amid the shoals of the nuclear age not on the basis of superstition, or guesswork, or wishful thinking, but in terms of realities, however harsh and disturbing they may be. In the non-Western world this fourth quality, exceptional in the leaders of any country, is possessed in high degree by Mr. Nehru among non-Communist rulers, and among Communist rulers by Marshal Tito.

The list of builders of emerging nations could easily be stretched into a long biographical dictionary. Here I have chosen for discussion those leaders who in my opinion—with which others may disagree—have in one way or another made a particularly significant contribution to the development of their countries since World War II. One or two, like Kemal Ataturk and Ramon Magsaysay, are, although dead, still directly affecting the actions of their countrymen. Some of these leaders I have had the privilege of meeting in their own countries. Others I have discussed with experts who know them personally. Varied as these men are, they have two things in common. Aristocrats or workers on land or in workshops, wealthy or poor, sophisticated or ill-educated, they are all rebels, each with a cause; and they have all been profoundly affected by the ideas of nationalism, whether or not they came under the influence of communism.

The major books and articles which I have found of particular value in the preparation of this book are listed in the selected bibliography. I want to acknowledge my debt to The New American Library, publisher of *The Nature of the Non-Western World* (Mentor) which I wrote with the aid of three colleagues, and a few of whose themes, presented there for the first time, I have carried forward in this book; to the Harvard University Press, for some points I made in my book *New Patterns of Democracy in India*; to Scott, Foresman for passages I have used from my chapter in their book, *Contemporary Civilization*; to faculty friends and students in the Non-Western Civilizations Program I have been directing at the University of Rochester since 1954 for many ideas developed during our discussions; and to the Foreign Policy Association for the use of some material which first appeared in the *Foreign Policy Bulletin*.

I want particularly to thank my friends, Virginia and Richard Adloff, who for years have conducted extensive studies of Asia and Africa and have embodied the results of their research in many valuable books, for sharing their knowledge with me, and most of all for their generosity in making it possible for me on several occasions to pause in a busy life and find in their Mediterranean home peace and beauty which encourage writing.

—V. M. D.

Villa Eze-les-Roses
Eze Bord-de-Mer
Alpes Maritimes, France

# 1
# The Men

# Ingredients of Change

"ARMY takes over rule in Turkey. . . ." "Students riot against Rhee government. . . ." "Castro defies U.S. . . ." "Nasser nationalizes Suez Canal. . . ." "Congo tribes clash as independence nears."

Here are some of the top stories that telegraph keys have been clicking off around the globe in the past decade. Here are some of the bold headlines that have shrieked at us from the pages of the world's newspapers. The stories, and the headlines they inspire, act as seismographs which register tremors—not in the earth's crust, but in the depths of human existence.

What do these tremors portend? When the ground stops heaving beneath our feet, when "the dust settles," shall we still recognize once-familiar landmarks? Or will the universe that emerges from this upheaval seem frighteningly strange to us, as strange as the moon might appear to a future astronaut?

Depending on individual temperament, change can be welcomed or feared, encouraged or opposed. But whatever one's reaction, it is impossible to avoid the realization that the twentieth century is permeated, riven, and kneaded into new shapes by changes of all kinds and of many different orders of magnitude. There is no more escape from change than there is from typhoons and earthquakes. For like typhoons and earthquakes, change is an inescapable element of nature and thus of man.

The French economic statesman Jean Monnet, who has labored unceasingly to remold old Europe to new patterns, contends that stability can be achieved only after the world has attained an equilibrium of change. "The Soviet Union is changing," he said after the collapse of the 1960 summit conference in Paris. "America is changing and Western Europe is beginning to change. A détente has no significance unless it represents facts. This process of change will go on until it produces new unity and strength in the West—then and only then will it be possible to negotiate an accommodation with Moscow."

But of all the seismic changes of our times, the most spectacular and far-reaching in its consequences is the emergence on the world scene of the peoples of the Middle East, Asia, Africa, Latin America—peoples who until the middle of the twentieth century had seemed voiceless and helpless spectators of, but not participants in, the global drama whose lines were written, spoken, and, one might add, often thrown away by the nations of the West, at that time acknowledged by all (or nearly all) as the center of the universe. And to this list must be added Russia, which, although it had been a great power for centuries, found its power inadequate in modern times when matched against the technologically more advanced nations of the West.

Are the changes in this vast sector of the globe portents of doom for the West? Does Khrushchev literally mean to "bury" us? Will Communist China court the risk, to us—and now also to Moscow—inconceivable, of nuclear war in order to destroy "imperialism," with the expectation of building on its ruins a "beautiful society" superior to that created by "capitalism"? Or are these changes harbingers of a new and happier era for the underdeveloped lands and their relations with the West? Are we witnessing, as some believe, the twilight of Western civilization? Or are we, as others aver, about to salute the dawn of a new world community, where West and non-West will meet as equals in a partnership dedicated to the achievement of common ends?

Few are so bold as to dare decipher the signs of the times. But if we are to essay the role of prophets, we must first try to identify the ingredients of change. We must discover what is basic and constant beneath the world's heaving surface, and what are the aspects of existing, often ancient, institutions which are being permanently discarded, as monarchy was discarded in the French Revolution or Britain's rule over its New World colonies in the American Revolution.

When we see the past crumbling around us before the shape of the future has been given time to emerge, we tend to identify with what we call "communism" some changes that would have come anyway as a result of the adaptation of all societies to modern technology. Yet in any realistic appraisal of the future it is important to distinguish those aspects of human endeavor which are essentially Communist from those which would in any case have emerged in non-Western countries even if Karl Marx had never written *Das Kapital* and Lenin had never seized power in Russia.

Once the non-Western peoples had won independence from the rule of Western democracies—and sooner or later democracy would have had to admit that it is incompatible with colonialism which, by its nature, is authoritarian—they would have established one-party governments (with the important exceptions of India and Japan, whose experiences differ in significant respects from those of other non-Western countries). And these one-party governments would have been inspired in the first instance not by Marxist doctrine but by the fact that a single—and single-minded—nationalist party, formed to combat the foreign ruler, had taken over power as soon as freedom was won.

Irrespective of Marxist doctrine, the new governments would have had to make plans for economic development, not because Russia and later Communist China made planning an article of Communist faith, but because at that stage a system of unbridled competition between private interests would have impeded the growth of weak economies in need of rapid and strongly directed modernization. The new governments would have had to use the machinery of the state in preparing the take-off of technologically backward countries from dead center, and this without necessarily having to consult oracles in Moscow or Peiping. They would have had to introduce technical training for the masses into an educational system hitherto dedicated to the teaching of the humanities for a small elite. They would have faced the harsh choice of concentrating their efforts and resources on economic development, with military defense relegated to secondary place, or sacrificing the immediate satisfaction of their peoples' bare needs in order to build up their defenses—although this choice would undoubtedly be made harsher by the exigencies of the cold war.

Thus, whether communism existed or not, authoritarian, or at least highly centralized, governments would have emerged, with three- or five- or six-year plans and government-directed, if not government-controlled, enterprises. Also, out of a feudal society of princes and landlords, priests and craftsmen, peasants and moneylenders, a new class would have arisen, produced by and attuned to industrialization through the application of modern science and technology.

If communism, as practiced in different circumstances and by different methods in Russia and China, is regarded as a unique and peculiar phenomenon, completely alien to and separate from the experience of the West, then the development of the emerging countries of Asia and the Middle East, Africa and Latin America, must also be viewed as unique and peculiar. And if this be the case, we shall have to accept the prospect of a prolonged, if not permanent (for what is permanent in human affairs?) division between the West and the non-West—a great divide which might with good fortune be kept from provoking nuclear war, but which would also prevent fruitful intercourse between different civilizations.

Communism, however, can also be viewed in a different light. To quote Robert L. Heilbroner in *The Future as History,*

> ... communism, as a major economic movement of today, is playing the same role as did capitalism in the seventeenth and eighteenth centuries. For the Western "socialist" nations have also gone through their periods of repression and severity in the course of their own transitions from agrarian to industrial societies. These periods were considerably milder than present-day communism because the transitions began at a higher level of well-being and because they were then the vanguard and not the rearguard of advance. But one who recoils at the rigors and suffering of the Chinese and Russian transformations would do well to compare these travails with those of the West in its early capitalist throes. He will then find striking—and perhaps discomfiting—similarities between the movement of the Western pre-industrial world into capitalism and that of the East into communism.

Where communism differs profoundly from the experience of the Western democracies (and even from that of Western dictatorships in our time like those of Spain and Portugal, but not from Hitler's regime in the most technologically advanced country of Europe) is not in the economic and social development it has inspired and carried out, but in its totalitarian system and the harsh rigidity with which this system has been applied in all fields of human endeavor. Even in this respect, however, we have to ask ourselves whether totalitarianism is an ineradicable feature of communism or a passing phase in the development of countries great in ancient civilizations, in territory, in spiritual and material resources, but backward industrially as compared with the West.

We must also determine the extent to which the experience of Russia and China has been affected by Marxist doctrine transplanted to an agrarian environment, or by their own historical traditions.

". . . Surely the hope of the future," says Heilbroner, "rests in the possibility that with communism, as with capitalism, the completion of the industrial transformation may soften and mellow the rigors of the transitional phase." And President Charles de Gaulle, a staunch anti-Communist who is a distinguished historian as well as a distinguished soldier, went further when he said in his May 31, 1960, address to the French nation that France believes "that by virtue of the modern rate of activity, the condition of men tends to become alike everywhere and that the virulent opposition of the various regimes is destined to diminish."

Thus what now seems a great ideological divide between West and non-West may one day prove to be an easily bridged gap between the industrialized and hitherto nonindustrialized sectors of the world.

The speed and effectiveness of this gap-bridging will depend both on the willingness of the West to accept change as a fact of life and on the ideas and policies of the emerging nations. For the West it is essential both to know and to understand—and knowledge is by no means always synonymous with understanding—the hopes and fears, the suspicions and aspirations, of the men engaged in the grueling task of building the new nations.

What are the sources of these men's ideas? Under what circumstances did they come into contact with the West, and what impression did such contact make on them? What do they hope to gain from the West? And what about the West do they dislike or reject?

Are these men in conflict with each other about the ultimate goals of their nations and of the modern world? Or, in spite of their widely differing backgrounds, are there common denominators between them? Is there a meeting ground between Nehru, the aristocratic Brahmin; Khrushchev, the tough coal miner, son of a miner, and Tito, son of a blacksmith; military men such as Kemal Ataturk, Nasser, Ayub Khan; U Nu, teacher and devout Buddhist; Julius Nyerere, teacher and devout Catholic; Tom Mboya, trade-union leader; Castro, born to comfort in a landowning family; and Mao Tse-tung, of peasant origin, whose top associate, Chou En-lai, has been described by one writer as a "Marxist mandarin"? On what points do they agree? On what points do they differ? What factors cause their agreements or differences?

For those charged with the task of forging the policy of the West, answers to these questions could ultimately prove more important than information about nuclear weapons which, we must still hope, will remain unused. For the forces at work in non-Western societies are potentially more explosive than atomic bombs. The builders of the emerging nations are the architects of our future as well as theirs. Let us take a look at their lives and at the blueprints of the world they seek to make.

# 1

# Russia and Yugoslavia

To a westerner it may seem strange that Russia and Yugoslavia should be included among the nations of the non-Western world. For Russia, under the Tsars, was long regarded by the West—and regarded itself—as a European power. As late as 1960, President de Gaulle of France expressed the hope that the day would come when Russia would return to the West, defining his geographic view of Russia by the remark that then Europe would stretch from the Atlantic to the Urals—that is, exclusive of Russia's territories in Asia. Yugoslavia, too, which like European Russia is in Eastern Europe, has been considered a member of the European community since its creation in 1919 as a South Slav state through the merger of Serbia, Croatia, Montenegro, Bosnia, and Herzegovina.

Yet Russia has for centuries also qualified for the adjective "Eurasian," not only because it spans two continents, Europe and Asia, but because about one quarter of its population (estimated in mid-1960 at 214 million) is Asian in origin. Unlike de Gaulle, Adolf Hitler in *Mein Kampf*, far from planning to welcome the Russians back to Europe, asserted that they should return to where they came from (meaning Asia) and leave the resources of their European domain to exploitation by the Germans. He sneeringly described the Slavs as "slaves," capable only of serving the German "master-race."

True, Russia both under the Tsars and under the Commissars has claimed a voice in the affairs of Europe and has participated as an equal in the Congress of Vienna (1815); the Congress of Paris (1856), which ended the Crimean war; and the Congress of Berlin (1878), which marked the defeat of Russia in the Balkans. Russia was not included in the Paris Peace Conference of 1919, which brought World War I to a close, because the Communist regime had not yet been recognized; in fact, at that time Communist Russia was sealed off by a *cordon sanitaire* of Eastern European countries. But in the 1940's, as one of the Big Three with Britain and the United States, Russia was present at the Yalta and Potsdam conferences, which laid the foundations for the World War II settlement in 1944-45 and gave Moscow a role in Berlin.

But the imprint of a non-European experience lay heavy on Russia, which in its early history had been invaded and dominated by the Tartars from Central Asia, and then, in the nineteenth century, turned about and established its imperial rule in Central Asia and the Far East. It would be difficult to demonstrate that the forces which molded Western civilization had by 1914 affected more than 10 or 15 per cent of the Tsarist Empire's population, or approximately the same percentage as had come under Western influence in undivided India before independence in 1947 and in China before the Communists took power in 1949.

Westerners who have read Turgenev and Chekhov, Tolstoi and Dostoevski, or heard the music of Tchaikovsky or Scriabin, or in recent times have come to know the ideas of Boris Pasternak, assume that the Russian people as a whole had shared in that potent decoction of ideas which Western Europe had absorbed over two thousand years from Greece and Rome, from Catholic (as distinguished from Byzantine) Christianity, the Renaissance, the Reformation, the English and French and American revolutions, and the impact of the Industrial Revolution. It is true that a small minority of the Russian people who could read French or German or English, who could afford to travel abroad and in some cases study in European universities (one of them was Lenin), did share, often with great sympathy and even enthusiasm, in this heritage. It is true, too, that some of Russia's leaders (Peter the Great, German-born Catherine II, Alexander I, who in 1812 pursued Napoleon's fleeing armies from Moscow to Paris) had a lively interest in the ideas and practices of Western Europe, but their impact on their contemporaries, significant as it was, did not transform Russia into a Western European country. For neither they, nor the intellectuals of the eighteenth and nineteenth centuries, reached the majority of the population—the peasants, who had been serfs until 1861, who were illiterate and untutored, who lived in poverty in Russia's "dark villages" or after liberation sought work in the new factories of the cities, where they often faced a life even grimmer than that of the countryside, a life depicted by Maxim Gorki in his play *The Lower Depths*.

In effect, before 1914 there were two Europes on the Continent, as the French economist, François Delaisi pointed out before World War II in his book *Les Deux Europes*. One was the Europe which had been permeated by ideas of many revolutions, religious, political, and economic, and had translated the concepts of modern science into the instruments of modern technology. The other Europe, east of Germany, although it had had many fruitful contacts with the first, still had religious, political, and economic institutions ranging from the Middle Ages to the early nineteenth century, and had only begun to make use of industrial techniques. The question may well be asked even today whether stabilization of the Continent can be achieved, as Delaisi suggested, only when the Europe of the East has reached the technological and economic—and conceivably the political —level of the Europe of the West.

Yet sensitive Western observers, had they been alert to Russia's condition, might have detected omens of a gathering storm in a society where a wide gap existed between the few rich and the many poor; where industrialization was still in its harsh early stages; where political liberty had not yet begun to flourish; and where a weak economic structure was ultimately strained to the breaking point by the burdens first of the Russo-Japanese war (1904-05) and a decade later of World War I. The tensions of this society, after three years of disastrous war, erupted in the March, 1917, revolution, led by the aristocracy and the middle class, who overthrew the rule of Tsar Nicholas II, and eight months later in the Bolshevik revolution of November 7, led by Lenin and Trotsky at the head of peasants and workers. Tolstoi and Dostoevski, and many a poet, from Aleksander Pushkin to Aleksander Blok, sensed the Russians' growing unrest and deep-seated grievances, and wrote of them with profound concern and passionate fears and hopes.

Into this society, undergoing transition from semifeudal to modern times now familiar to us in Asia, the Middle East, Africa, and Latin America, the Communists, in the midst of a shattering war, came on the scene with a numerically small but highly organized leadership, armed with carefully worked-out, precise plans for far-reaching internal changes. To many Westerners the Communists of Russia looked like wreckers of an established order, whose seeming stability and survival until then had made it appear worthy of retention and outside support. But the old order had been slowly undermined long before November, 1917, by economic and social changes which had created a desire for new political forms, and had then been shaken beyond reconstruction during World War I by military defeats, resulting administrative and economic chaos, and the overthrow, in quick succession, of the monarchy and the antimonarchist aristocracy and middle class. It was as if in France of 1789, within a few months, the king and the nobles, toppled by the third estate, had barely disappeared from the stage before the middle class followed them into oblivion, to be replaced by a completely new caste of political characters—the Communist leadership drawn from gentry (Lenin) and lower bourgeoisie (Trotsky and Stalin) and backed by factory workers and peasants.

Within less than a year Russia had thus lived through the revolutionary experience which had taken a century or two in France and England. But while the Communists looked both to Western observers and to those whom they had swept out of power in Russia like destroyers—and indeed they did destroy the religious hierarchy, the aristocracy, the landowners, private business and industry, and the role of the individual in literature and the arts—they were also builders of new institutions. What is more, far from trying to carry Russia back to its non-Western past, they proceeded to Westernize it as no one except Peter the Great (with whom the Communist leaders have an affinity they frequently acknowledge) had tried to do in previous centuries.

The Communists, it is true, did not bring Western-type democracy to Russia—but neither had the Tsars, except for the short-lived and limited experience of the Duma, the parliament forced on Nicholas II by the revolution of 1905, which had been precipitated by Russia's defeat in its war with industrially advanced, militarist Japan. But now that we know from conditions in Asia, the Middle East, Africa, and Latin America that democracy cannot develop without an environment created by economic and social changes, the nonexistence of democratic institutions in Russia after 1917 does not appear as unique as it seemed forty years ago when Russian conditions were measured solely by the experience of the West. What the Communists did was to rein in Russia until it rose up "on its hind legs," to quote Pushkin's famous verse about the statue of Peter the Great on a rearing horse, which overlooks the Neva in Leningrad (once his own city of St. Petersburg). Between 1917 and 1953 the Communist leaders, although differing among themselves on crucial points, profoundly altered the character of agriculture and industry through the complete collectivization of farms, developed large-scale heavy industry capable of producing both machinery and military weapons, and reorganized the educational system to foster the training of technologically skilled men and women.

This transformation was accomplished without consideration for the freedom or comfort of the human beings involved. They had to work long and hard for minimum rewards in terms of pay and what that pay could buy out of purposely limited supplies of consumer goods and even bare necessities, and frequently with imposition of forced labor on those who in one way or another incurred the displeasure of the state. In the absence of free elections, popular discontent was made known only in two ways: First, through differences of opinion within the supposedly monolithic Communist party. These were called "deviations" from the party line—regarded as the revealed truth for all Communists—the critics were either driven out of the party, condemned to forced labor, or executed. Second, through passive resistance such as the peasants displayed in the 1930's when they refused to sow, or if they sowed refused to reap, despite pressures by the government which ranged from exile and forced labor to executions.

Yet in spite of these repressions, a spirit of opposition has persisted during the past forty years. It found a variety of expressions after the grueling Second World War, which took at least 20 million lives and destroyed valuable resources, and the death in 1953 of Stalin, who had grown more and more tyrannical in his latter years. Subsequently a "thaw" set in with the coming to power of Nikita S. Khrushchev, who by 1956 had assumed the two roles formerly played by Stalin—Chairman of the Council of Ministers of the USSR and secretary general of the Communist party. In February of that year, at the Twentieth Congress of the Communist party of the Soviet Union, Khrushchev delivered his celebrated denunciation of Stalin and derided the dictator's "cult of personality" when he said:

> Stalin acted not through persuasion, explanation and patient co-operation with people, but by imposing his concepts and demanding absolute submission to his opinion. Whoever opposed this concept or tried to prove his viewpoint and the correctness of his position was doomed to removal from the leading collective and to subsequent moral and physi-

cal annihilation. . . . The cult of the individual acquired such monstrous size chiefly because Stalin himself, using all conceivable methods, supported the glorification of his own person. . . . Comrades! We must abolish the cult of the individual decisively, once and for all . . . and . . . return to and actually practice . . . the main principle of collective leadership.

Khrushchev did not attack the principles and practices of communism, only what he regarded as their wrong application by Stalin, particularly criticized for his ruthless purges of Communist leaders who disagreed with him. Khrushchev emphasized that, henceforth, "collective leadership"—that is, rule by the party Presidium—would succeed one-man rule by a dictator addicted to the "cult of personality." The use of violence was opposed. Legality was restored through the abolition of the secret police. Greater latitude was encouraged in the arts and literature.

Most important for the rest of the world, both Communist and non-Communist, the view proclaimed by Marx, elaborated by Lenin, and implemented by Stalin, that war between communism and imperialism is inevitable, was rejected with increasing emphasis.

A culminating point was reached in the June, 1960, review by *Pravda*, the organ of the Communist party, of Lenin's book *Left-Wing Communism: An Infantile Disorder*, written in 1920, whose fortieth anniversary was thus celebrated. In this article, published after the fiasco of the Paris summit conference of May 16, 1960, *Pravda* asserted that changed conditions in the world required new policies, calling for a reinterpretation of Lenin's views on the "inevitability of war." Khrushchev's often-repeated view that nuclear war would destroy communism as well as capitalism was here presented in vigorous form. War, said *Pravda*, not only can, but should be avoided. Belief in the inevitability of war, now that nuclear destruction is possible, is a "leftist deviation," said *Pravda*. This does not mean that communism will not win. On the contrary, it can win by peaceful means—through propaganda, trade, and aid—which will assure the victory of communism because of the weaknesses of "capitalism" and the growing strength of the masses. Khrushchev thus took issue with the Chinese Communists, who had been asserting that war is not only inevitable, but desirable so that imperialism can be defeated, and then, on its ruins, "socialism" can build a "beautiful" future.

Throughout the period of Communist rule the Soviet government—

first alone while it was "building socialism in one country," to use Stalin's phrase, then after World War II, as leader of the Soviet bloc in Europe—had, in world affairs, combined the national policy of Russia with the international policy of communism. By 1945 over fifty countries in all the continents had been brought within the ken of Communist influence radiating from Moscow. Thus, often at one and the same time, but on occasions keeping Russian nationalism in a separate compartment from international communism, Moscow was able to pursue a flexible and wide-ranging set of policies and to conduct a variegated propaganda adapted to given circumstances in each country with which it dealt. In spite of this dramatic combination of nationalism and communism the Soviet government by no means always achieved its goals, even when it was most feared by its opponents.

Russia's weakness became most apparent in its relations with other Communist countries: first in Eastern Europe after Moscow had established its influence over Poland, Czechoslovakia, Hungary, Bulgaria, Rumania and Albania and had developed relations with Tito's Yugoslavia, and then, after 1949, with Communist China. This became particularly evident in the case of Yugoslavia after the latter had decided to set off on a road different from that of Russia.

Yugoslavia, like Russia, had been only in part exposed to Western influence. In contrast to Croatia (which had been included until 1919 in Austria-Hungary), Serbia, Montenegro and Herzegovina had lived for many years under the rule of the Ottoman Empire. At first, after World War II, Marshal Tito tried to follow the example of Russia both at home and abroad by promoting farm collectives and rapid industrialization. However, he found it difficult to maintain the stringent program of collectivization and heavy industry development for which the Yugoslavs were not equipped either by traditions of individual or, as in the case of Croatia, co-operative farming, or by their limited raw-material resources. Nor was Tito willing to accept Russia's domination which, to his surprise, he found just as demanding and oppressive as the "imperialism" of the West, at a time when he had come to believe in "national socialism" rather than in an international communism directed from Moscow.

Having defied Stalin and withstood his pressures, Tito, after the Russian dictator's death, welcomed Khrushchev's thaw, hoping that a more flexible relationship would be initiated among Communist states. He found that Poland was eager to follow his example in easing the burdens of a Communist economic system, and he welcomed Mao Tse-tung's statement at the time of the Poznan revolt in Poland that there are "many roads to socialism." By 1958, however, when the Communist countries at Moscow's command adopted a harsher policy toward dissidents, the Chinese leader had rejected his own statement.

In that year Yugoslavia, once more at odds with the Communist bloc, published a draft party program containing two assertions that orthodox Communists could not but regard as heretical. The Yugoslavs pointed out that a "swelling wave of state capitalist 'tendencies' was developing in the West and that Western nations were moving toward 'socialist organization.' " This was interpreted to mean that communism was no longer the only answer to the aspirations of underdeveloped countries for Socialist development. The Yugoslavs also criticized the bureaucracy of the Soviet system which, in Tito's view, threatened to dominate society instead of serving it. (Milovan Djilas, former close associate of Tito, had earlier denounced bureaucratization of Yugoslav communism in his book, *The New Class*—and for this was jailed, being released only in 1961.) The remedy, said the Yugoslavs, was to reduce the power of socialist states and to permit more direct democracy, a statement which seemed to bring Belgrade closer to Western political concepts.

Moreover, Yugoslavia, while still expressing its solidarity with other Communist countries, claimed the freedom to accept aid from both sides, a position which both the West and the USSR regard as "neutralist." Tito has not only rejected the idea of the inevitability of war between capitalism and communism, but has gone beyond that and believes that "peaceful coexistence" means not only a temporary Communist tactic but genuine co-operation with non-Communist as well as Communist countries. Although steadfastly refusing to enter into military alliances with either of the two blocs, Yugoslavia has accepted economic aid and some military assistance from the West, and in July, 1960, announced its intention to free its trade from government control, and to join the General Agreement on Tariffs and Trade (GATT), and possibly the Common Market (the trade group of six European countries—France, West Germany, Belgium, Luxembourg, the Netherlands and Italy), which has been denounced by Khrushchev. Tito's position is regarded by the USSR leaders as a "rightist" deviation from communism.

By contrast Communist China has, according to Moscow, shown a tendency toward a "leftist" deviation. Mao Tse-tung has argued that there should be unity between Communist countries but diversity in their policies, although, after a short-lived 1956 promise to "let a hundred flowers bloom together, let a hundred schools of thought contend," Peiping once more resorted to totalitarian suppression of opposition in 1957. Even more than Moscow, Peiping insists on "the dictatorship of the proletariat," in contrast to Tito's emphasis on "socialist democracy." The policies in which Mao Tse-tung shows the most dramatic diversity from the USSR are his determination to build "socialism" at a faster pace than was done by Stalin, through the creation of agrarian "communes," and his belief, in spite of Khrushchev, that war is not an unmitigated evil but an expected boon for the "socialist" countries which, the Chinese contend will survive to see a better day, presumably because of the vast numbers of China's population as compared with the Western nations and with Russia.

Thus Tito and Mao Tse-tung, each in his own way and in terms of his own country's past experience and present circumstances, have emphasized that there are different means of achieving communism, thereby challenging Moscow's supremacy in the Communist world. The example of Yugoslavia has been watched with interest by other Communist countries, notably Poland, which is geographically less well placed than Yugoslavia to challenge Moscow's leadership, yet has been moving toward a Polish "communism" of its own. Non-Communist countries, too, which follow a policy of "nonalignment," like India, or of "positive neutralism," like Egypt, have developed close relations with Yugoslavia. Russia, however, with its success in applying science and technology to the development of what was forty years ago a predominantly backward agrarian economy, has made a profound impression on many non-Western countries—not because they want to follow the road of communism, but because they hope that they can benefit by Russia's techniques without having to adopt its ideology. In the future, Communist China may also have a strong impact on the still newer countries of Asia, Africa, and Latin America with its policy of a communism still more rapid and more total than that of Russia—and in Eastern Europe little Albania is reported to favor the Chinese, rather than the Russian brand of communism.

Meanwhile, Khrushchev increasingly regards his form of Communist ideas as the middle course, from which Yugoslavia has deviated to the right and China to the left. His views were reflected in the declaration of the ruling Communist parties adopted in Moscow in November, 1957, which stated: "The experience of the U.S.S.R. and other socialist countries has fully confirmed the correctness of the tenet of Marxist-Leninist theory that the processes of the socialist revolution and the building of socialism are governed by a number of basic laws applicable in all countries embarking on a socialist path. These laws are manifested everywhere alongside a great variety of historically formed national features and traditions which should be taken into account without fail."

Western observers believe that Mr. Khrushchev intends to maintain the strength and security of the USSR but to avoid a nuclear war with the United States or any situation that could lead to such a war; to fight the "cold war" in the underdeveloped countries of Africa, Asia, the Middle East, and Latin America on the basis of "anti-imperialism" and "anti-colonialism"; and to continue the expansion of industrial production and the improvement of living conditions in the Soviet Union. To achieve these objectives, Mr. Khrushchev, it is thought, is ready to overlook strict adherence to Communist dogma, not only by other Communist countries, but by his own government. To the extent that he becomes more pliable in the interpretation of Communist doctrine he may find himself, by coincidence, if not by design, far closer to Marshal Tito, who has been ahead of the Russians in adapting Marxism-Leninism to changing domestic and world conditions, than to Communist China. The differences between the USSR and Communist China were bridged over but not reconciled in the Communist manifesto published on December 5, 1960, as pointed out in the last chapter. But both Moscow and Peiping joined on that occasion in denouncing the "revisionism" of Yugoslavia.

What were the different conditions in the USSR and in Yugoslavia which produced the contrasts between Khrushchev and Tito—and what may now bring them closer in the future?

## NIKITA S. KHRUSHCHEV—

## USSR

The chairman of the Council of Ministers of the USSR and secretary general of its Communist party, heir of Lenin and Stalin, was born on April 17, 1894, in the village of Kalinovka in the Ukraine, to the family of a coal miner. In his youth Khrushchev worked first as a herdsman, then as a metal worker in the factories and mines of one of the areas of Russia particularly rich in raw materials—in this case coal and iron—the Don Basin or Donbass.

In 1918, soon after the Bolshevik revolution of November, 1917, Khrushchev joined the Communist party, and he was an active participant in the ensuing civil war, fighting on the southern front. Once the war was over, Khrushchev, like his father, worked in a coal mine, then studied at the Donetz industrial institute. He was active in the party, was repeatedly elected secretary of his party cell, and played a leading role in the party's work in the Donbass and subsequently in Kiev, capital of the Ukraine.

Eager for more education, Khrushchev in 1929 began to study at the J. V. Stalin Industrial Academy in Moscow, and was elected secretary of the party committee there. He rose rapidly in the party, becoming between 1932 and 1938 secretary of the Moscow city and regional committees. During this period he carried out important party and government plans for developing public services in Moscow and improving the living conditions of factory workers and office employees.

In 1938, twenty years after he had joined the Communist party, he was elected first secretary of the Central Committee in the Ukraine and, after a brief term as chairman of the Council of Ministers in the Ukraine SSR, was again elected secretary of the Central Committee in December, 1947, serving until December, 1949. He had also been a member of the Central Committee of the party since 1934 as well as of the Politburo since 1938.

Meanwhile, during World War II he had served with the army in the field, as a member of the Military Council of the Special Kiev Military District and in other posts. He actively participated in the defense of Stalingrad while continuing his work with the Central Committee.

During the postwar period Khrushchev resumed his steady rise in the Communist party, and in September, 1953, the party Plenum elected him first secretary of its Central Committee.

In this top position Khrushchev, who at Stalin's death had been regarded as only one of the dictator's successors, with Malenkov, Bulganin, and Mikoyan more in the spotlight, gradually gathered power into his hands. His famous 1956 report, "On the cult of personality and its consequences," in which he scathingly attacked Stalin's one-man rule proved a milestone in his spectacular career. He stood off all his competitors for Stalin's mantle, and in June, 1957, returned hurriedly to Moscow from a visit to Finland to check, with Marshal Zhukov's aid, a revolt within the party led by Malenkov, Molotov, and others who were banished from Moscow but given government assignments in the provinces. And then, in October, 1957, while Marshal Zhukov was on a tour of Yugoslavia, Khrushchev deprived the popular warhero of his position. On March 27, 1958, Khrushchev reached the peak of the Soviet ruling hierarchy when he became premier of the USSR as well as secretary general of the Communist party. He has shown himself skilled in the game of politics, which in Stalin's day, for top Communist leaders, as for lesser folk, was often a game for survival. To the west, Khrushchev looks stubborn, even intransigent. Yet, although he displayed impressive courage at the front during World War II, he himself admitted in 1956 that when Stalin said, " 'Dance...' I danced."

To Western observers Khurshchev, who received little formal education, and has had little opportunity to acquire the elaborate courtesy of an aristocrat or the manners of a top businessman, often seems crude and ill-bred—and many, particularly during the fifteenth session of the United Nations General Assembly in New York (1960), when he indulged in table-thumping and interruptions while smiling broadly, described him as a "buffoon." At sixty-seven, after an arduous life during which, under Stalin's rule, he must have constantly faced the danger of disgrace, demotion, or even death, he is a vigorous and buoyant man, who can maintain an impressive dignity when he so wishes, but can also make broad jokes and scatter around Russian proverbs. Contrary to rumor, he is not a heavy drinker and holds a glass in his hand more often than he imbibes its contents. He is at ease in all types of conversation, whether with foreign statesmen or with Russian peasants, and has an encyclopedic memory. Some observers think that he is a boor by nature. Others contend that he puts on an act, turning from simulated rage to simulated cordiality, depending on his shrewd calculations of given circumstances. He has a steely will, but can also be flexible, as he has been in his dealings with Marshal Tito, depending on the ends he is seeking to achieve. After he came to supreme power, he began to patronize a well-known Italian tailor, although, in keeping with Communist custom, he never wears evening dress even when it is required by protocol.

When away from the glare of publicity, the formidable Khrushchev, whose first wife died in the 1920's, enjoys a peaceful existence with his second wife, Nina Petrovna. She is a former schoolteacher, motherly in appearance, unassuming in manner, but said to be well-read and interested in many subjects, among them music. They have been married for twenty-three years, and Mme. Khrushchev brought up her husband's children by his first marriage, as well as their own children. Khrushchev's eldest son, Leonid, a pilot in the Soviet Air Force, was killed in World War II. A second son, Sergei, is an electronics engineer; as a hobby he collects butterflies. One daughter, Yulia, is married to the director of the Kiev Opera and Ballet Company. Another, Rada, is the wife of Aleksi Adzhubei, editor of *Izvestia*. The Soviet Premier has five grandchildren.

A veteran American newspaperman, Thomas P. Whitney, who during his six years of service as Associated Press correspondent in the USSR (1947-53) had ample opportunity to observe Khrushchev, gives this portrait of the Soviet ruler in "Has Russia Changed?" a *Headline Series* published by the Foreign Policy Association in 1960:

> First and foremost, Khrushchev is a Soviet organization-man. He is a creation of the Soviet Communist party. He has dedicated his life to this organization and it has given him his position and his power. He is well aware of this fact. Why did Khrushchev triumph over his adversaries in the fight for succession to leadership? In considerable part probably because he, among all the leaders, was more familiar at first hand with the problems and personnel of the party organization. Alone among the top leaders under Stalin it was Khrushchev who worked closely with local Communist bosses and understood their needs and desires. While

others among the leaders were confined by Stalin to the Kremlin, Khrushchev was busy in both the Ukraine and in the Moscow region working with local party chieftains. His politics were grass roots politics. He knew the men of the machine and they knew and trusted him.

Second, Khrushchev is a born politician of great talent. He loves the limelight. He loves to persuade people, to get them to do what he wants. He loves the adulation and attention that go with being a political leader. It is bread and butter to him—his profession and career—and he is good at it. If Stalin was an introverted personality, a sadist, a person who wanted to hide behind the Kremlin walls and govern by intrigue and conspiracy, Khrushchev is a man who loves to work out in the open. He loves to be among people, to talk to them, to make a good impression on them, to be liked by them. He is no stranger to conspiracy, but it does not make up the main theme of his political career. His great gift is that of persuasion. Garrulous and prolix to a fault, he enjoys talking and sometimes cannot stop. But at any rate he does not attempt to conceal his views, attitudes, prejudices and plans.

The essence of Khrushchev is that he likes and enjoys people. The essence of Stalin was that he hated and feared people. This is a difference of decisive importance.

But not all of the personality traits of Khrushchev constitute positive factors in Soviet and world affairs. For example, it is amply clear that Khrushchev has marked inferiority feelings about persons or classes who are, so to speak, wellborn or of the aristocracy. He is ever conscious of his lowly origin and his dirty hands, figuratively speaking. He is fearful lest those of better background with whom he comes in contact find him ridiculous. Beneath what appears to be the thickest of skins he is in reality a very sensitive person. He tends to mistrust, even hate, all those of higher class origin than himself. The worst of this is that he tends to extend this mistrust and hate to entire nations, like the United States, which have a higher standard of living than Russia.

Khrushchev is clever—in the way Russian peasants are clever. He is adept at dissimulation, at playing the fool when in reality he is calculating ahead and knows exactly what goes on. This has always been an important political asset with him. One can say that he has made a career by inducing other people to underestimate him.

Khrushchev is impulsive. He is capable of taking sudden action. Interestingly enough his actions are quite often likely to coincide with his own best interest. This is a part of his cleverness. But he is genuinely impulsive. This does not mean he is the man, necessarily, who will press the buttons to set off World War III out of caprice. But, when dealing with him, it does mean one should take into account the fact that he is capable of reaching important decisions on the spur of the moment and that he will quite possibly stick to these decisions. He is not a person to be fooled with or teased. This is fundamental, and must be kept in mind even at times when he seems to invite ridicule or even contempt by his conduct.

This analysis of Khrushchev's character was amply borne out by the Soviet leader's reaction to the U-2 incident, his behavior at the abortive Paris conference, and even more in the months that followed his decision not to negotiate with President Eisenhower but to await the inauguration of a new president in the United States.

The significance of Khrushchev as a member of the Soviet trinity with Lenin and Stalin is that in contrast to Lenin, who generated ideas for the transformation of Russia, and Stalin, who implemented these ideas, and carried them forward by force, Khrushchev, coming to power nearly forty years after the Bolshevik revolution, is the man who has consolidated material gains in spite of wartime destruction of men and resources, who has eased the strains of Soviet society through his policy of "thaw," and who has found it possible to adapt what had been hitherto regarded as untouchable Communist dogma to the conditions of the nuclear age, which neither Lenin nor Stalin could have anticipated. In this sense, although obviously lacking the glamour and dash of Napoleon, he is the leader who has absorbed the ideas of a great revolution and has carried them around the world through incessant travel, which Stalin, who refused to leave Russia, had never undertaken. By exposing himself to non-Communist ideas and practices from Britain to India, from the United States to Austria, Khrushchev has acted not with the fanaticism of Stalin and other early old Bolsheviks, but with a realism that combines hardheaded nationalism with flexible communism, thereby qualifying for the title of communism's "new man."

In all these respects Khrushchev, although in age belonging to the old guard, has reflected the thoughts and aspirations of the younger generation of the USSR, who are more interested in practical achievements than in metaphysical disputations about Communist theories. Although attached to the values of their own country and to the system under which they have been brought up, these young people are at the same time curious about the life of the West and willing, in fact eager, to learn from Westerners what they regard as pleasant or useful for themselves—from jazz and abstract painting to automation and the operation of chemical plants. To a generation whose most prominent leaders are industrial managers and nuclear scientists, agronomists and astronauts, Khrushchev, with his quick grasp of scientific and technological problems, has opened the doors to the future instead of rehashing the bitter ideological past, as Stalin did in his day.

## JOSIP BROZ TITO—
## YUGOSLAVIA

The president of Yugoslavia, like the premier of the USSR, is of lowly social origin. He was born in May, 1892, in the village of Kumrovec in Croatia, near the border of Slovenia, the seventh of fifteen children. His father, who drank heavily, farmed a dozen or more acres and also earned a little by doing odd jobs as a blacksmith. The family led a hard life in two rooms and half of a kitchen of a house which they shared with cousins.

In a Catholic family, Josip Broz (who during the fighting of World War II acquired the nickname Tito) at first liked to go to church, but he lost interest when the priest boxed his ears. He attended the village school, but left it at the age of twelve. His school report stated that he was good at gymnastics, gardening, and scripture, and that his conduct was "excellent"—in school.

When he was fifteen, Josip was sent to Sisak to work as a waiter. Disliking the job, he apprenticed himself to a locksmith for three years. His employer, however, hit him one day for reading instead of working, and he ran away and got a job at a brickworks. He was jailed for breaking his contract, but the locksmith had him released and took him back.

Having finished his apprenticeship in 1910, at the age of eighteen, Josip set out for Agram (now Zagreb) and found work as a mechanic. He became a member of the Metalworkers' Union and joined the Social-Democratic party of Croatia-Slovenia. But soon he was on the road again, often going hungry. In spite of work difficulties, he studied German and Czech, improved his engineering knowledge, and, for lighter moments, learned to dance.

In 1913, on the eve of World War I, he was called up for his two-year military service in the army of Austria-Hungary, of which his native Croatia formed a part. He made a good soldier, became a sergeant-major, and distinguished himself at fencing. During the war he proved effective at conducting raids behind enemy lines, and soon came to be regarded as a natural leader; men gladly followed him.

In 1915 he was seriously wounded and taken prisoner by the Russians, spending a year in an army hospital. He used that period of leisure to learn Russian, and the next year he was sent to work in a mill, and later was put in charge of a gang of prisoners working on the Trans-Siberian Railway. When the Bolshevik revolution broke out, he sided with the revolutionaries, and was arrested several times. During this period he married a Russian girl, Palagea Byelusnova (Polka) who bore him two sons, Hinko and Zarko, and a daughter, Zlatica. Hinko and Zlatica died in early childhood. Zarko spent his youth in Russia, but later came to Yugoslavia during World War II and fought at his father's side.

When peace came in 1919 Josip returned to Croatia. By that time he had become a Communist. In 1927 he was named secretary of the Zagreb branch of the Metalworkers' Union. From that time on he devoted his whole life to the Communist party. He was imprisoned in June, 1927, and again in November, 1928, when he was condemned to five years in jail. Like other Communist leaders under the reign of the harshly dictatorial, strongly anti-Communist King Alexander, Tito studied Marx and Lenin during his prison terms and became more than ever a believer in Communist doctrine.

In 1934—the year King Alexander was assassinated by Yugoslavs in Marseilles as he disembarked for a state visit to France—the party sent Josip to Russia, and in January, 1935, he settled down to work at the Communist International (Comintern) headquarters in Moscow, where he became known as "Comrade Walter."

His experience with the Comintern brought about a cooling-off in Josip's former enthusiasm for Russia. In 1936 he became organizing secretary of the Communist party in Yugoslavia and, after another visit to Moscow in 1937, he returned to his country the following year and established party headquarters there—a new development for

Yugoslavia. More visits to Russia followed in 1938 and 1939. In the meantime his Russian wife had divorced him, he had married a Slovene girl, Herta, and they had one son.

In April, 1941, Hitler, aided by Mussolini, attacked Yugoslavia, established his sway over the country, and then invaded Russia in June. Outwardly Josip Broz, known as engineer Slavko Babic, was a respected citizen with a vineyard near Zagreb. But under the name of Tito, he began to form guerrilla bands to fight German and Italian forces which had conquered the land. However, he did not go into action until Nazi Germany invaded the USSR in June 1941. The men who followed him, the Partisans, fought a civil war with the Cetniks led by General Draga Mihajlovic, who counseled caution in opposing the invaders. This was in contrast to Tito who sought to oust them, but was unable to obtain much aid from the USSR while Mihajlovic was receiving support from Britain. The British, however, eventually found Mihajlovic of doubtful assistance, and when in 1944 he failed to take action against the Germans and Italians, they transferred their support to Tito, who left Yugoslavia and went to the island of Vis off the Dalmatian coast with the help of the Royal Air Force.

In the complex political and military situation of the war years, when Yugoslavs fought each other as well as foreign invaders, Tito made his own position clear on April 11, 1945, when he signed the Soviet-Yugoslav treaty of friendship and mutual assistance in Moscow. On June 11 he withdrew from Trieste, a territory to which both Italians and Yugoslavs had laid claim. On July 17, 1946, Tito had Mihajlovic executed, and thus removed a great potential danger to his regime. Another of Tito's wartime foes, Archbishop Stepinac of Zagreb, who had supported Mihajlovic, and thus, according to Tito, fascism, was arrested on September 18, 1946. Three weeks later Stepinac was sentenced to sixteen years in prison with hard labor, but this was later commuted to house arrest in his native village. Thus he, too, was eliminated as an adversary of Tito. Stepinac died in 1960, and with the government's approval was given a religious funeral.

As soon as peace had come, Tito turned his thoughts to economic reconstruction. On November 29, 1946, Yugoslavia announced its first Five-Year Plan, which was started in January, 1947. In 1947 Tito also signed an agreement with the USSR under which Yugoslavia was to receive $135 million for the purchase of capital goods from Moscow. In reality, however, it received only equipment valued at $800,000.

It soon became clear that Stalin was not strongly predisposed in favor of his fellow Communist Tito, who, in his opinion, was too inclined to negotiate with Western nations. In 1949 the USSR denounced the 1947 financial agreement. Meanwhile, Yugoslavia had refused in 1948 to attend the Comintern meeting, and on June 28 of that year it was expelled from the Comintern.

Stalin's break with Tito marked the beginning of Yugoslavia's period of "national socialism," which has persisted since that time in spite of brief formal reconciliations between the two Communist countries. Tito's system, which contended that there are "different roads to socialism," and each nation should be free to choose its own was anathema to Communist doctrinaires in the USSR. It emphasized the national, in contrast to the international, character of communism as developed by Moscow and implemented by the Comintern; and a pragmatic adjustment of Communist doctrines both to the economic and social conditions of Yugoslavia and to changing world circumstances. Tito's views, labeled by his opponents as "Titoism," were regarded by the Russians, as well as by other leaders throughout the Communist world, as a betrayal of Lenin and Stalin. Tito, for his part, maintained that he, and not the Russians, was a "simon-pure" Communist and a true follower of Lenin and Marx, although he repudiated Stalinism.

As evidence of his independent position, Tito began to accept economic aid from Western countries, and in 1950, after the outbreak of the Korean War, he also accepted Western military aid. Contacts with Western non-Communist nations multiplied. In 1952-53 Britain's prime minister, Sir Anthony Eden, and Marshal Tito exchanged visits. On February 28, 1953, Tito signed a treaty of friendship and co-operation with his neighbors, Greece and Turkey, both of whom he had bitterly opposed in the past. Most important of all for the stabilization of an area which had long been in a turbulent condition, Yugoslavia, through the friendly intervention of United States Ambassador Llewellyn E. Thompson, reached an agreement with Italy over Trieste in 1954.

Meanwhile, on the home front, Tito had released Archbishop Stepinac from jail in December, 1951, confining him to residence in his native village. A year later, however, Tito broke off formal relations with the Vatican which, in the opinion of Yugoslavs, had intervened in the country's internal affairs during World War II by supporting Stepinac. In January, 1953, a new state constitution was adopted, modeled to some extent on that of the United States, instead of the previous, Soviet-inspired constitution. Political, economic, and social restrictions previously imposed under a harsh Communist regime were eased or abandoned. Yet in spite of this "thaw," which preceded that of Russia by some five years, Milovan Djilas, once a close friend of Tito, and vice-premier of his government, was expelled from the Central Committee of the party in 1953. Djilas resigned his government posts and returned his party card; and the next year not only Djilas, but his close friend, Vlado Dedijer, Tito's official biographer, was condemned to prison.

Sir Fitzroy Maclean, a former British diplomat who parachuted behind the enemy's lines into Yugoslavia and from 1942 to 1945 was Brigadier Commanding the British Military Mission to the Partisans in German-occupied Yugoslavia, describes in his biography of the Yugoslav leader, *The Heretic*, the reaction of Tito, whom he knew well, to Yugoslavia's expulsion from the Comintern. The scene is the Fifth Congress of the Yugoslav Communist party on July 21, 1948:

The Congress was attended by over two thousand delegates from all over the country, representing a total of some half a million party members. Almost every man and woman present had fought under Tito's command as a Partisan during the war.

Tito opened the proceedings with a speech lasting no less than eight hours. The first seven and a half of these were taken up with a detailed historical survey of Jugoslav Communism from its earliest beginnings down to the present time. . . . He told them how, on June 22, 1941, the day of Hitler's attack on the Soviet Union, the Jugoslav Politburo had issued a proclamation calling for a general armed uprising to "help the righteous struggle of the great, peaceloving Country of Socialism, the Soviet Union, our dear Socialist Country, our hope and beacon." He recalled the years that had followed, those "three and a half years of bitter strife" in which almost every man and woman there had taken an active part. He recalled their defeats and their victories, the hardships they had endured and the sacrifices they had made. He reminded them of those comrades of theirs who with their last breath had cried: "Long live the Soviet Union and Comrade Stalin." He also told them how, when the war was nearly over and the Western Allies had been helping them for some considerable time, the Russians had eventually given them some help in taking Belgrade and had sent them a certain amount of war material, for which, he was careful to say, they were duly grateful. Finally he spoke of the party's achievements since the war, of the good progress it had made with the liquidation of capitalism and the building of Socialism, of the success it had achieved with its Five Year Plan, of the benefits it had derived from the People's Front, of its fundamental ideological soundness, of its strength and unity and of its determination to continue in the same path in future.

It was only in the last twenty minutes that he "turned briefly" to the Cominform communiqué, with its "monstrous accusations against our party and its leaders"; with its "call to civil war" and its "call to destroy our country." "Those who attack us," he said, "the leaders of the Communist parties in the countries we have helped most, should at least have the decency not to resort to such lies, to such shocking slander. . . . Our critics," he continued, "now dispute the fact that we are Marxist-Leninists. But on what ideological basis did we achieve so much? Was it because we were Trotskyists that we entered the war on the side of the Soviet Union in 1941? Or out of loyalty to Marxism-Leninism, as practiced by Comrade Stalin himself in the U.S.S.R.? We entered it because we were Marxist-Leninists not only in words but in deeds. . . . 'Our teaching,' " said Tito, quoting Lenin quoting Marx and Engels, " " is not dogma, but leadership for action' . . . that is what Lenin said and taught. And now *they* want us to confine ourselves to certain narrow formulas in building Socialism." After which he went on to declare his firm intention of doing everything in his power to restore good relations with the Soviet party and once again extended to them, this time publicly, a cordial invitation to come and see things for themselves on the spot.

At the bottom of the Yugoslavs' dispute with the Kremlin, Maclean points out:

lay Tito's claim that "The Jugoslav brand of Communism was not something imported from Moscow but had its origin in the forests and mountains of Jugoslavia," the contention, in other words, that Marxism-Leninism was not unalterable dogma, but "leadership for action," something they could adapt to suit their own particular needs. It is easy to see how this line of thought soon led them, as the controversy grew more embittered, to criticize the way in which the Russians had adapted Marxism-Leninism to meet *their* own particular requirements. Instead of gradually withering away, as Marx had intended it should, the Soviet State, they pointed out, had under Stalin become more and more powerful, more centralized and more bureaucratized, until in the end it dominated everything. Soon, the original ideas from which it had sprung had been lost sight of or perverted; today its guiding motives were "bureaucratism," state capitalism, and in relation to other countries, the most brutal kind of imperialism. They, for their part, were determined henceforward to avoid these mistakes in Jugoslavia. The term "Titoism," with its hint of deviation, they indignantly rejected. They were no deviationists, but were guided by the purest Marxism-Leninism; what they were building was the only true Socialist state in the world. It was Stalin who was the deviationist. Indeed, as a rough rule of thumb, there was much to be said, when in doubt, for finding out what line the Russians were taking on any given subject and then doing the opposite.

In 1955, two years after Stalin's death, the Soviet government made an unprecedented move to achieve a reconciliation with Yugoslavia in the hope of eliminating an intraparty conflict. On May 14, 1955, Khrushchev, Nicholas Bulganin, Soviet premier, and Anastas I. Mikoyan, Foreign Trade Minister and a confirmed world traveler, were invited to Belgrade. There, following a public apology which caused some observers to compare the Russian leaders' visit to the humiliating experience of Emperor Frederick when he went to bow to the Pope at Canossa, relations between the two countries were resumed. This time, however, the two leaders dealt with each other not as superior and inferior, but as equals, as Tito had always insisted they should.

Meanwhile Tito, who had divorced his second wife Herta, had married the handsome and statuesque Jovanka Budisavljevic. A Serbian girl in her twenties, she had been a Partisan and has since played an important role as his hostess in Belgrade, at his summer residence in Bled, and in his retreat on the beautiful island of Brioni in the Adriatic, developed before World War II by rich Italian and Austrian industrialists as a pleasure retreat, where the Marshal prefers to receive visitors.

From that time to the present, Russo-Yugoslav relations have seesawed from cordiality to bitterness, depending on the internal problems of each country and the state of world affairs. Thus in September, 1955, Khrushchev again arrived in Yugoslavia, and Tito returned the visit at the end of the month. Yet by the end of the year there was so much anti-Yugoslav propaganda in Russia that Moscow blamed the Hungarian revolt of 1956 on Tito, causing another serious rift. Yugoslavia continued to receive economic aid from the United States. But in the midst of eased tensions Djilas was rearrested in 1954, and remained in prison until early 1961.

In October, 1957, the United States decided to suspend all economic and military aid, following Tito's recognition of the East German regime—yet a week later Tito said he would not take part in the ceremonies of the fortieth anniversary of the Bolshevik revolution. In spite of his criticism of Soviet internal methods, on December 4, 1957,

Yugoslavia adopted a new Five-Year Plan, the first time since Tito's break with Stalin that Yugoslavia had returned to long-term planning on the Soviet model. Five days later, on December 9, 1957, Tito asked the United States to discontinue military aid to Yugoslavia.

Moscow, not to be outdone on boycotts, arranged for the Soviet-bloc boycott of the Yugoslav Seventh Communist Congress. In a matter of days Tito, elected to a third term as President, told Moscow on April 22, 1958, to stop meddling in his country's internal affairs; and in June arrested some 100 former agents of the Communist Information Bureau, who, it was stated, had been working on Yugoslav soil. By December, 1958, Tito was urging coexistence with the West—not a revolutionary policy, since, at that time it was also advocated by Mr. Khrushchev—and sought additional financial aid from the United States. At the same time, Tito cultivated relations with "neutralist" countries on a three-month journey, January–March, 1959, during which he toured Asia and Africa, and met, among others, Nasser and Nehru.

While retaining Yugoslavia's ties with other Communist countries—including mainland China, which had seemed to agree with Belgrade on national communism, but then made its political and economic institutions increasingly harsh just when Belgrade was liberalizing its regime—Tito has often differed with the USSR on basic issues of Communist doctrine. Above all, he has opposed Soviet intervention in Yugoslavia's internal affairs, which in his opinion resembles the "imperialist" methods once attributed exclusively to Western capitalist countries.

At the age of sixty-nine Tito, with his erect figure, dynamic energy, and zest for life, looks at least ten years younger, in spite of the hardships he has undergone in jail and during the war. He works hard, eats well, and likes to dress for important occasions; he looks particularly striking in his white uniforms, and his array of medals. He loves the country, and spends as much time as he can on the island of Brioni. He shoots, rides, and swims, likes to experiment with mechanical things, enjoys the company of his children and grandchildren, and likes dogs and horses. Endowed with indomitable courage, a good sense of humor, mellowed since his Partisan days, resolute, realistic, and ruthless, but also keenly aware of the problems of the modern world, he has demonstrated that, without dogmatic preconceptions or ideological intricacies, he can hold his own with other statesmen of his time. He can prevail over his Communist opponents, and can retain his integrity, which in his own mind is inextricably linked with that of his small country—poor in some of the resources needed for modern industry, but rich in its ancient heritage of independence from foreign rule whatever its source, Ottoman, Hapsburg, or Stalinist. Some who know him well believe that his gifts far surpass the capacity for action of his country—that he is a great statesman on a small stage. To show how times have changed, Tito, once denounced in the West as a "bandit" and a "firebrand," was described by *The New York Times* as a "dignified revolutionary" when he came to the United Nations General Assembly in 1960, and was received by President Eisenhower.

How can one explain the marked differences in views between two Communist leaders of Eastern Europe—Khrushchev and Tito? A psychologist might discover important differences in temperament; he might also conclude that two men who have shown great ambition for power, tremendous tenacity, a capacity for independent thought and action within the totalitarian framework of communism, would find it no easier to bow to each other's ideas than Tito did to accept the dictation of Stalin, more inflexible than that of Khrushchev. A political scientist could point out that at least one area of Yugoslavia—Croatia—had been in contact with Western ideas through its inclusion in the Austro-Hungarian Empire. An economist would note that Yugoslavia, with its limited natural resources, could not hope to follow the pattern of vast industrial development set by the USSR, but would have to accept a less grandiose future and rely more both on the initiative of its people and on foreign aid, including aid from the West—a situation that would dictate a policy of mild liberalization at home and of nonalignment abroad.

But perhaps the most important factor in determining the estrangement of Yugoslavia from the Soviet bloc has been Tito's growing awareness that a Communist great power is no more free of "imperialist" aspirations than "capitalist" great powers had been in their prime. This factor, which goes to the very heart of the Communist contention about the superiority of communism as against capitalism on the world scene, first noted by Tito, convinced the Yugoslav leader of the value of "positive neutralism" between the camps of Russian communism and Western anti-communism. His conviction led him to seek the co-operation of other countries which had chosen nonalignment, notably India and Egypt.

As a result, Tito played a major role in building the "third force" of uncommitted nations, a group which has grown rapidly with the admission of newly independent nations of Asia and Africa to the UN. Thus Titoism, which challenged Russian communism, and was in turn challenged by Communist China's Maoism, also challenged—with success—the initial resistance of the United States to "neutralism." At the same time, as Tito made clear during the 1960 UN Assembly, he independently supported some major policies backed by Khrushchev, notably admission of Peiping to the UN and independence for Algeria.

# 2

# The Middle East

$L$ IKE Asia, the Middle East has produced great civilizations during its millenial history—the civilizations of Sumer, Mesopotamia, Egypt, Persia. Like Asia, too, the Middle East has been the cradle of great religions—the monotheistic faiths of Judaism, Christianity, and Islam. And, like Asia, the Middle East has been the battleground of bloody struggles between new conquerors, seeking to oust or dominate conquerors of the past, and between men of different faiths, most recently Hindus and Muslims in India, Arabs and Jews in the Middle East.

Western nations—Britain and France—have won and lost colonial possessions in the Middle East, as well as in Asia and Africa and Latin America. And in the twentieth century the United States, in its new role of leader of the non-Communist coalition, has entered the arena of the Middle East as contender for influence with Russia which, under the Communists as under the Tsars, has taken a strong interest in the area, implementing this long-time national interest by the international policies of communism.

Comparable conditions have over the centuries produced comparable results in our own times. Memories of past glories—of great Egyptian dynasties, of the Jews as a "chosen people," of Allah's prophet Mohammed, of Muslim prowess in defending Islam against the "infidel" Crusaders, and then carrying their holy war (*jihad*) from the Arab peninsula through North Africa and across the Mediterranean, leaving their imprint on the culture of Spain and, through Spain, even on Latin America, of the achievements of the Ottoman Empire— all these aroused aspirations to new successes in the modern world. Yet these aspirations, as in other technologically underdeveloped lands, seemed thwarted at every turn by the economic backwardness of the Middle East as compared with the West. This sense of backwardness, of inferiority not in terms of historical experience, ideas, beliefs, art, and literature, but of modern tools for peace and war, made the leaders of the Middle East both hostile to the West, which threatened their interests and even their security, and grimly determined to emulate those aspects of the West which symbolized its material superiority— weapons and machines. Napoleon at Cairo, Disraeli at Suez, were at once foes and models.

With the weakening of the Ottoman Empire in the latter years of the nineteenth century, and its eventual disintegration during World War I, Britain, France, and Italy acquired fragments of its widespread realm. The British ruled Egypt under various forms of administration from 1881 to 1956. Italy acquired Libya and Tripoli as World War I spoils. From the League of Nations, founded in 1919, Britain obtained as mandates, Iraq, Jordan, and Palestine, while France was granted mandates over Syria and Lebanon. Turkey, keystone of the Ottoman Empire, having fought in World War I alongside Germany and Austria-Hungary, shared their losses and found itself reduced to its territory outside Europe and to the Arab Middle East. Earlier in the century Persia, although remaining technically independent, had had to accept the decision of Britain and Russia to acquire spheres of influ- ence on its soil—Britain in the south, which turned out to be rich in oil, and Russia in the north, which gave it a strategic position although no oil resources to add to those of its Baku oil fields.

As was true of other non-Western peoples, foreign rule, whether administered in the form of colonies or of League of Nations mandates, aroused national sentiments which had either been long dormant, as in Egypt and in Iraq, heir of ancient Mesopotamia, or nonexistent, as in Jordan, an artificial state carved out by the British after World War I. Palestine, historical homeland of the Jews who had been set wandering over the face of the earth through centuries of vicissitudes, scattering over all the continents and settling in many lands yet pre- serving the dream of ultimate "in-gathering," became once more the focus of emotions combining age-old religious beliefs with a new sense of nationhood. During World War I Britain, in the Balfour declara- tion, had promised the Jews a "Jewish home" in Palestine, although four-fifths of Palestine's population were Arabs. This was in direct contradiction to its promises of independence for the Arabs if they for- swore aid to the Central Powers and supported the Allies.

No need arose immediately after World War I to implement Brit- ain's pledge to either Jews or Arabs, since the territories inhabited by both became League of Nations mandates. But the relentless drive launched by Hitler in the 1930's, first against the Jews of Germany and then of all European lands conquered by the Nazis, created a tragically urgent need to find a haven for those of his victims who had gone into exile early in the Nazi period or who had survived Dachau and Belsen. By the end of World War II it was evident that the Jews of Europe, wanderers once more, would seek by all means in their power to create a state of their own on what was to them the sacred soil of Palestine.

Meanwhile, the Turks had been rallied from their World War I defeat and territorial breakup by Kemal Ataturk, a military leader who at one and the same time forged them into a nation-state and undertook to modernize their Islamic society by far-reaching reforms in religious practices, education, political institutions, economic conditions, and social customs. The tranformation of Turkey served as an example to other Muslim peoples of what could be accomplished by energetic, reform-minded military leaders. Its influence can be seen in the post-World War II policies of General Naguib and Colonel Nasser in Egypt and of General Abdul Karim Kassim in Iraq after these countries had been freed of colonial and League mandate status. In other Arab states, however, independence, far from spurring modernization, strengthened the rule of feudal kings, emirs, and chieftains, as in Saudi Arabia, Yemen, and Kuwait, whose oil wealth, developed by Western corporations, was used primarily to enhance the luxury and power of a small ruling group, while the masses of the poor, still living in primitive poverty and illiteracy, remained at the mercy of harsh authoritarian rulers.

The postwar decision of the UN in 1947, strongly urged by the Western powers—Britain, France, and the United States—to create the new state of Israel in Palestine and admit to it an unlimited number of Jews not only from Europe, but from the entire world, precipitated a Middle East crisis between Jews and Arabs which, although less critical today, remains unresolved.

The crux of this crisis is that the new nationalism of the state of Israel whose people, cemented by Judaism, are drawn from many lands, clashed head on with the new nationalism of the Arab states and particularly of Egypt which, although not an Arab country, shares with its neighbors the common faith of Islam and, recalling its glorious past, aspires to the leadership both of the Arabs and of the Muslim world, embracing, at its maximum, 300 million peoples in the arc from Morocco to the Philippines.

This clash was further sharpened by the conviction among Arabs that Israel was a creation of the West, and thus a Western outpost in the Middle East, designed to reinstitute a colonial relationship which had appeared to have been ended by Britain's gradual relinquishment of its claims in Egypt after World War II and by the termination of League of Nations mandates held by Britain and France. Apprehension about the intentions of Israel and the West seemed confirmed by the Anglo-French and Israeli attacks on Suez in 1956.

A clash already charged with dynamite was given a new dimension by the sharp contrast between the store of scientific and technological skills brought to Israel by immigrants from the advanced countries of Europe and other continents and the lack of such skills in Arab lands. In addition there was the generous aid given to the new state by Jews throughout the world, particularly the United States. The resulting technological and financial differential revived the feeling of inferiority which Egypt and the Arabs had experienced when first confronted by the West on their own soil at the turn of the eighteenth century, with the added grievance that, in the meantime, the already wide gap between them had grown still wider.

The disadvantage, and even danger, which this gap spelled for Egypt and the Arabs were concretely demonstrated in 1948 when Egypt, having assumed the leadership of a military coalition determined to defeat Israel and "drive it into the sea" suffered prompt defeat at the hands of the numerically smaller but better-organized and better-equipped Israeli state. This defeat Egypt's young military officers, notably Naguib and Nasser, attributed to the superior weapons of Israel, provided by Western countries. Their profound humiliation and resentment at the outcome were vented both against king Farouk, accused of having squandered Egypt's financial resources on his own pleasures instead of assuring the country's military strength, and on the Western nations which had sponsored Israel and had given it the capacity to resist Arab attack.

These explosive emotions were envenomed by the realization that the 600,000 Arabs who had either fled from Palestine for fear of the Israelis or had been urged by Egypt and its Arab neighbors to leave Israel and return there later with their own victorious armies, would find it difficult, if not impossible, to recover their former homes. Faced by this Arab exodus and by the prospect that the Jews, themselves once victims of an exodus, would replace the Arabs with new Jewish immigrants who would reinforce Israel's strength and make its ouster from the Middle East still more difficult, Egypt and the Arab states took the adamant position that they would not offer a haven to the ousted Arabs, even if Israel paid compensation for land and other possessions left behind and the West provided financial resources for their resettlement.

Instead, they insisted that the Arabs should remain in the no man's land of refugee camps in Jordan, unemployed, living on a pittance distributed through the United Nations Arab Refugee Administration, out of funds supplied in large part by the United States, and increasing in number from year to year. There are now over one million, with no hope for the future. Israel, on its part, has made it clear that beyond token readmission of Arab refugees who are relatives of the Arab minority which refused to leave in 1948, and now lives in relative tranquility and comfort, it does not plan to accept the bulk of these refugees. Their place has since been filled by new Jewish settlers, many of whom have come from Arab lands, notably Yemen, Tunisia, and Morocco, not to speak of fresh immigrants from Europe and other parts of the world.

The continuance of a state of war between Israel and the Arab states has meanwhile been invoked by Cairo as justification for refusal to permit the passage of cargoes bound from or to Israeli ports through the Suez Canal, which Nasser nationalized in 1956. By this measure Egypt has imposed a severe burden on the trade, and thus on the economic life, of Israel, which even Israel's best friends have not succeeded in removing through action by the UN. This same refusal to consider peace with Israel has blocked all other constructive projects proposed by the United States and the UN, notably development and joint use of the Jordan River waters through the creation of a Jordan Valley Authority. It has also foreclosed for the present the possibility, often urged by Israel, of making available to Egypt and the Arab states the scientific and technological skills of the Israelis, which have been used to great advantage by other underdeveloped countries, among them Burma and Ghana, and have been accepted by the still newer nations of Nigeria and the Congo.

Into this welter of clashing nationalisms and conflicting political and economic interests, the USSR, which had previously remained aloof from the Middle East, entered in the 1950's as a competitor with the United States, which had replaced Britain and France in the role played by the West during two centuries.

Using two of the most powerful weapons at its command—communism and economic aid—Moscow, depending on the circumstances in each country at a given time, either backed local Communists, as in Iraq in 1956, or played down Communist activities, as in Egypt, but offered to both nations economic and technical aid, irrespective of their attitude toward communism. The United States responded to the entrance of Russia on the Middle East stage with the Eisenhower Doctrine, under which it offered military assistance to any country requesting it. There was a move to give such aid to Lebanon in 1956 after Iraq, under Kassim, had overthrown the regime of King Faisal (assassinated along with his pro-Western prime minister, Nuri-Said), and had terminated its relationship with the Baghdad pact alliance previously forged with Turkey, Iran, and Pakistan.

The USSR, in spite of earlier threats, refrained from military action, but accelerated its offers of economic aid, the most spectacular of which was its pledge to help Egypt build the High Aswan Dam—a project Nasser had placed at the top of his list for modernizing Egypt and for which he had failed in 1956 to obtain aid from the United States, Britain, and the World Bank. It was this failure that triggered the nationalization of the Suez Canal he had already been contemplating. While the Western nations denounced this action, prophesied doom for the canal when operated by the Egyptians, and in a dramatic thrust by Britain, France, and Israel at Suez sought to oust Nasser, Egypt succeeded in maintaining the canal's operation without major difficulties, and subsequently obtained aid from the World Bank to dredge and widen it.

As the passions aroused on both sides by the West's rejection of Nasser's High Aswan Dam plans and by his nationalization of the canal began to cool, the United States, Britain, and France accepted the compensation offered by Nasser during a series of negotiations, resumed their economic relations with Egypt, and offered technical aid. The net result of great power actions in the Middle East had by 1961 produced a balance of forces. Egypt assumed a policy of "positive neutralism" between the West and the USSR, imposed a check on Communists within the United Arab Republic (UAR) which it had formed with Syria in 1958 and accepted aid from both sides. Iraq, which after initial toleration of Communist activities had sponsored a "national" Communist group, became reconciled with the Western nations but refused to accept further military aid or to join alliances with them, thereby establishing its own form of neutralism. Neither the Soviet bloc nor the West could claim a clear-cut victory, but neither had to admit defeat. Meanwhile, Egypt was the recipient of aid offers not only from the two blocs, but also from the two Germanys, West and East, which vied for its trade and for participation in its new industrial projects. And an uneasy peace was maintained by a small UN force, led first by a Canadian, then by an Indian general, which policed the Gaza Strip, a no man's land that serves as a buffer between Egypt and Israel.

There was little prospect of a peace settlement between Israel and its neighbors, but neither was there a serious threat of new warfare. The best hope for the future seemed to be that, through the industrialization of Egypt and the Arab states, economic equality might eventually be achieved between Israel and the countries which had previously threatened to drive it into the sea. This sense of equality, not felt by the Middle East with respect to the West since the end of the Middle Ages, might then permit Egypt and the Arabs to accept the presence of Israel, which itself, through the admission and modernization of Jews from non-Western lands, and their greater fertility as contrasted with Europeans, is rapidly becoming a Middle Eastern, rather than European-dominated, country. And today the younger generation of Israelis, who have grown up in their own country, free from the tensions imposed on their elders by dispersion and anti-Semitism, would welcome the opportunity of reaching an understanding with Egypt and the Arab states.

## MUSTAFA KEMAL ATATURK—
## TURKEY

Mustafa Kemal Pasha, who became known as Ataturk (Preceptor of the Turks) in his role of President of Turkey, was born in Salonika in 1881 to a family we would now describe as lower bourgeoisie. His father, who went into trade in another town after losing his job as a petty official, died when Mustafa was a small boy. His mother, although a peasant, was eager to educate her son, and sent him to Salonika, where his father's family arranged for continuance of his studies. After passing the required examination he entered the government's military secondary school at the age of twelve, and was thus assured of a career in the Ottoman system.

The name Kemal (excellent) was given to Mustafa by one of his teachers to indicate the quality of his school work. Like other young men of that period in the Ottoman Empire he came in touch, through his studies, with Western ideas which were being circulated underground by Ottoman intellectuals. In fact, he was regarded as a young man of "radical ideas," but actually, as pointed out by Lewis Thomas in *The United States and Turkey and Iran*, "His role in the Young Turk revolution was active but relatively modest; he never figured prominently in the inner councils of the party. On the contrary, his relations with the party's leaders were poor." What brought him to public notice was not his political activity, but the outstanding military talent he displayed, particularly at Gallipoli, in World War I, during which Turkey, traditionally anti-Russian, fought at the side of Germany and Austria-Hungary.

This war ended in disaster for the Central Powers, a disaster made all the more bitter for the Turks by the Greek invasion of western Anatolia, under the sponsorship of the Allies. Amid the chaos precipitated by the defeat of the Ottoman Empire, its withdrawal from the war, and the disintegration of its possessions in the Middle East, Allied ships on May 14, 1919, landed a Greek occupying force at Smyrna. "In so doing," says Professor Thomas, "the Allied Powers fully betrayed their basic ignorance of the foundation realities of the situation and of the area. What they were acting upon was the old, soft-headed philo-Hellene asumption that the Greeks were a 'superior' and 'European' people who could bring law, order, and light to the 'barbarian Turk' and who could at the same time 'redeem' at least those sections of western Anatolia which contained sizable Greek populations. Every item in that assumption was proved false in the next four years."

In this confused and, for the Turks, tragic situation Mustafa Kemal —thirty-eight years old, on May 19, 1919, five days after the Greek invasion at Smyrna—landed from an Istanbul ship at the Black Sea port of Samsun, and started on his career of forging a "Turkey for the Turks." To this task he brought ideas and methods which have profoundly influenced not only his own people but also the military leaders of other countries in Asia and the Middle East, notably Ayub Khan of Pakistan and Gamal Abdel Nasser of Egypt.

A man trained for military service, Kemal Ataturk displayed a remarkable comprehension of the revolutionary changes a traditional Muslim society like Turkey had to carry out if it was to become a modern state capable of dealing on equal terms with the Western powers, which at that very time were dividing among themselves portions of the Ottoman Empire in the Middle East—Palestine, Jordan, Syria, and Lebanon—assigned by the League of Nations as mandates to Britain and France. By mind and character he was well prepared for the complex task, fraught with many risks, of transforming the Turks into a people of the twentieth century. According to Professor Thomas, "he was ideally endowed to carve out a future and a destiny for himself and for his people. When ruthlessness was required, he was ruthless indeed. When circumstances required him to be politic or to dissemble, he excelled at these."

Ataturk had no intention of creating a military or even military-ruled state (and this has proved true also of Ayub Khan and Nasser). He assumed personal leadership, but he was determined to bring the "whole people"—and this meant not just the officers, but the peasants, then and still today 85 per cent of the population—into the operation of the state. He united conflicting groups and leaders under his rule, and on April 23, 1920, less than one year after his Samsun landing, he established a nationalist provisional government at Ankara, then the railhead of the line from Istanbul, now Turkey's capital. Although the Sultan still nominally reigned over what was left of the Ottoman Empire, Kemal Ataturk became the spokesman not for the Empire, but for the Muslim Turks of Anatolia and Thrace. Rallying them to the cause of defending their homeland against the Greek invaders, Ataturk, following a year's military campaign, captured Smyrna, September 9-11, 1922, and "the Greeks from Greece" were literally driven into the sea. Many Ottoman Greeks were also forced to leave during this struggle. At the end of the war Turkey and Greece carried out an exchange of populations which, painful as it was at the time for the human beings involved, is regarded as one of the most successful operations of its kind. Its completion cleared the way for subsequent co-operation between the two countries in the North Atlantic Treaty Organization and in more limited regional arrangements.

The removal of the Greeks and the pre-World War I expulsions of the Armenians, by force or otherwise, left Turkey with a highly homogeneous population. This, in turn, made it possible for Ataturk to carry out the four major reforms through which he fulfilled his goal of creating a "Turkey for the Turks."'These reforms were the establishment of a nation-state with a common language; the transformation of a Muslim society into a secular community; a series of measures concerning education, social customs, and the expression of ideas which altered the physical appearance as well as the intellectual content of Turkish life; and the development of the country's economy through measures taken or initiated by the state, known as *Etatism* (the term used for industrialization of the country through state initiative).

Ataturk's closest collaborator in this far-reaching transformation of his people was Ismet Pasha (later Inonu), a fellow officer, who had also become westernized but, unlike Ataturk, had preserved his belief in the traditional spiritual, and cultural values of the Turks. Inonu negotiated with the Allies after World War I, and under the Treaty of Lausanne, July 24, 1923, obtained recognition of Turkey as a state. Subsequently he served as prime minister from 1925-37, when he retired. He returned as president of Turkey after Ataturk's death in 1938 and remained in office until he lost the elections of 1950. In May, 1960, he played a key role in the overthrow of his successor, Adnan Menderes, by General Cemal Gursel.

The achievement of sovereignty by Turkey within its present boundaries was accepted by the Western powers at Lausanne, and the Turks, for their part, abandoned all claims to the Ottoman Empire. The Western powers relinquished the system of capitulations, under which Westerners had to be tried not under Turkish law, but by their own courts in Turkey. Today foreigners resident in Turkey are subject to Turkish law. The remaining minorities—Greeks, Jews, and Armenians—have been guaranteed basic civil rights. And under the Montreux Convention of April 11, 1936, which revised the Lausanne treaty, the Straits of the Dardanelles, the subject of centuries-old disputes between Turkey and Tsarist Russia, involving frequent intervention by Britain and France, were placed under the full control of Turkey, with the right to fortify them.

On October 29, 1923, three months after Turkey had achieved its sovereignty at Lausanne, Ataturk proclaimed the country an independent republic. This, says Thomas, "marked the formal starting point of the real Turkish Revolution; the systematic attempt quickly to evoke enough New Turks to ensure New Turkey's continuing survival." The first step toward that goal was the rapid westernization of the 15 per cent of the population—in business, the professions, the government, the army—who could be expected to lead the country toward the ultimate achievement of a Western-type society. Ataturk, unlike Inonu, had carried away from his own contacts with Western ideas and practices "disillusionment with and finally contempt for most of the old." Like Peter the Great of Russia two centuries earlier, he wanted to lose no time in westernizing Turkey's leadership. He started on this assignment by transferring the government from Istanbul, an international port city, to Ankara, then a dusty small town in the heart of Anatolia. The Turkish state, Ataturk proclaimed, would be a republic, modeled on Western parliamentary governments, with a unicameral legislature, the Grand National Assembly, which was to be responsible only to the voters. The legislators were to choose from their own ranks a president who would serve a four-year term, the same term as the members of the Assembly. The president, in turn, was to select a member of the Assembly as prime minister, who was to choose his cabinet from among the deputies, and who would remain in office as long as he commanded majority support.

The constitution of the new republic abolished the sultanate, but not yet the caliphate. To this extent, it retained the concept, basic to Islam, that the Koran is the foundation stone of the political order and Islam is not only a religion but also a way of life and of governance. This, however, proved a short-lived compromise. In 1924 the caliphate was abolished and the Ottoman dynasty went into exile. In 1928 the article which named Islam as the state religion was removed from the constitution, and Turkey became a secular state. The revolutionary character of this change can be understood only if one bears in mind that in 1947 the issue of secular versus religious state was one of the fundamental conflicts in India between the Hindus, who believe in secularism, and the Muslims led by Mohammed Ali Jinnah, who sought to create a state of Pakistan based on the Muslim faith.

The success of the secular republic appeared to have been demonstrated in the orderly elections of 1950, in which the ruling Republican party of Ataturk's successor, Inonu, was defeated by the Democratic party led by Adnan Menderes in a direct poll in which 87 per cent of the registered voters participated. By 1960, however, the Republicans increasingly complained against alleged undemocratic measures by the Menderes government (from censorship of the press and interference with education to suppression of the opposition's legitimate activities), and in a dramatic coup on May 27 General Gursel, backed by Ismet Inonu, took over power and proposed a series of governmental reforms. An important result of Ataturk's secularization of the state was that the Turks, unlike the Egyptians and the Arabs, relinquished all dreams of participation in a Pan-Islamic movement.

The third important step taken by Ataturk toward transforming Turkey into a modern state was a series of measures designed to alter the appearance and reorient the ideas of the Turks. The most dramatic of these were prohibition of the fez, traditional headgear of the Mussulman, which was to be replaced by a Western-type hat; and the injunction that religious garb was not to be worn in public, a final step in the downgrading of the Muslim Brotherhood, which had once played a key role in Islamic society.

These, however, were outer changes. A revolutionary inner change was the abolition, proclaimed by Ataturk at a public meeting in an Istanbul park in 1935, of the old Arabic script, which was to be replaced with a specially devised version of the Latin alphabet. The alphabet reform, vigorously carried out, has had the effect, as pointed out by Professor Thomas, of cutting off contemporary Turks from ancient works written in Arabic script, and thus from the sources of old Islamic ideas. But it has also had the effect, desired by Ataturk, of bringing the Turks into the mainstream of the writings, and thus of the ideas, of the West. The Turks, by abandoning the usage of other Muslim countries which still employ the Arabic script, found themselves able to make use of the vocabulary of the West, with its science and technology, and of such mechanical aids to government and business as European typewriters.

Through the new alphabet, Thomas writes, "the younger generation has had its own cultural past burnt for it. . . . Ataturk would have rejoiced at this, for he was out to kill the past." And the new alphabet, it is hoped, will accelerate literacy, which is still estimated at only about 50 per cent. Turkey's alphabet reform recalls the efforts of the Indian government, so far relatively unsuccessful, to introduce an arti-ficial language, Hindi, based on Hindustani, as the official means of communication between the states of India with their fourteen major languages; and the change in the alphabet of China, as radical as that of Turkey, made by Peiping in 1958.

The fourth basic reform launched by Ataturk was *Etatism*. The government, since the 1930's, has not only built a network of roads, designed primarily for military purposes and at present not used to any extent by private citizens because of the lack of cars, but has started a number of heavy industries, such as steel, and light industries, such as cement, boots and shoes, textiles, matches, and so on. Some of these have been sold to private owners, particularly during the regime of Menderes, who believed in private enterprise far more than did Ata-turk and Inonu.

The policy of *Etatism* has been subjected to more criticism by both Turks and Westerners than any other measure undertaken by Ataturk. These criticisms are summed up as follows by Thomas:

> Thanks to efforts exerted by the Republic since the early 1930's, Turkey now has a small heavy industry, poorly designed and poorly operated, plus a relatively small scattering of light industries, most of which are also poorly operated and designed. All this plant has been erected and is maintained at an incredibly heavy cost to the ultimate taxpayer, which is to say the peasant. Those few light industries which do pay a profit—especially the textile mills—are deliberately run at an excessive profit in order to help cover the losses of the other state enter-prises of *Etatism*. . . . [Moreover,] By financing this venture from the sweat of the taxpayers' and the consumers' defenseless brows, *Etatism* has had the lion's share in keeping Turkey a consistently expensive country in which to live, and so in helping keep the standard of living of almost all of its inhabitants extremely low.

Other commentators, however, point out that in Turkey, as in other underdeveloped countries, it is unrealistic to expect that the small minority who have any capital at all (usually land) will take the initiative in starting industrial enterprises which in their early stages present serious risks. Professor Thomas points this out when he says that "even its most rabid critics cannot claim that *Etatism's* accomplishments to date, faulty as they are, would have been duplicated or even faintly approached had the government not taken the initiative in some such fashion as it did." And the construction of industries, expensive and unsatisfactory as it may be, does satisfy the nationalist aspirations of the Turks for a Western-type economy, which Ataturk was determined to encourage. "Turkey," says Professor Thomas, "at least has a small industrial elephant, white though it is. The sensible thing is neither to kill the beast nor to spend time berating its past keepers, but rather to doctor it into health and the proper elephant color."

Whatever criticisms may be made of Ataturk's many-pronged reform program, it had the intended result of pulling Turkey up by its "bootstraps" into the ranks of modern nations. The "Preceptor of the Turks" in his private life had indulged in excesses of many kinds, from women to drink, which hastened his death on November 10, 1938, only a few days after the celebration of the republic's fifteenth birthday and less than a year before World War II. But he had the satisfaction of seeing the results he had envisioned achieved, and achieved with a minimum of internal conflict and violence. That the spirit of his reforms is still alive in Turkey is shown by General Gursel's dedication of his regime twenty-two years later to the ideas of Ataturk.

## DAVID BEN-GURION—
## ISRAEL

The prime minister of Israel was born in Plonsk, Poland, in 1886. His mother died when he was eleven years old. His father, Avigdor Green, a scholar who practiced law, had been an early adherent of Zionism.

Young David went to school first in Plonsk, then in Warsaw. At the age of fourteen he and other contemporaries formed a Zionist youth society called "Ezra." He gave up his studies four years later and traveled around Poland making speeches, organizing Zionist workers and directing strikes. As a student he had been arrested for his Zionist activities, but his father got him out of jail.

By that time, the early 1900's, thousands of Jews were emigrating from Eastern Europe to escape the ghetto conditions imposed on them in countries with predominantly Catholic and Russian Orthodox populations. David, deeply influenced by the ideas of Theodor Herzl, who spearheaded the Zionist movement and urged the return of dispersed

Jews to their ancient homeland, went with some of his friends to Palestine through Russia, enduring harsh conditions—near-starvation and malaria—which left him at twenty with a streak of gray in his hair.

After working first in Judea, then in Galilee, he settled down in Jerusalem in 1910 as a Zionist Workers' official and one of the editors of the magazine *Unity*. At that time he adopted the name of Ben-Gurion, a Jewish hero who had fought the Romans in the period shortly after the death of Christ. This name is derived from the Hebrew word for "young lion," which well symbolized the unflagging courage of the future prime minister in his determination to create a home for the Jews of the world. As Seth A. King of *The New York Times* said in his article, "A New Battle for Israel's 'Happy Warrior,'" in *The New York Times Magazine,* July 19, 1959, Ben-Gurion pitted himself "against anyone who stood in the way of his determination to help create a state of Israel or anyone since then who has opposed Israel's development or what Ben-Gurion believes must be done for her."

When World War I broke out Ben-Gurion was jailed, then expelled from Palestine, which at that time formed part of the Ottoman Empire. Undismayed, he went to the United States, where he married Paula Munweis, of Russian parentage, and in 1918 enlisted in the Jewish Legion, with which he trained in Canada. He was sent to Palestine with the rank of corporal, and served there under Lord Allenby. After the war his wife and small daughter joined him in Palestine.

Ben-Gurion rapidly rose to the leadership of Jewish organizations. In 1921 he founded the labor organization, Histradut; in the early 1930's he became the head of the Mapai party, a moderate socialist group, which he still leads in Israel; in 1933 he was made president of the Zionist Congress; in 1935 he was chosen chairman of the Jewish Agency, which played the role of "shadow government" for Palestine, with Ben-Gurion cast in the part of prime minister.

Throughout this period Ben-Gurion, basing himself on the Balfour Declaration in which Britain, during World War I, had promised the creation of a "Jewish home" in Palestine, pursued undeviatingly his dream of founding a Jewish state. He did this in spite of such setbacks as the failure of the 1939 conference of Arabs and Jews in London sponsored by Britain which, in the opinion of Jewish leaders, sought to appease the Arabs. When World War II broke out Ben-Gurion returned to London to press the Jewish cause. Always a voracious reader of history, he taught himself Greek in an air-raid shelter between raids because he wanted to study Thucydides on military strategy in the original.

During the war years Ben-Gurion shuttled from London, to Palestine, to New York, lining up support for the Jewish state which with the persecution of Jews by the Nazis had become the longed-for refuge for thousands of exiles and concentration-camp survivors. He hoped to persuade Britain, which ruled Palestine as a League of Nations mandate, of the urgency of admitting Jewish refugees in spite of growing Arab resistance, and to do so by peaceful means. But he found himself defied by terrorist groups, Irgun and the Stern Gang, whose leaders were convinced that force alone would gain Jews admission into Palestine.

On November 29, 1947, the efforts of Ben-Gurion, and of Chaim Weizmann, Russian-born British citizen and distinguished scientist who had also become deeply committed to the idea of a Jewish state, appeared to be about to bear fruit when the UN, with the support of the Western powers as well as of the USSR, created in Palestine two states—Jewish (Israel) and Arab (Arab Palestine, which never achieved the status of a state and parts of which were incorporated into Jordan in 1950). In 1948, however, Egypt and the Arab states (Jordan, Syria, Lebanon, and Iraq) with 30 million people, invaded Israel, with a population of 650,000. Following a military victory over the combined Egyptian-Arab forces, Ben-Gurion proclaimed Israel's independence in Tel Aviv on May 14, 1948, and became the new state's prime minister, thus achieving the goal he had sought since his boyhood in Poland of ending two thousand years of Jewish dispersion.

But strenuous years of building the new state still lay ahead, so strenuous that in 1953 Ben-Gurion resigned as prime minister, declaring that he was "tired, tired, tired." He moved away from Jerusalem and Tel Aviv to a *Kibbutz* at Sed Boker, in the Negev desert, where he lived and worked with other members of the collective settlement. Two years later, however, he was asked to return as minister of defense, and in November of that year he once more became prime minister. He remained unshaken by Israel's 1956 military campaign against Egypt, which ended with the intervention of the United States against the efforts of Israel, Britain, and France to defeat and overthrow Nasser after his nationalization of the Suez Canal, and the creation of a UN force to police the Gaza Strip, a buffer area between Israel and Egypt.

Today, the short, stocky, robust seventy-five-year-old Ben-Gurion, his massive head framed in a halo of thick white hair, looks back with pride at more than a decade of achievement by the new state. In 1919 there had been 60,000 Jews in Palestine. By 1947 their number had grown to 650,000 through immigration, mostly from Europe. In the decade 1947-57 Israel's population trebled, with a total figure of nearly two million, of whom about 1,800,000 were Jews from seventy-nine countries of Europe, the Middle East, Asia, Africa, the Americas, and over 200,000 Arabs. This large-scale immigration, which still continues, was the principal goal of the new state at its birth. The 1948 proclamation of independence said, "The State of Israel will be open to the immigration of Jews from all countries of their dispersion."

Ben-Gurion has led this multiracial population, ranging in experience from the most primitive (Yemenites and Moroccans), to the most technically skilled (Western Europeans, Americans, and South Africans), in the building of a secular state of Jewish faith which has achieved an outstandingly modern technological economy. Drawing on the world's most up-to-date scientific discoveries Israel has given its people living standards and welfare conditions comparable with those of the most advanced nations of the Western world. At the same time it has built up military defenses capable of withstanding attack by Egypt and the Arab states, and except for its brief Sinai war on Egypt in 1956 has abstained from resorting to open hostilities with its neighbors, which have so far refused to terminate the state of war technically ended in 1948. Ben-Gurion has repeatedly offered to make peace with Egypt and the Arab states, but Israel's neighbors have persisted in refusing to accept the situation created by the establishment of the Jewish state and the departure from Palestine (which they regard as an ouster) of Arabs now living as refugees around Israel's borders.

Not content with these achievements, Ben-Gurion looks forward with ever-fresh energy to Israel's future political, economic, and social development. In a CBS "Small World" television conversation on November 8, 1959, with Burma's Prime Minister U Nu, who counseled "meditation," Ben-Gurion said, "But meditation, my dear U Nu, is not enough. Meditation is merely a personal thing. Everyone of us must do something for the world, for humanity, and this cannot be done by meditation alone. The 'I' is not so bad in itself. The question is whether it's a selfish 'I' or a human 'I.' "

What Ben-Gurion still plans to do for the world he outlined in an article in the April 20, 1958, *New York Times Magazine,* in which he summed up Israel's first decade and looked ahead to the future. Here is what he said:

> In our second decade we must complete a number of tasks which we began in the first decade, and carry out several tasks which have yet to be begun.
>
> The main goal of our settlement work in the next ten years is to populate the South and Negev and establish agricultural and industrial settlements in Central and Upper Galilee. The first thing that is required for this purpose is the completion of the Jordan project so that the waters of the River Jordan may flow to the South and Negev and enable us to double the number of our agricultural settlements in those areas.
>
> From now onward, however, the concept of settlement must not be limited to agriculture. Israel's shipping, to the expansion of which there is hardly any limit, must occupy an important place in our constructive work, and the same applies to the development of mining and industry. During the next decade we shall develop and exploit solar and atomic energy and we may succeed in desalting sea water by a cheap and economic process. . . .
>
> During the next ten years we shall raise the standards of elementary, secondary and higher education, foster scientific research, and do all we can to attract men of intellect and science from all countries to Israel and to establish Jerusalem as a world center of science and culture.
>
> In the second decade we must complete the absorption and integration of all the immigrants who arrived during the decade, as well as taking in and absorbing several hundred thousand additional immigrants from the centers of distress in Europe, Asia and Africa and tens of thousands of pioneering youth from the prosperous countries of Europe, America and South Africa. From the Western countries we shall receive, in the main, a select and pioneering immigration. The driving force behind this

latter immigration will not be distress—for it is to be hoped that the Jews of the Western countries will not suffer from economic or political disabilities—but Israel's power of attraction.

During the next ten years we must enhance our scientific and technical skills, and our capacity and efficiency in work. Increased stability, strength, security and survival itself are possible only if we raise our high standards of quality in all spheres; the quality of our work in field and factory; the quality of our military service; the quality of our science and technology; the quality of the internal social relations among our people. . . .

If the Arab states understood the benefits to be obtained from peace and cooperation between neighbors, Israel would be ready to cooperate with them in the political, economic and cultural fields on a basis of equality and mutual assistance. I am convinced that not only would this be an important contribution to world peace, but it would be of advantage to the Arab peoples. . . .

In the meantime, Israel is determined to strengthen her military preparedness and to persevere in her work of rebuilding and redemption; to bring in Jews from the lands of oppression and misery; to conquer the desert and make it flourish by the power of science and the pioneering spirit, and to transform the country into a bastion of democracy, liberty and universal cultural values based on the teaching of Israel's prophets and the achievements of modern science.

This is Ben-Gurion's dream. But, while offering to help Israel's neighbors in the Middle East, Ben-Gurion has made it clear in another statement that the one fate he hopes to avert for Israel is that of becoming a "Levantine" country, that is, of becoming like Egypt and the Arab nations. In an address at the opening session of the Knesset (parliament) on October 24, 1960, Ben-Gurion said that Israel faced a graver danger from its own growing Levantine atmosphere than from the hostile Arab states that lie at its frontiers. He pointed out that almost 55 per cent of those who migrated to Israel since its beginning came from Africa and Asia. Jews in Islamic countries on both continents, he said, "lived in a society that was backward, corrupt, uneducated and lacking in independence and self-respect, and the damage done over hundreds of years cannot be repaired in a day." The older of these immigrants, Ben-Gurion declared, will not change basically, but the younger ones must be imbued with the "superior moral and intellectual qualities of those who created the state. . . . If, heaven forbid we do not succeed, there is a danger that the coming generation may transform Israel into a Levantine state." To ward off this danger, Ben-Gurion, in a much-discussed address before the twenty-fifth Zionist

Congress in Jerusalem on December 28, 1960, said that all Jews living in the Diaspora—outside Israel—should leave their countries and come to Israel, bringing the capital, skills, and knowledge urgently needed by the new state; and in support of his plea quoted the passage in the Talmud which says, "Whoever dwells outside the land of Israel is considered to have no God."

Meanwhile, there is another, also powerful, dream in the Middle East—the dream of Muslim identity expressed on behalf of Egypt and the Arab states by Gamal Abdel Nasser.

## GAMAL ABDEL NASSER—
## EGYPT

The president of Egypt—and of the United Arab Republic (UAR) in which Egypt has been joined with Syria since 1958—is a striking example of a man born in modest circumstances in an underdeveloped country who, amid social turmoil, rises to power by reason of training and success in the armed forces—like Ayub Khan in Pakistan, Ataturk in Turkey, and a roster of military men in Latin America.

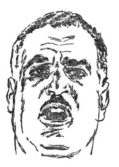

Gamal Abdel Nasser, of Arab origin, was born on January 5, 1918, in the thriving port city of Alexandria, famous in ancient as well as modern times for its luxury and in past ages for its intellectual leadership. His family came from Beni Mar, a small dusty village on the Nile where he spent most of his boyhood. Nasser's father was a post-office clerk; his mother, the daughter of a businessman. The future president displayed revolutionary tendencies and an interest in politics at an early age. He attended the Renaissance Secondary School in Cairo, studied law for a time, and then decided on a military career. He entered a military college in 1937, received his commission in 1938, and for a brief period served in the Sudan.

According to his autobiography, *The Philosophy of the Revolution,* Nasser became increasingly preoccupied with what he and some of his fellow officers regarded as Egypt's grave problems: the inadequacy of the monarchy under King Farouk, the domination of the country by Britain since 1882, the economic plight of the people. This concern was sharply increased after World War II, when the state of Israel was established in 1947 on the territory of Palestine, administered by Britain as a League of Nations mandate since the breakup in 1919 of the Turkish empire, which in World War I had been aligned with the Central Powers, Germany and Austria–Hungary, against Britain and France. At one time Nasser had been guided by extremists, notably Hadj Amin El Husseini, Grand Mufti of Jerusalem, who had supported the Nazis against the British. He had been an early member of the Muslim Brotherhood, a fanatical religious group, one of whose members made an attempt on the life of General Naguib in 1953. For a while Nasser flirted with the idea of assassinating Farouk. And once, as member of a youth group, Misr el Fatah, he took part in a murder plot against a Cabinet member which miscarried, much to his relief.

Egypt's failure to defeat Israel in the war the Arab nations waged against the new state in 1948 crystallized Nasser's conviction that King Farouk was unable to defend the country and to maintain its prestige. Like many other young officers, Nasser believed that Farouk and his government had grievously injured the country by squandering money on their own enhancement and amusement, instead of being concerned with the welfare and the security of the people, and had neglected to provide the army with the weapons it needed to defeat Israel.

Inspired by these ideas Nasser took the lead in organizing the Free Officers' Committee, out of which eventually grew the Council of Revolutionary Command, composed of nine officers. Naguib, who in 1952 led the movement for removal of Farouk and his expulsion from Egypt, was not a member of this committee. But by July, 1953, Nasser, who had not previously been known outside inner government circles, became Naguib's deputy prime minister and minister of interior. Six months later, in January, 1954, the Muslim Brotherhood, uneasy over the social changes being made or contemplated by the young officers, began to agitate against the government. On February 25, 1954, Naguib was forced to resign all major posts, and Nasser became premier and chairman of the Council of Revolutionary Command.

Then, for a brief period, due to fierce resistance in Cairo and from the Sudan, Nasser was forced to give up his government posts. On March 8, Naguib became premier again, while Nasser resumed the presidency. On March 27 a state of emergency was declared in Cairo. In October some of the members of the Muslim Brotherhood attempted to assassinate Nasser. The government moved swiftly to crush the Brotherhood, and six of its members were eventually hanged. The seesawing struggle for power between Naguib, who had sought prompt return to a normal parliamentary regime, and Nasser, who wanted to press forward with the revolution started by the ouster of Farouk, reached a climax in November, when Nasser removed Naguib from office and restricted him to living in his Cairo villa, a restriction which persists to this day.

Having thus disposed of his only important opponent, Nasser not only started to reorganize Egypt along the lines about which he had dreamed since his adolescence, but also, himself an Arab although Egypt is not an Arab country, asserted his leadership in the Arab world, as well as in Africa, and through union with Syria expanded Egypt into the UAR. Nasser, moreover, assumed an important role as a neutralist leader who, since his nationalization of the Suez Canal in 1956, commands one of the world's strategic waterways, and strives to maintain a balance of power between the USSR and the West, at the same time opposing Communist influence not only in the UAR but also in Iraq, Egypt's rival in the Middle East. In addressing his own people, Nasser often invokes the glories of ancient Egypt, and speaks of himself as the modern reincarnation of Saladin, the Muslim leader who held back the Crusade of Christian kings and princes. He is implying, of course, that modern Egypt must remain girded for the crusade now waged against it by the Western powers which support Israel, regarded by Egypt and the Arabs as an outpost of the West.

In spite of the dramatic role Nasser has assumed in Egypt, in the Middle East, and in the world, he is unostentatious in private life. A devout Muslim, he carefully observes the ritual of Islam, and never drinks. His wife, Tahia Mohamed Kazem, a talented pianist, never goes to the Koubbeh Palace, the president's official residence. Both she and her husband are known to enjoy the privacy of their house, with their five children, three daughters and two sons. It is at home that Nasser does most of his work. Six feet tall and weighing two hundred pounds, he has enormous energy, and can work for long stretches without sleep. He finds relaxation in watching movies and playing chess.

Those who know Nasser well describe him as disarmingly modest, but quick to lose his temper, and as a believer in the doctrine of "an eye for an eye." But most of all he impresses those around him with his dedication to the cause of advancing his country, which he has expressed in *The Philosophy of the Revolution*.

This small book is a distillation of the thoughts not only of Nasser as an individual, but of similar ideas held by many other Egyptians, as well as by leaders of other non-Western peoples, notably Sukarno of Indonesia and Ayub Khan of Pakistan. Its significance thus far exceeds the confines of one personality or one country.

*The Philosophy of the Revolution* was first published in 1953 as a pamphlet in an informational series sponsored by the Revolutionary Council under the general title, "We Have Chosen for You." This little book does not pretend to be a program for Egypt's future. As John S. Badeau, former president of the American University in Cairo, now president of the Near East Foundation, has pointed out in his introduction to the Economica edition of this book: "One reason why later political developments are not forecast in *The Philosophy* is because the Egyptian revolution has been largely pragmatic in character. As *The Philosophy* frankly states, the Free Officers started out without any very clear idea as to where they were going. Nasser likens them to an 'advance vanguard' storming the 'walls of the fort of tyranny.' But once the fort had fallen and the unlamented King had taken his unlamented farewell, there was no clear plan of action. Subsequent revolutionary policy—both internal and external—developed in response to immediate situations on a pragmatic basis, rather than as parts of any master plan."

Nasser himself declares that he does not "pretend to be a professor of history." He believes, however, that the July 23 revolution "is the realization of a hope that the people of Egypt, in modern times, have aspired to since they began to think of governing themselves and since they decided to be the masters of their fate." It was by his expression of frustration over Egypt's weaknesses—which he attributed both to

foreign domination and to misgovernment by Egyptian monarchs—
and of idealistic faith in the country's potential strength and success,
that Nasser became the spokesman of his people. As Dr. Badeau makes
clear, Nasser, to students of his generation, has been "both the symbol
and substance of the national regeneration that is their confused concern"— and this not only in Egypt, but also in Egypt's Arab neighbors.
At the height of the Palestine war, when officers' cells were meeting in
trenches and army posts for study and soul-searching, Nasser reports,
"Our bullets were aimed at the enemy lurking in the trenches in front
of us, but our hearts were hovering round our distant Mother Country,
which was then a prey to the wolves that ravaged it."

But, he asks, why did the duty of carrying out the changes needed
in Egypt "fall upon the army?" And he answers: " 'If the army does not
move,' we said to ourselves, 'who else will?' " Yet when the military had
taken the action they regarded as necessary, they found the task of
national regeneration had only begun. "We needed discipline but
found chaos behind our lines. We needed unity but found dissensions.
We needed action but found nothing but surrender and idleness. It
was from this source and no other that the revolution derived its motto"
(Unity, Discipline, Work).

Nasser's motto is based on the ideas of the Egyptian thinker and
reformer, Sheikh Muhammad 'Abduh (1849-1905), who believed,
according to Richard H. Nolte, that only a "just dictatorship, persuasion and force, could unite the community and instill healthy ideas. . . .
Fifteen years would be enough to build the necessary foundations for
free representative government. But without such a sound authoritarian regime, fifteen centuries would not suffice."

Nasser contends that he and his fellow officers had no desire to implement the revolution they had staged. He reports that in discussing
the future with "men of learning" at a university ("Many spoke and
spoke at length. Unfortunately not one of them presented a new
idea"), he said to them, "Do not look up to us. Circumstances have
compelled us to leave our posts to perform a sacred task. We sincerely
wish the country had no further use for us save as professional soldiers
in the army. There we would have remained."

But the prevailing state of affairs made the army the only force
capable of action. Here Nasser gives a description of the role of the
military in a technologically underdeveloped non-Western country
which could be applied to Argentina and Cuba, to Pakistan and Sudan:

"The situation demanded a homogeneous force. Its members should have faith in each other and should have in their hands such elements of material force as to ensure swift and decisive action. Such conditions did not prevail except in the army. It was not the army, as I mentioned, that determined its role in the events. The opposite is nearer the truth. It was the events and their evolution that determined for the army its role in the mighty struggle for the liberation of the country."

In the absence of other leadership, Nasser and his young officers proceeded to carry out the two revolutions which, he says, "Every nation on earth undergoes. . . . One is political, in which it recovers its right for self-government from an imposed despot, or an aggressive army occupying its territory without its consent.

"The second revolution is social, in which the classes of society would struggle against each other until justice for all countrymen has been gained and conditions have become stable." But, as Nasser points out, other nations have "passed through the two revolutions but not simultaneously. Hundreds of years separated the one from the other." What makes the situation of Egypt (and, one can add, of all non-Western countries) different from those of the West, is that "In the case of our nation, it is going through the two revolutions together and at the same time, a great experiment, putting us to the test." The two revolutions had to be wrought together. "The day we marched along the path of political revolution and dethroned Farouk we took a similar step along the path of social revolution by limiting the ownership of agricultural land." (On August 12, 1952, the new government announced its decision "in principle" to limit land ownership to 200 acres. The Agrarian Reform Law of September 9, 1952, embodied the 200-acre rule.)

As Nasser looks back on Egypt's ancient and glorious history, he sees the Crusades, led by Western Europeans, as "the commencement of the dark ages in our country," and thinks of himself as a modern defender of Islam against assaults from the West, symbolized today on Middle East soil by Israel. In contrast to European countries, which passed through their revolution in an orderly manner, in Egypt "everything was sudden . . . torrents of ideas and opinions burst upon us which we were, at that stage of evolution, incapable of assimilating. Our spirits were still in the Thirteenth Century though the symptoms of the Nineteenth and Twentieth Centuries infiltrated in their various aspects. Our minds were trying to catch up the advancing caravan of humanity." But the tasks of modernizing a country which lives in many centuries at one and the same time did not overwhelm Nasser. "I can comprehend," he writes, "the bewilderment and the confusion that assail us. Then I say to myself, 'This society will crystallize; its component parts will hold together; it will form a homogeneous entity; but this necessitates that we should strain our nerves during the period of transition.'"

As Nasser looked outward from Egypt, he saw his country facing three circles: the Arab circle, to which it is joined by religion and geography; the circle of the continent of Africa, where Egypt, a Middle East nation, also lies; and "the circle that goes beyond continents and oceans . . . the circle of our brethren in faith," the Muslims of Indonesia, China, Malaya, Thailand, Burma, Pakistan, the USSR.

What is to be Egypt's role with respect to these three circles? Nasser, recalling the play of the Italian dramatist and novelist, Luigi Pirandello, *Six Characters in Search of an Author,* imagines that "in this region in which we live, there is a role wandering aimlessly about seeking an actor to play it. I do not know why this role, tired of roaming about in this vast region which extends to every place around us, should at last settle down, weary and worn out, on our frontiers beckoning us to move, to dress up for it and to perform it since there is nobody else who can do so." This role, he contends, is not a leading role. "It is one of interplay of reactions and experiments with all these factors aiming at exploding this terrific energy latent in every sphere around us and at the creation, in this region, of a tremendous power capable of lifting this region up and making it play its positive role in the construction of the future of humanity."

With fervent belief in Egypt's destiny and potential power, Nasser declares, "Such is the role, such are its features and such is its stage. We, and only we, are compelled by our environment and are capable of performing this role."

In the performance of this role, Nasser has so far sought to lead the Arabs in unyielding opposition to Israel, and to all countries, great or small, which have shown friendship for that country.

# 3

# Asia

THE WESTERNER, on his first visit to Asia, may experience one of two reactions. He may become enraptured with the color and movement of Asian life, with the beauty of ancient monuments—the Ellora temples carved out of rock in India and the colorful temples of Bangkok reflected in the turbid River Menam; with the purity of the Muslim Taj Mahal; with the mysterious ruins of Angkor Vat hidden deep in the Cambodian jungle; with the shrines of Japan amid well-tended groves, against a backdrop of snow-capped mountains; and, if he was fortunate enough to travel before China became *terra prohibita,* by memories of the magnificent palaces of imperial Peking. He may be held in thrall by the fluid Indian dance; Japan's Kabuki theater with its stately ritual, controlled passions and magnificent costumes; the arts and crafts redolent of centuries-old skills. Or he may, instead, be appalled by the poverty, disease, and filth which he cannot fail to see in village mud huts and in the slums of Calcutta, Hong Kong, and Singapore, and succumb to a feeling of despair at the thought that it is useless to try to alter man's terrifying fate in Asia. If he can maintain a balanced view, he may depart with both impressions, for both are true.

Yet had the Westerner lived a thousand years ago he would have felt at home in Asia, at home with both its beauty and its poverty. For at that time it was not Europe, which Nehru has called "a peninsula of Asia," but Asia which was the center of the universe. Here is how Nehru describes Asia and Europe one thousand years ago in his book, *Glimpses of World History,* written in the form of letters to his then teen-age daughter Indira during one of the many periods he spent in jail under British rule:

> Asia. The old civilizations of India and China still continue and flourish. Indian culture spreads to Malaysia and Cambodia and brings rich fruit there. Chinese culture spreads to Korea and Japan and, to some

extent, Malaysia. In western Asia, Arabian culture prevails in Arabia, Palestine, Syria and Mesopotamia; in Persia or Iran, there is a mixture of the old Iranian and the newer Arabian civilization. Some of the countries of Central Asia have also imbibed this mixed Iranian-Arabian civilization, and have also been influenced by India and China. In all these countries there is a high level civilization; trade and learning and the arts flourish; great cities abound; and famous universities attract students from afar. Only in Mongolia and in some parts of Central Asia, as well as in Siberia in the north, is the level of civilization low.

Europe now. It is backward and semi-barbarous compared to the progressive countries of Asia. The old Greco-Roman civilization is just a memory of the distant past. Learning is at a discount; the arts are not much in evidence; and trade is far less than in Asia. . . . Over the greater part of Europe there is frequent disorder and, under the feudal system which prevails, each knight and lord is a little king in his domain. Rome, the imperial capital of old, at one time had been hardly bigger than a village, and wild animals had lived in its old Colosseum. But it is growing again.

So if you compared the two, Asia and Europe, one thousand years after Christ, the comparison would have been greatly to the advantage of Asia.

But, as Nehru points out, at that very moment India and China were on the verge of decline, while Europe was entering a period of stirring development during which, after mastering science and technology, it advanced economically and socially through the Industrial Revolution, politically through the English, American, and French revolutions, and reached out overseas to build empires in Asia, Africa, Latin America, and the Middle East.

Asia, left far behind, was subjected to encroachments by the Western powers through trade (the British East India Company in India, the penetration of Western commerce into China), through military pressures (Western gunboats traveling up the Yangtze River), and through political intervention (with the United States reinforcing Japan against Russia at the end of the Russo-Japanese war of 1904-05, only to see Japan later become the invader of China whose territorial integrity Washington had sought to preserve in the hope of maintaining there an open door for the commerce of all nations). Memories of past glories—of great religions which swayed Asia—Hinduism, Buddhism, Confucianism; of art, music, and literature; of successful administration by dedicated rulers like India's Emperor Asoka, who would have well fitted Plato's ideal of the philosopher–king—made contemporary abuses at the hands of Western colonial invaders all the more intolerable. Memories of grievances affected the attitude of Asian peoples toward Western nations, whom they accused of "imperialism," until, with the rise of military fascism in Japan, after World War II of communism in China, and the rapid withdrawal of the West, it became evident that imperialism is a concomitant not of race or color, but of a given stage of national development and nationalist desire for expansion.

Events in the non-Western world have been moving at such a breath-taking pace since World War II that current trends in Africa become merged in the mind of reader or viewer with earlier developments in Asia. Yet a closer look reveals not only comparisons but also significant contrasts between the two continents.

Africa with its "lost cities" has few monuments, and an ancient experience still being slowly reconstructed by anthropologists and archaeologists. Asia, with its millennial history recorded in holy books, epics, laws graven on rocks and iron pillars, and vast stores of art and architecture, lives today among the riches of past ages. Asia's heritage of belief and custom may slow down its modernization, as in India or in static-appearing Thailand. By contrast Africa's lack of living mementos may leave the way clear for rapid new growth into twentieth-century conditions.

While both Asia and Africa have experienced Western colonial rule, this experience shows significant differences. Some of the Asian countries have been ruled by Western nations for long periods of time. This was true of India, with two hundred years of East India Trading Company administration, followed by nearly one hundred years of rule by the British Crown; and of Indonesia, where the Dutch governed for three hundred and fifty years. Under the best of circumstances, Western rule brought benefits to Asia. India, for instance, after independence, freely acknowledged its indebtedness to Britain. This, however, was not true when the Western ruler did little or nothing to advance Asian subjects toward self-government, as in the Dutch East Indies and French Indochina.

In Africa the Western powers, most of whom had ruled for less than one hundred years before the wane of colonialism, had little opportunity, even had they so desired, to prepare their subjects for self-government; and the white man's disdain toward Africans (far greater than toward Asians, whose cultural contributions were recognized at least by the discriminating) made a relationship of equality between white and nonwhite more difficult to achieve than in Asia.

Moreover, the Western powers' haphazard division of Africa into areas carved out for strategic or economic or communications purposes, but with little or no concern for tribal affiliations, left Africa with a multiplicity of small units. Compare this with the vast, relatively intact territories of great nations—India and China—and the cohesive Japanese islands, with a homogeneous population insulated from the rest of the world until 1854; not to speak of Thailand, once Siam, which escaped foreign rule altogether, and succeeded in maintaining its character relatively unchanged into our own times.

The preservation of territorial integrity by several of the Asian nations served them well when the twilight of colonialism set in. Japan, once it had admitted foreigners, voluntarily selected those Western political and economic institutions which it regarded as worth integrating with its own, and promptly acquired the aspect and technological capacity of a modern Western state.

China, after suffering encroachments by several Western powers, as well as by Russia, both Tsarist and Communist, withdrew under communism behind the Bamboo Curtain and, by tremendous effort, is transforming its primarily agrarian economy into an industrial economy which may soon be capable of matching Britain in the output of steel—but for a population 600 million larger.

India, having acquired under British rule an experience in administration which greatly eased the reorganization of the subcontinent into a nation-state, is now intent on catching up to China in the modernization of its economy without abandoning its democratic practices.

The long political experience of Japan, China, and India has no counterpart in Africa. There, peoples newly emerging from Western colonial rule are struggling to improvise political institutions to meet their practical needs. The most crucial of their immediate political problems is that of welding many tribes (for example, in the Belgian Congo) into viable national states. If we in the West think this task intractable, we should recall the difficulties experienced by Burma with its restless border tribes, and remember, much further back, that in Europe the Germanic tribes were not welded into a nation until 1871.

Beset with the many tasks of the first stages of independence, the African nations may sometimes appear more impatient, less tolerant of the Western powers, more insistent on a faster pace of action by the West and by the UN, on questions which deeply affect them (Algeria, South Africa, France's nuclear tests in the Sahara) than the Asian nations, which are a few years ahead of them in experience. In the

Asian-Arab-African bloc, India, Burma, and Ceylon often sound like elder brothers restraining the younger, more impassioned African nations. This appears to have been true, for example, in the South Africa debate of the UN Security Council on April 1, 1960, during which India and Ceylon spoke with statesmanlike moderation, in spite of the fact that India has intervened again and again in recent years to defend the rights of Indians in the Union of South Africa, who are listed, and treated, as "coloreds." But even the African countries, aroused as they were over the ill-treatment of Africans in Capetown and Johannesburg, showed unexpected restraint. Ethiopia, Ghana, Tunisia, Guinea, and Liberia, all indicated their desire not merely to deplore the actions of the white man, but to make it possible for him to reform his ways—"to build a bridge and not a wall," as Henry Cabot Lodge, former head of the United States delegation to the United Nations, put it in his speech to the Security Council.

In part this restraint is due to the influence of Asia's elder nations. In part it is also due to the new realization in Africa, as well as Asia, that colonialism is no longer a monopoly of white nations, and may also be imposed by nonwhites. This was indicated by delegates from nineteen Asian and African nations who gathered in New Delhi on April 9-11, 1960, at the Afro-Asian Convention on Tibet and Against Colonialism in Asia and Africa. The convention discussed Algeria and racial violence in South Africa, but its main focus was on Tibet.

In dealing with the countries of Asia we must recognize that the peoples of this area (like those of Russia, sections of Eastern Europe, the Middle East, Africa, and Latin America) have not shared the experiences of Western Europe and the United States. They have long and glorious histories of their own; they have forged great civilizations based on Hinduism, Buddhism, Islam; they have made distinguished contributions to the cultural heritage of the world through their religions, philosophies, architecture, art, literature, music. But their political, economic, and social development, for a variety of historical reasons, has been profoundly different from that of Western peoples.

It is therefore unrealistic to expect that, merely because in the last decade the peoples of Asia have achieved independence from the colonial rule of Western powers—Britain, France, the Netherlands—they will simultaneously bridge the gap of centuries which separates them from Western Europe and the United States and establish political institutions familiar to the Western democracies. We must show understanding of the myriad difficulties faced by the technologically underdeveloped peoples of Southeast Asia in achieving what we call democracy. Nor should we urge them to set up democratic institutions which may prove merely a façade for continued authoritarianism, as proved to be the case in Japan before Pearl Harbor.

Instead, we should face the fact that the peoples of Asia, who are wrestling with tremendous problems of population growth, demand for land reform, shortages of food, tensions and maladjustments resulting from the early stages of industrialization, and internal stresses between various political, racial, and linguistic groups, need today and probably for many years to come strong governments capable of maintaining the unity of newly independent nations, of modernizing their economies, of carrying out necessary but often harsh reforms, and of protecting their territories against encroachments by their neighbors.

This means that we shall have to accept the existence in Asia of authoritarian governments of one kind or another, whether they be the military dictatorship of Ayub Khan in Pakistan, or the military rule of General Ne Win in Burma (terminated in the spring of 1960), or the "guided democracy" of Sukarno in Indonesia, or the military dictatorship of Thailand. The best we can hope for in this area is authoritarianism without totalitarianism. Such a government assumes the authority to take whatever measures it regards as desirable without consulting the citizens, but at the same time assures civil liberties and does not seek to brainwash or indoctrinate the people, as has been done by Communists in China and Russia.

In our relations with these authoritarian governments, we should avoid criticizing them for not being democratic in the Western sense of the term. Instead, we should commend them for all steps they take to improve the welfare and protect the personal freedom of their people. The governments of Asia, whatever their political label, find themselves forced to take measures which many Americans may criticize as tantamount to "socialism," if not to "communism," for the simple reason that they must control and direct, more or less strictly, their countries' economic and social development. Otherwise they risk stagnation and hence continued misery, which produces rising discontent threatening internal upheavals. We must therefore rid ourselves of fear about "socialism" in Asia, and accept the fact that even governments we regard as "conservative" cannot escape intervening in the operation of their countries' economies. However, we should not hesitate to point out the features of our own democratic institutions of which we are particularly proud, and at the same time do everything in our power to correct defects in our society which weaken our arguments abroad on behalf of democracy, notably with respect to our Negro fellow citizens.

In this over-all picture of nontotalitarian authoritarianism in Asia, two countries appear as exceptions: India and Japan. India, like other Asian countries, lacks the elements which the West usually regards as prerequisites of democracy: 1. a homogeneous population of manageable size; 2. natural resources sufficient for a viable economy, with a balanced ratio of resources to population; 3. a strong middle class; 4. large-scale industrialization; 5. universal literacy. In spite of this, India, through an exceptional combination of its own religious and philosophical traditions, its political experience under enlightened rulers such as the Hindu Emperor Asoka and the Muslim ruler Akbar, and the comprehension of the basic concepts of Western democracy which it absorbed from the British during the period of colonial rule, has developed new patterns of democracy in which Western ideas and practices have been adapted to Indian traditions. The success of the Indian form of democracy, as contrasted with the totalitarian system of Communist China, may determine whether other countries of Asia will, in the future, choose India as a model in preference to China. But even in India the stupendous task of transforming a premedieval village society into a modern state capable of making use of atomic energy for peacetime purposes has been carried out under the direction of an outstanding "charismatic" leader, Jawaharlal Nehru, who, however, in contrast to the leaders of other Asian nations, has respected and made effective use of democratic institutions.

In contrast to India, Japan, having made an early start on modernization a century ago, has succeeded in creating a modern industrialized economy, has achieved a high degree of literacy, and has developed a significant and influential middle class. It has not, however, succeeded in solving the many problems created by its large population which, although now subject to various forms of regulation, continues to press dangerously on its resources. Following their military defeat in World War II, the Japanese established a parliamentary democracy and reduced the role of the once-dominant emperor to that of a ceremonial head of state.

But it is not clear whether the Japanese have absorbed the ideas of Western-type democracy, either in their political life or in their relations with each other. Experts fear, particularly after the June, 1960, riots against the government of former Premier Nobusuka Kishi that, in the foreseeable future, Japan, while outwardly a two-party state, will continue to be ruled by one party, the Conservatives, much as West Germany, although a two-party country, has long been ruled by the conservative party of Chancellor Konrad Adenauer. Should the possibility of political change continue to be blocked, it is not impossible that communism may make greater gains in Japan than in India, where a more flexible political system and a greater degree of self-criticism permit the existence of a variety of smaller parties which can, and do, challenge the ruling Congress party. Given these circumstances, it is particularly important that the United States should be acquainted and maintain contacts with the nonconservative groups in Japan, and not give the impression that it is committed solely and irrevocably to the conservatives as the bastion of our security in Asia.

The countries of Asia now, and for years to come, will require substantial aid both in terms of money and of technical know-how of all kinds. This can come from several sources: the United States; the industrial nations of Western Europe, primarily Britain and West Germany; Japan; the USSR and the industrial nations of Eastern Europe, notably Czechoslovakia; the Colombo Plan, under which Commonwealth countries led by Britain, in co-operation with the United States, work jointly with Asian nations for the latters' development; international financial agencies such as the World Bank, the International Monetary Fund, and the newly created International Development Loan Association; specialized international agencies such as the Food and Agriculture Organization and the World Health Organization; and the UN technical assistance program.

In planning future aid to Asia, the following considerations should be borne in mind:

1. It is estimated that aid will be required for some fifty years if the countries of Southeast Asia are to reach the point of "take-off" for modern economic development. Of all the countries in this area India alone is regarded as being at the take-off stage; because of this India is in particularly urgent need of expanded aid so that it will not lose the momentum already achieved. Thus the United States should make long-term plans for aid to this area.

Long-term planning is essential for the Asian governments, which are trying to map out their economic needs and set their targets in stated periods, usually of five years. The practice followed by the United States of voting foreign-aid appropriations on an annual basis (with uncertainty every year both on the part of the Executive and of the nations requesting aid as to what will be the final outcome of Congressional debates) should be replaced by a system under which long-term (preferably five-year) appropriations would be voted, subject to Congressional review at the end of every fiscal year.

2.  Aid is needed for several purposes: for the modernization and diversification of agriculture; for the building of each country's infrastructure—roads, dams, transportation facilities, irrigation projects, and so on, which are essential to create a base for industrialization; for the construction of industrial enterprises, whether light or heavy industries, depending on available raw materials; for the training of personnel in modern science and technology; for the creation of educational facilities; and for the expansion of community development projects, which have the triple purpose of accelerating the transformation of village life, of increasing agricultural productivity, and of encouraging grass-roots self-government.

Private investors and philanthropic foundations can and do make a valuable and welcome contribution to some of these tasks. At the present stage of development, however, the bulk of aid will have to come from governments or international agencies, either because the projects to be undertaken cannot bring the financial returns which private investors legitimately expect, or because the size of the funds required is beyond the resources of private investors and philanthropies —or both. Experience shows that contributions by our government cannot be effectively replaced by private investment or by private charity, although both should be encouraged to the utmost.

3.  The scope and variety of aid required by Asia are so vast that there will be plenty of room for every country and every agency which can be enlisted in this task. The United States should not oppose aid by the USSR and the countries of Eastern Europe; on the contrary, it should welcome such aid. If our objective is to speed up the technological development and the welfare improvement of Asia, aid from any quarter can prove useful. We should not fear competition by the Communist countries; we should invite it by challenging them to outdo us in generosity, efficiency, and quality of performance. Unless

the United States economy suffers grave retrogression, this country should be able to succeed in such a competition.

Nor should we refuse aid to Communist countries if it is requested. We are already giving aid to Communist countries in Eastern Europe —Poland and Yugoslavia. The emergence of new Communist regimes is not at present anticipated in Asia. However, the United States might make a powerful impression on countries in this area by declaring that—once Peiping has been admitted to the UN—it would be ready to give aid to Communist China, which now relies almost exclusively on financial and technological aid from the Soviet bloc.

4. In the long run, however, national aid, whether by individual countries or by countries grouped in some new agency (such as the one proposed in 1960 by then Undersecretary of State C. Douglas Dillon for Western Europe, Canada, and the United States) may prove less desirable and less effective than the channeling of aid through world-wide international agencies, and particularly through the UN technical assistance program, as urged by Paul G. Hoffman, managing director of the UN Special Fund. Competition in aid to underdeveloped countries by the West and by the Soviet bloc has many advantages for the recipient countries, which are now in a position to play one side off against the other; but such competition, although clearly preferable to the cold-war struggle, continues to have political overtones. If all the technologically advanced nations (and this group now includes the USSR in addition to the United States, Canada, the Western European nations, and Japan) could be persuaded to pool their resources and place them under the administrative supervision of the UN, three gains would be achieved:

a. The pooled aid could be allocated to the nations requiring aid at periodic meetings attended by both donors and recipients, as is now done under the highly successful Colombo Plan. The psychological tensions created by the recurring need of each country to go hat in hand to Moscow or Washington, London or Bonn, for one kind of aid or another, would be eliminated, and a genuine partnership between the "have" countries and the "have-nots" would be created.

b. The pooling of aid would permit long-term planning on a regional basis, thereby eliminating the dangers of duplication of requests for aid, overemphasis on individual projects, and nationalistic demands for developments which may contribute to a country's prestige but not enhance its over-all development. The success achieved by Western

Europe in pooling its resources to develop Euratom (European Atomic Community) is an example of what might be done in Southeast Asia.

c. The administration of aid by the UN would permit strict supervision of the use made by each country of the funds allocated for its development, without the danger that such supervision—essential to the honest and efficient operation of all aid programs—will be denounced by the recipient as an act of "imperialism" or "intervention" or "strings attached" by the contributing nation. Then distressing episodes such as the alleged mismanagement of United States aid to Laos and South Vietnam could be avoided.

It must therefore be hoped that the United States will overcome its present reluctance to channel the bulk of its aid funds through international agencies, and instead take the lead in urging this method of administering aid for underdeveloped countries.

The economic position of Japan is in sharp contrast to that of the countries of Southeast Asia. Japan is a highly industrialized and technologically competent nation. In spite of its population problem, it is a "have" nation, with a standard of living infinitely superior to that of any of its Asian neighbors. Because of its financial and technological resources it is in a position to give aid to less developed countries. However, the Southeast Asian countries which suffered from Japanese conquest during World War II—particularly the Philippines and Indonesia—do not share the enthusiasm of the United States for Japan, and while eager to obtain reparations for war damages inflicted by the Japanese, are not always eager for aid or trade with Japan if other sources of assistance and other markets are available. Channeling aid through the UN would make it possible to use contributions by Japan, a member of the UN, without the stigma of the national label.

Meanwhile, Japan itself needs aid, but of another kind. To maintain its present standard of living and, hopefully, to improve it, the Japanese will need to find expanding markets overseas for their varied manufactured goods. Unless the United States can enlarge its purchases of Japanese products such as textiles, cameras, stainless-steel cutlery, and so on, Japan will have to look elsewhere for customers. While the countries of Southeast Asia need the consumer goods as well as the heavy-industry products of Japan, they do not always have the foreign currency to make purchases there, and some find it necessary to buy from Communist China on a barter basis. Meanwhile India and Communist China now compete with Japan in the export of various goods: India particularly in textiles, Communist China in a wide range of products, from textiles to bicycles and flashlights. The presence in several Asian countries (Thailand, Indonesia, the Philippines) of large Chinese communities totaling 12 million people, facilitates Peiping's export drive in the area. The one important exception to this situation is India, which was not invaded by Japan in World War II. Japan now obtains there some of its raw materials, notably iron ore, and enjoys a market for machinery and other manufactured goods. In the long run, however, the Japanese may have to seek markets in Communist China, and they can be expected to do so if and when Peiping is admitted to the UN, or even before.

A new and highly controversial question about foreign aid has been raised in connection with the problem of population growth in the underdeveloped countries, including some in Asia, notably India. A population explosion, as is well known, results from a sharp decline in the death rate due to medical improvement and public-health measures, with no corresponding decline in the birth rate. The 1959 report of the Draper Committee, entrusted by President Eisenhower with the task of reviewing United States military and economic aid, stated that "no realistic discussion of economic development can fail to note that development efforts in many areas of the world are being offset by increasingly rapid population growth." The Committee recommended that, in order to meet more effectively the problems of economic development, the United States should, among other things, "assist those countries with which it is co-operating in economic aid programs, on request, in the formulation of their plans designed to deal with the problem of rapid population growth."

The Draper report brought a strong statement on November 25, 1959, by the Roman Catholic Bishops of the United States opposing birth-control aid by government agencies. So far as can be ascertained, no country has requested the United States for information about birth control, which is now a matter of common knowledge throughout the world. What several underdeveloped countries, notably India, seek are two things: increased economic aid so that they can allocate more of their own resources to population-regulation measures they have chosen to undertake (in India, as well as in Japan, the governments support programs of birth control and sterilization, and abortion is widely practiced in Japan); and intensification in the United States of research, such as is being conducted in Puerto Rico on a limited scale, for the discovery of a contraceptive which might be useful under conditions existing in underdeveloped areas.

The views of all religious groups are entitled to respectful consideration. The question must be faced, however, whether the United States can continue to assist death control, through aid to public health and improved welfare in the Asian countries, without taking some responsibility for the resulting population pressures which arise in the absence of birth control. If the United States government is precluded from adopting the measures proposed by the Draper Committee, then American political leaders have a responsibility to urge increased efforts by private organizations and individuals in this country to bring nearer, through research and other means, the day when underdeveloped countries can, of their own free choice, and with the support of leaders of their own religious faiths, deal effectively with population growth in their territories.

In Asia, as in other non-Western areas of the world, the United States since the onset of the cold war has been confronted with three categories of nations: those which, like North Vietnam and North Korea, support the Communist bloc; those which, like India, Burma, Ceylon, and Indonesia, have chosen not to become aligned with either of the two blocs—the non-Communist bloc led by the United States or the Communist bloc led by the USSR; and those which, like Pakistan, Thailand, the Philippines, South Korea, and South Vietnam, have chosen to take a strong stand against the Communist bloc and to accept military aid from the United States.

For many years after the Korean War the United States was highly critical of what it first called "neutrality," and later "neutralism," although official statements on this point did not always harmonize. (Thus in 1956 Secretary of State John Foster Dulles, referring to India, said "Neutralism is immoral," while at approximately the same time President Eisenhower declared that he understood the policy of India, which made him think of the no-foreign-commitment policy of the United States under George Washington.) Many American spokesmen continued to ask Mr. Nehru: "Are you with us or against us?" If they meant that India had to decide for or against democracy this was a futile question, since India had answered it immediately after achieving independence when it voluntarily joined democratic Britain in the Commonwealth. Meanwhile, in the South East Asia Treaty Organization (SEATO) the United States backed the countries of the area which had pledged themselves to oppose Communist aggression and gave each of them military aid.

During 1959 this policy underwent a noticeable, and in 1960 explicitly formulated, change. By 1961 the United States had accepted nonalignment as a position worthy of respect, and no longer subject, as in the past, to criticism and derision. President Eisenhower, during and after his spectacular visit to India, indicated that he was deeply impressed by that country and by its leader, Mr. Nehru, and in 1960 urged increased aid to India. Neutralism has become not only respectable, but desirable, as President Eisenhower made clear in his September 22, 1960, address to the UN General Assembly. In fact, the United States may find that, with the decrease in emphasis on the military aspects of the East-West struggle, military commitments in Asia need to be de-emphasized.

Three facts are coming to be generally recognized:

1. Military aid given by the United States may be a burden, rather than a boon, for underdeveloped countries; they need every ounce of their resources, in terms of money, trained manpower, and raw materials, to develop their economies as rapidly as possible. In order to utilize United States military aid they have to expend a considerable portion of their own limited resources; for example, Pakistan allocates 70 per cent of its budget for defense. As a result, United States aid often leads to inflation, which causes economic maladjustments and political unrest. The question therefore arises whether it would not be wiser for the United States to increase its economic aid and decrease its military aid, in the hope that the recipient country will then strengthen itself through internal development and resulting political stability, both of which may have to be held in abeyance if attention continues to be focused on defense.

2. Assuming that both power blocs agree to impose a permanent nuclear test ban and initiate phased disarmament, the United States may find that it will no longer need bases around the periphery of the USSR and Communist China, but that instead it should place its chief reliance on long-range missiles to be delivered from its own territory or from mobile platforms, for example, Polaris submarines. Should such a decision ultimately emerge from the debate about United States defense policy, this would sharply reduce the value of military installations in Southeast Asia. It might then be advisable to give only minimum military aid in the form of experts and a limited range of non-nuclear weapons to the governments in this area for the training of local troops to be used primarily for the maintenance of law and order, possibly under UN supervision, as the United States has proposed doing in Africa.

3. If such a decision is reached, it would reduce the tensions between some of the countries of Asia which have hitherto feared that United States military aid given to one of them would be used eventually not against the USSR or Communist China but against a neighbor (as in the case of India and Pakistan). Such reduction of tensions would, in turn, lead to political stabilization in the area and encourage long-term economic development.

4. Once the military aspects of the East-West struggle are de-emphasized, nonalignment, instead of being a threat to the United States, might be an advantage, for while the nonaligned countries would not be committed to the United States, neither would they be committed to the Soviet bloc. Thus the nonaligned countries would in effect form a demilitarized, denuclearized zone between the two blocs hitherto arraigned against each other.

Such a change in our policy about military pacts and military aid would involve a review of our attitude toward Japan, now regarded as our principal ally in Asia. Many Japanese have had reservations about their country's military alliance with the United States, even after we accepted in 1959 a number of modifications of the United States-Japanese security treaty favorable to Japan. Nor are the Japanese, shocked by their experience in World War II and impressed by our arguments against their future participation in war, eager to rearm. Under these circumstances, the question arises whether, in an emergency, the security of Japan would be more effectively safeguarded by the use of United States long-range missiles than by the presence of American troops and/or weapons on Japanese territory.

The future of Asia, and of Asia's relations with the United States, is being shaped both by leaders now living, and by some no longer alive whose memory continues to inspire their countrymen. Who are, or were, these men?

## U NU—

## BURMA

U Nu, premier of Burma, described by an English writer, Hugh Tinker, as "the Serene Statesman," was born on May 25, 1907, at Wakema, in an area of rich paddy fields. His father was a small trader. After completing his studies at a local school and at the Myoma

National High School in Rangoon, one of the independent institutions established by the Burmese nationalists after their 1920 boycott of schools and colleges operated by the British, U Nu took his B.A. degree at the University of Rangoon. He then turned to teaching, and served as superintendent of the National School at Pantanaw, in the Delta district. He also joined a new political group, *Do Bamà Asi-ayon* ("We Burmans"), also known as the Thakins, who opposed British rule.

In 1934 U Nu returned to the university to read law, and became active in student affairs, being known to his fellow students as *Ko* (elder brother). Elected vice president of the university Students' Union for 1934-35, he became president the year after. The Union was then determined to overthrow British rule, by violence if necessary. After a series of clashes with university authorities, in the course of which U Nu was suspended, the students staged a strike and the British authorities yielded to their forceful methods.

During his student days U Nu became known for his gift as an orator. In contrast to his early emphasis on violence, he later became deeply devoted to Buddhism, the principal tenets of which are humility and love of peace. The extent to which U Nu's attitude altered after his stormy university days is indicated by the apologies, later made public, which he offered to the former British principal of University College during his visit to England in 1955, when he said he "now realized that the strike was a grave mistake, a disservice to the university and to Burma."

In the interval, however, U Nu had continued his attacks on the British, first through political pamphlets and books published under the auspices of a literary and political organization, *Naga Ni* (Red Dragon Society), and later through the activities of the Thakins, who organized a "private army," stirred up industrial unrest in the oil fields, and established contact with Japanese agents. On the eve of World War II the British in Burma interned U Nu, along with other Thakin leaders, and put him in jail in Mandalay. Subsequently released, he unsuccessfully attempted to flee to China, then returned to Rangoon— a hegira he described in his autobiography, *Five Years' Season in Burma.*

On his return U Nu served as foreign minister in the puppet government headed by Ba Maw, set up by the Japanese who had conquered Burma and driven out the British. This experience altered U Nu's ideas in important respects. According to his own account, he learned "What it means to be a puppet. . . . How we detested those days." The resistance he had once led against the British now turned against the Japanese. He participated in the secret establishment of the Anti-Fascist People's Freedom League (AFPFL) late in 1944, headed by Aung San, who eventually set up an "underground" in the jungle and supported British troops advancing against the Japanese. U Nu did not join the underground; instead, he was evacuated by the Japanese with the remnants of the Ba Maw government to the border of Thailand.

Once the war was over, U Nu retired to his native village and turned to literary work. He did serve as vice president of the AFPFL, Burma's united front, but did not come forward as a candidate in the elections for a Constitutional Assembly held after Britain had promised Burma immediate independence. Then, when a by-election vacancy arose, U Nu yielded to the pleas of Aung San, won the seat and was unanimously elected on June 11, 1947, as president of the Constituent Assembly. Any hope he might have had of abstaining from active participation in politics was shattered on July 19 when Aung San and six other ministers were assassinated, another act of violence which belied Buddhist dedication to peaceful means. The AFPFL was threatened by disintegration. But then the governor of Burma summoned U Nu to the office of premier.

This opened a new stage in the life of the Burmese leader. After an abortive attempt to bring the Communists into the AFPFL in the hope of achieving national unity, U Nu formed a cabinet composed largely of the Socialists, the PVO (the paramilitary wing of the AFPFL), and of representatives of the Frontier peoples (Shans, Kachins, Chins) and pro-AFPFL Karens (the second largest community in Burma), whose support U Nu won by his promises of fair play. Through his efforts the Constitutional Assembly adopted the constitution, and U Nu, in London, signed a treaty by which Britain, then ruled by the Labor party under Prime Minister Clement Attlee, formally recognized the independence of Burma on October 17, 1947. As Tinker puts it, "This accomplished, any bitterness that U Nu may have previously entertained towards the former colonial power now evaporated. Henceforward, whether in public or in private, he voiced a warm regard for Britain, while towards Clement Attlee and the British Labor Party his attitude was unfeignedly fraternal."

As in other newly independent non-Western countries, the achievement of independence was only the first stage in the arduous process of building a nation. U Nu was promptly confronted by the violent opposition of the Communists and of the PVO. On March 27, 1948, and on subsequent occasions, U Nu offered to resign the premiership if this would achieve reconciliation. But when the Communists called for the overthrow of the government, he ordered the arrest of the Communist leaders who, however, escaped and plunged the country into civil war. The Socialist party, which by then dominated the government, demanded supreme authority. U Nu sought to comply with this demand by resigning on July 16, but pressure of the Frontier peoples and the Karens forced him to resume office ten days later.

He then faced not only the revolt of the Communists and the PVO, but also that of the newly formed Karen National Defense Organization (KNDO) which sought to create a separate Karen national state. The countryside was in turmoil. Rangoon was faced with dissension, strikes, fighting, and defeatism. During a flying visit to Upper Burma in March, 1949, to discuss plans for the recapture of Mandalay, U Nu learned that several Socialist leaders had decided to hand over power to the Communists, with the proviso that U Nu would remain prime minister. The Communists had rejected these terms. The Socialist and PVO ministers handed in their resignations, and U Nu reorganized his cabinet with the co-operation of Independents. U Nu continued to invite the co-operation of the Communists provided they abandoned force, but when they refused to do so he declared the Communist party illegal in 1953. After failing to negotiate an armistice with KNDO, U Nu, with the aid of loyalist Karen leaders, stemmed the tide of separatism and gradually rebuilt the unity of the country.

Like many of the leaders of the Indian National Congress, notably Nehru, the Thakins had been influenced first by Marxism, which led them to seek changes by revolutionary methods, and then by the Fabian Socialists of Britain, whose ideas, implemented by the Labor party when it came to power in 1945, emphasized political gradualism and the welfare state. As Mr. Tinker points out, "In a broadcast delivered in April, 1948, U Nu explained that his government rejected Soviet methods in favor of 'the circle of democracy.' The programme which was announced simultaneously was based upon the principle of State control, the nationalization of foreign enterprises such as the Irawaddy Flotilla Company and the great teak firms, the transfer of the rice export trade to National Marketing Board, and (potentially the most radical of all these measures) the nationalization of agricultural land."

Civil war prevented the realization of this program. By the time the country had been more or less stabilized in 1949, the government was no longer enthusiastic about Marxism and, because of its own experience with communism, was opposed to the use of force in reorganization of the economy. U Nu favored voluntary local self-help, rather than government intervention, for such tasks as the building of roads, schools, wells, reading rooms, and so on. The concept of good works, which had previously guided Buddhist religious activities had thus been transferred to works for the good of society under the name *Pyidawatha*.

Religious belief has also inspired U Nu's attitude toward other aspects of building the new state. According to him, "the power of things spiritual can alone save Burma—and the world—from Desire, Hatred, and Delusion." He has encouraged the spread and strengthening of Buddhism in Burma, and fostered world Buddhism through the Sixth Ecumenical Council held near Rangoon from 1954 to 1956. A devout Buddhist, U Nu has also shown interest in and respect for other faiths. When challenged by some Buddhists for his religious tolerance, particularly toward Islam, he has invoked the example of India's Emperor Asoka of the third century B.C., a convert to Buddhism, who urged nonviolence and mutual understanding.

In spite of the power he commands and the influence he wields, U Nu has again and again expressed his desire for retirement from public life to a life of contemplation. Simple and warm in his relations with all people, no matter how great or how humble, and praised by many for his sincerity, he has been known to show a quick temper when angered, and has been accused of gullibility. Yet what some regard as naïveté has endeared him to many people both in Burma and other countries. Inspired by Buddhist concepts of tolerance, he defined his foreign policy at the 1955 Bandung conference as follows: "Mistrust begets mistrust, and suspicion breeds suspicion. . . . We cannot afford to live in mistrust of our neighbors. We have to learn to live with them in mutual trust and confidence, and when this happy state of affairs has not existed in the past, someone has to break the ice. For trust also begets trust and confidence begets confidence." U Nu had read Dale Carnegie's *How to Win Friends and Influence People*, and on his official visit to the United States in 1955 asked to meet Mr. Carnegie who, however, was unable to accept because of illness.

But U Nu's religious tolerance does not go so far as to accept any and all pressures applied to Burma by its neighbors, notably Communist China. In December, 1954, on his first visit to Peiping, U Nu assured "my esteemed friend, Premier Chou En-lai, that we will under no circumstances be stooges of any power." On his second visit, in November, 1956, he said more bluntly, "The Chinese people would defend to the last the preservation of their honour and dignity. The Burmese would do likewise, and any infringement would be resisted."

Like Mr. Nehru, U Nu places great emphasis on the UN as a world forum where concepts of international morality can be forged by all peoples, irrespective of their ideologies. Under his leadership Burma, although in "the circle of democracy," has accepted economic aid from the Communist bloc, and in 1960 negotiated with Peiping a settlement of its borders regarded by the Burmese as favorable to their territorial claims. It has combined nonalignment with a democratic outlook and reliance on the moral influence of the world community.

With his deep-seated longing to leave the arena of public affairs for a life of religious contemplation, U Nu has sought again and again to lay down his official duties. On June 5, 1956, he resigned as premier to become president of the AFPFL, only to resume the former post in December of that year. After a long struggle within his party he was deposed on June 22, 1958, as its president, and expelled for "the persecution of political enemies, plotting to split the party by subversion and public slander, violation of the country's constitution and refusal to call meetings of the executive or Supreme Council."

Faced once again with the harsh realities of having to unite disparate elements into a viable state without resort to force, which would have violated both his Buddhist faith and his belief in democracy, he threatened to resign from the premiership on September 26, 1958, declaring that free elections could not be held under existing conditions. He carried out his threat on October 29, when he called on all Burmese to support the successor he had named, General Ne Win. The general, according to well-informed observers, succeeded in stabilizing political and economic conditions and rooting out corruption, but his firm methods antagonized U Nu and other political leaders, who saw his military rule as spelling the end of democracy.

Reluctantly, U Nu again returned to the political scene early in 1959, and urged his supporters to begin passive resistance against "oppression" by followers of General Ne Win. In the national elections held a year later, in February, 1960, U Nu's party won an unexpectedly impressive victory, and he returned to the premiership without open resistance on the part of General Ne Win and the army.

The miracle of Burma is that this small country, racked by controversies and a struggle for power among many parties and by conflicts between various racial groups, has succeeded in surviving the onslaughts of Burmese Communists, the pressures of Peiping, encroachments by Chinese Nationalists and the economic tug of war between East and West. Throughout these conflicts and vicissitudes U Nu has remained the charismatic leader around whom otherwise disparate groups have managed to rally as around a flag, and has persisted in his efforts, often thwarted and sometimes seemingly defeated, to create a united nation. Some regard him as a skillful politician, others as naïve. At the conference of the World Federation of Buddhists at Yegu in December, 1954, marking the thousandth anniversary of Buddhism, U Nu was greeted by the president, scholarly Dr. Malalaskerara of Ceylon, as "unique amongst the world's statesmen by his unparalleled piety," and as "the ruler who is also a sage."

## JAWAHARLAL NEHRU—
## INDIA

The man who became the first prime minister of independent India was born in Allahabad on November 14, 1889, the only son, and for eleven years the only child, of a wealthy Kashmiri Brahmin, Motilal

Nehru, a successful lawyer, and of his second wife, who was fifteen years old at the time of her marriage.

Nehru's father, although distant from him during his youth, had a profound influence on him, but not so great as the influence of Mohandas Gandhi whom Nehru met at the annual conference of the Indian National Congress in Lucknow in 1916, and introduced to his family, all of whom became devoted supporters of the Mahatma. Motilal Nehru, his son Jawaharlal, and Gandhi were known irreverently as the Father, the Son, and the Holy Ghost. Nehru's sister, now Madam Pandit, born when he was eleven, became one of his closest associates, serving the Indian government in one important diplomatic post after another, notably as permanent head of India's delegation to the UN and as High Commissioner to Britain.

Following the practice of many wealthy families in India, Nehru's parents sent him to Britain for his school and university education. At Harrow his schoolmaster described him as "a very nice boy, quiet and refined. Never gave much trouble." In 1907 he went to Cambridge University, where he studied chemistry, geology, and botany, winning a second-class honors degree in the Natural Science Tripos in 1910. Even in those days Nehru demonstrated his capacity for broad-gauged thought and varied interests. For the next two years he studied at the Inner Temple and in 1912 was called to the Bar. In all that time he returned to India on only two occasions. During his stay in England he became deeply imbued with Western ideas of liberalism and Fabian socialism, which shaped his thinking and later his policies during the struggle for India's freedom from British rule and in the turbulent years of building independent India.

In March, 1916, Nehru married a seventeen-year-old girl, Kamala Kaul, like himself a Kashmiri Brahmin, and the next year their daughter and only child, Indira Priyadarshini, was born. Indira, now the wife of a newspaper publisher, Pheroze Gandhi (no relative of the Mahatma), was very close to her father, particularly after the death of her mother in 1936 from tuberculosis, aggravated by imprisonment in the cause of independence which Kamala, a shy, retiring woman, had espoused under Nehru's influence. Indira not only has been her father's confidante and hostess, but also has played an important role in her own right as an active member of a group of younger men and women—"the Ginger" group—who, dissatisfied in the late 1950's with corruption, apathy, and nepotism in the ruling Congress party, sought to "ginger" it up by self-criticism and reform. In 1958 Indira was elected president of the Congress party, the only woman to be chosen for that post and, as successor to her grandfather Motilal Nehru and her father, the third generation of Nehrus to hold it. Ill-health and the weight of responsibilities in her father's home caused her to relinquish this office in 1960.

To Indira her father, during two of his several terms in jail under the British, wrote letters which were subsequently gathered into a book, *Glimpses of World History*. In these letters he vividly described for his teen-age daughter the main phases of the world's development over the centuries, and set forth his thoughts on the role India had played in its glorious past and the contributions he foresaw it could make in the future. Nehru here revealed himself as a perceptive and brilliant, if not trained, historian, with an extraordinary grasp of the wide range of developments experienced by peoples of many faiths, varied traditions, and contrasting ideologies, and with an abiding faith in man's capacity to achieve progress.

Nehru started his national political career in 1918, when he became a member of the All-India Congress Committee, rising to the office of general secretary in 1923. In that year he was imprisoned by the British in Nabha State for inciting Akalis to perform a religious ceremony in defiance of official objections, and served a three-year term. On his release he went to England to recuperate, and afterward spent considerable time in Switzerland because of his wife's ill-health. Re-elected president of the Indian National Congress in 1929, he was imprisoned for six months in 1930 for his participation in Gandhi's "march to the sea" campaign to make salt; and again was arrested for a seditious speech in 1934, serving a one-year term. In 1936 he became president of the Indian National Congress for the third time. Once more he revealed the breadth of his interests, visiting Spain in 1938, where he met the Republican leaders of the Civil War, and traveling in 1939 to China, where he met Chiang Kai-shek and his associates.

When World War II broke out, Britain brought India, its colony, into the war without its consent, thereby arousing deep resentment among Indians. Nehru, more convinced than ever of the need for independence, in 1942 joined India's distinguished Muslim leader, Maulana Abdul Kalam Azad, then president of the Indian National Congress in negotiations with a British mission headed by Sir Stafford Cripps regarding steps to achieve this goal. The Cripps mission, however, ended in failure. Negotiations were resumed in 1946 by a British Cabinet Mission. According to Azad's memoirs, *India Wins Freedom,* which were published in 1958 shortly after his death and caused a sensation in India, these negotiations could have brought about independence without partition of the Indian subcontinent. Azad proposed the creation of a central government with powers over defense, foreign policy, and communications, and three regions, one predominantly Muslim. Thus each region would have had broad autonomy over its own internal affairs.

The plan devised by Azad firmly opposed that of the Muslim leader Mohammed Ali Jinnah, who demanded partition and the creation of the separate Muslim state of Pakistan. Azad's plan had won the approval of the British Mission, had been reluctantly accepted by Jinnah, and had been made the basis of the Mission's proposal to the coalition government headed by Winston Churchill. However, according to Azad, Nehru, who in 1946 was once more president of the Indian National Congress, declared in a press interview that the Congress would not be bound in advance by any plans. This statement, in Azad's opinion, antagonized Jinnah, who then declared that he had resumed his freedom of action and reiterated his demand for Pakistan. Whether or not partition could in fact have been averted, given the passions aroused among Muslims by the prospect of an independent India where they would have been a minority and among Hindus by shocked awareness of Muslim opposition to a united nation, is a moot question. In later years Nehru expressed his profound regret at the partition of the continent and its tragic consequences of riots, murders, and loss of property on both sides, a bitter aftermath for the once-united peoples of India's two great faiths.

In spite of the wrenching experience of partition, Azad became minister of education and for a while the only Muslim member in the first cabinet of independent India organized on August 15, 1947, by Nehru, who served as prime minister and minister of external affairs, two posts he has occupied since that time. Azad remained in office until his death in 1958, after dedicating to Nehru, "dear friend and comrade," the book in which he expressed criticisms of the prime minister's attitude toward his plan for India's unification.

That Nehru, whose decision in a moment of crisis had wrecked Azad's fondest hopes, could nevertheless win his devotion is symbolic of the many facets which friend and foe alike have found in Nehru's complex, richly endowed, and often seemingly contradictory personality. These many facets are described by an admirer of Nehru, Acharya Krishna Kripalani, who writes: "He is at once personal and detached, human and aloof, with the result that now he appears fond, now cold, now proud, now modest. An aristocrat in love with the masses, a nationalist who represents the culture of the foreigner, an intellectual caught up in the maelstrom of an emotional upheaval—the very paradox has surrounded him with a halo."

Many observers see in Nehru a Hamlet who, like the melancholy Dane, eternally asks himself the never wholly answered question: "To be or not to be?" It is true that Nehru experiences dark moods such as he voiced when he wrote: "What then was one to do? Not to act was a complete confession of failure and a submission to evil; to act meant often enough a compromise with some form of that evil, with all the untoward consequences that such compromises result in." Yet he is also a man of decision and action. "The call of action has long been with me," he has written, "not action divorced from thought, but rather flowing from it in one continuous sequence." He has held the disparate elements of India—geographic, linguistic, political, economic—together in the first nation-state of India's millennial experience; he has striven to effect the transformation of India's premedieval agrarian economy through modernization of agriculture, community development projects designed to change the pattern of life in ancient villages, and a modest but expanding program of industrialization; and he has steadfastly practiced political democracy.

In the Hindu tradition of rejecting the idea that the world is all black or all white, and of seeking to reconcile conflicting concepts and practices through a pragmatic approach toward realities, Nehru has been deeply interested in Western democracy, in socialism, and in Marxism, without asserting that any one approach offers an absolute solution to India's manifold problems. "The real problems for me," he has written, "remain problems of individual and social life, of harmonious living, of a proper balancing of an individual's inner and outer life, of an adjustment of the relations between individuals and groups, of a continuous becoming something better and higher, of social development, of the ceaseless adventure of man. In the solution of these problems the way of observation and precise knowledge and deliberate reasoning, according to the method of science, must be followed. . . . A living philosophy must answer the problems of today."

An avowed agnostic, Nehru firmly believes in the secular state, as contrasted with the religious state of Islam, but at the same time supports "an ethical approach to life." In the 1920's, when the anti-colonialism of Lenin made a profound impression on the leaders of peoples ruled by Western powers, Nehru, like many of his contemporaries under comparable circumstances, became deeply interested in Marxism. But Marxism, he has said, "did not satisfy me completely, nor did it answer all the questions in my mind, and, almost unawares, a vague idealist approach would creep into my mind, something rather akin to the Vedanta approach."

He found Marxism rigid and dogmatic, as his biographer, Michael Brecher, points out in *Nehru: A Political Biography*. "Life is too complicated," Nehru wrote, "and, as far as we can understand it in our present state of knowledge, too illogical for it to be confined within the four corners of a fixed doctrine." He has found things to admire in both the USSR and Communist China, but he who, like most Hindus, believes in nonviolence, has been repelled by the Communists' resort to force to achieve the ends they seek and, an ardent individualist, has rejected their regimentation of personal freedom. "The ends," he said, "cannot be separated from the means."

In 1950, soon after the outbreak of the Korean War, he declared: "I don't like monolithic States. I don't like authoritarian States. . . . I do think that individual liberty, *i.e.*, normally considered political liberty, does not exist in monolithic authoritarian countries." And in 1952 he asserted: "I think Marx is out of date today. To talk about Marxism today, if I may say so, is reaction. I think Communists with all their fire and fury are in some ways utterly reactionary in outlook."

Nehru has undeviatingly opposed the activities of India's Communists, whom he regards as spokesmen not for their country but for world communism. The convictions of an ardent nationalist are reflected in the harsh words he used about the Communists in 1954:

"They have no moorings in the land of their birth, but always look to outside countries for inspiration and guidance. They are of the opinion that internecine trouble, violence, and bloodshed are the main things to be pursued." This, however, has not in any way prevented him from seeking to maintain friendly relations with the USSR and receiving economic and technical aid from the Soviet bloc. Similarly, it has not deterred his search for a peaceful settlement of India's conflict with Communist China over Chinese encroachments on its border, in spite of his outspoken disappointment with Peiping's violation of the five principles of peaceful coexistence (*Panchshila*) which China and India had agreed to observe in 1954.

Nehru, by his own avowal, has been deeply inspired by the concepts of Western liberalism with which he became acquainted during his student days in Britain. He believes in democracy. He also believes in socialism which, he is convinced, "will release innumerable individuals from economic and cultural bondage." He is an intellectual with a wide-ranging mind and myriad interests. Quick of wit and temper, he does not suffer fools gladly, and is often regarded as intolerant of criticism and arrogant toward lesser minds. Yet he is completely at ease among illiterate peasants, who are not overawed by this sophisticated aristocrat with a Western turn of mind and find in him the charismatic personality of a beloved leader, without being troubled by his agnosticism; he can be delightfully gay, and even impish when at ease; yet he is concerned with day-to-day problems, both material and spiritual. He deeply feels the sorrows of mankind, and constantly searches for ways to achieve peace. Yet he can easily turn for relaxation to art, the theater or literature. He is the brilliant author of two autobiographical books: *The Discovery of India* and *Toward Freedom*. In New York during the 1960 UN General Assembly he visited the Guggenheim and Metropolitan Art museums, saw a political play, *The Best Man*, and went to the World Series. In his well-cut *ashkan*, a knee-length coat, with a rose invariably in his buttonhole, he is a towering and elegant figure.

Of all the builders of emerging nations in the non-Western world Nehru comes closest to the ideal philosopher-king portrayed, but never discovered in actuality, by Plato. He is an intellectual heir to comparable leaders of India in past centuries: the Hindu Asoka who became a convert to Buddhism ("No orthodox religion attracts me," Nehru is reported to have told an old friend, "but if I had to choose, it would certainly be Buddhism"); and the Muslim ruler Abkar, who sought to achieve a synthesis between the great faiths of the world—Hinduism, Islam, Christianity, and Judaism.

Michael Brecher reports Nehru's extemporaneous reflections on "what constitutes a good society and the good life?" as follows:

> Broadly speaking, apart from the material things that are necessary, obviously, a certain individual growth in the society, not only the corporate social growth but the individual growth. For I do believe that ultimately it is the individual that counts. I can't say that I believe in it because I have no proof, but the idea appeals to me without belief, the old Hindu idea that if there is any divine essence in the world every individual possesses a bit of it . . . and he can develop it. Therefore, no individual is trivial. Every individual has an importance and should be given full opportunities to develop—material opportunities, naturally, food, clothing, education, housing, health, etc. They should be common to everybody. The difficulty comes in about the moral aspect, the moral aspect of religion. I'm not at all concerned about the hereafter. It doesn't worry me: I don't see why it should worry people whether the next world is or is not there. And I am not prepared to deny many things. I just don't know! The most correct attitude, if I may say so, is that of the Buddha who didn't deny it and didn't assert it. He said "this life is enough for me and when you don't know about something why talk about it." I do believe in certain standards. Call them moral standards, call them what you like, spiritual standards. They are important in any individual and in any social group. And if they fade away, I think that all the material advancement you may have will lead to nothing worthwhile. How to maintain them I don't know; I mean to say, there is the religious approach. It seems to me rather a narrow approach with its forms and all kinds of ceremonials. And yet, I am not prepared to deny that approach. If a person feels comforted by that, it is not for me to remove that sense of comfort.

Pakistan, a part of India before partition for several centuries, differs from the Republic of India in several important respects—and so does its leader Ayub Khan differ from Nehru.

## MOHAMMED AYUB KHAN—
## PAKISTAN

Like many other military men in non-Western countries, Marshal Mohammed Ayub Khan, president of Pakistan since October 7, 1958, had thought of politics as a field of activity rife with corruption and self-seeking, to be avoided by army men.

As commander in chief of the Pakistani army since 1951, Ayub

Khan used to tell his staff: "My task is to keep the army sound and intact and out of politics." As president of Pakistan he wrote in his article, "Pakistan Perspective," in *Foreign Affairs,* July, 1960: "The former politicians are no problem to us now or in the near future. We have taken good care to spare them the usual tragic fate of those overtaken by revolutionary upheavals. On the contrary, we are content to treat them as a big joke, just as they turned a perfectly sound country into the laughing-stock of the whole world. When they are confronted with skeletons collected from their cupboards, most of them wisely prefer to retire from public life for five to six years rather than face the risk of open trial. This saves a lot of dirty linen from being washed publicly, and decent folk prefer this quiet exit of errant politicians."

Son of a Pathan bugler in the pre-independence Indian army under the British, Mohammed Ayub Khan was born in 1908 in Hazara District of what was then called the North-West Frontier Province of British India. He studied at the Muslim University in Aligarh, then entered the Royal Military College at Sandhurst, England (which was also attended by General Kassim, president of Iraq). After a year with a British regiment, the Royal Fusiliers, he was transferred to the Fourteenth Punjab Regiment. During World War II he briefly commanded a battalion in Burma. With the partition of India in 1947, the Fourteenth Punjab Regiment became part of the Pakistani army.

Ayub Khan moved rapidly from brigade commander in Waziristan to adjutant general, then commander in chief and, for ten months in 1954-55, also minister of defense. He has traveled widely, and has been on various missions to the United States, Britain, Germany, Scandinavia, France, Turkey, and accompanied his old comrade-in-arms,

Iskander Mirza, on a Middle Eastern tour. Louis Dupree of the American Universities Field Staff, revisiting Pakistan after an eight-year absence, described in August, 1959, his impressions of Ayub Khan: "Physically impressive, President Ayub has the tall, big boned build of the Pathan, and he is an excellent athlete. He affects a distinguished mustache with twirled ends so popular with the officer corps." Other observers have commented that he looks more British than the British: "mustache, swagger stick, stiff upper lip and that sort of thing." He has an unusually forceful personality, likes hunting and fishing, and abhors desk duties.

Ayub Khan and Iskander Mirza, who had been minister of defense and then took over rule of the country from Prime Minister Suhrawardy in 1958, were disturbed by the political instability of Pakistan, particularly, writes a *New York Times* observer, by "the general unworthiness of political leaders who kept changing allegiance with the seasons and stuffing their pockets as long as they were in office." The politicians, in their opinion, showed no concern for the integrity of the country, only for their own personal interests. Their attitude toward politicians was similar to that of the young officers led by Naguib and Nasser in Egypt.

When Mirza became president of Pakistan, he did so with the support of the army, which was loyal to Ayub Khan. Mirza abrogated the new constitution adopted in 1956 and dissolved the political parties which were at odds with each other over internal affairs, particularly over the conflict of traditions and ideas between conservative West and liberal East Pakistan. However, Mirza apparently did not live up to the ideals of Ayub Khan who on October 7, 1958, in a well-planned, skillfully organized maneuver offered Mirza the opportunity of leaving the country peacefully for England, with a pension. When Mirza departed, Ayub Khan proclaimed martial law until December 31, 1960.

The function of martial law, according to Ayub Khan, was to provide a simpler, faster mechanism "to deal with such persons whose pernicious activities under the cover of politics, religion, or business brought about instability and very nearly jeopardized the security of Pakistan." This, however, he says in his July, 1960, *Foreign Affairs* article,

> . . . should not be taken to imply that we can do—or wish to do—without democracy. The revolution of October 7, 1958, was not aimed against the institution of democracy as such. No, it was only against the manner in which its institutions were being worked. There are two main reasons

why we in Pakistan cannot but adhere to a democratic pattern of life and government. In the first place, as Muslims, we are brought up on two basic ingredients of democracy, namely, equality and fraternity. Anything to the contrary would be the negation of our spiritual faith and practice. And, secondly, we have to fight a long and arduous battle for progress and development in which every man, woman, and child of Pakistan must participate to the fullest possible extent. Democracy provides the only healthy way for arousing the willing cooperation of people and harnessing it to a sustained national endeavor.

We must, therefore, have democracy. The question then is: What type of democracy? The answer need not be sought in the theories and practices of other people alone. On the contrary, it must be found from within the book of Pakistan itself.

To my mind, there are four prerequisites for the success of any democratic system in a country like Pakistan:

It should be simple to understand, easy to work and cheap to sustain.

It should put to the voter only such questions as he can answer in the light of his own personal knowledge and understanding—without external prompting.

It should ensure the effective participation of all citizens in the affairs of the country up to the level of their mental horizon and intellectual calibre.

It should be able to produce reasonably strong and stable governments.

To achieve these four prerequisites, Ayub Khan introduced a system of "basic democracies." In his own words, the two wings of the country, West and East Pakistan, "have each been divided into 40,000 constituencies with an average population of about 1,000. Every constituency elects one representative by universal franchise. In such a small and well-defined field of choice, voters of the meanest intelligence cannot go far wrong in putting their finger on the right type of candidate." These constituencies then form the base for a series of indirect rural elections to higher and higher councils. "Provision has also been made for nominated members to ensure, where necessary, the representation of special interests, like women, minorities, etc." A similar pattern is followed in towns and larger municipalities. The system "is designed to ensure a full sense of cooperation between the official and elected agencies at all stages of public administration."

The first elections to basic democracies, held in December, 1959, were, in Ayub Khan's opinion, "quite heartening." Those elected "came from the real hard core of the country, the majority of them being middle-class and lower middle-class agriculturists, lawyers, medical practitioners, businessmen, retired government workers, and artisans. One great lesson which these elections brought out was that for the first time in Pakistan, it seemed possible for an average citizen to seek election purely on his or her personal merit without the help of any financial, social or political backing. Also for the first time, the elected candidate finds himself in a position to participate effectively and directly in the affairs of the country as they exist immediately around him."

The next step in the search for a form of democracy suitable for the needs of Pakistan was the creation in February, 1960, of the Constitution Commission, composed of "eminent judges, lawyers, and other interests." This commission is

> to examine the progressive failure of parliamentary government in Pakistan leading to the abrogation of the Constitution of 1956 and to determine the causes and the nature of the failure: To consider how best the said or like causes may be identified and their recurrence prevented: And, having further taken account of the genius of the people, the general standard of education and of political judgment in the country, the present state of a sense of nationhood, the prime need for sustained development, and the effect of the constitutional and administrative changes brought into being in recent months, to submit constitutional proposals in the form of a report advising how best the following ends may be secured: a democracy adaptable to changing circumstances and based on the Islamic principles of justice, equality and tolerance; the consolidation of national unity; and a firm and stable system of government.

Ayub Khan has stated that he does not prejudge "what sort of a constitution we shall have, though I naturally have my personal views. Two things, however, we must agree on. First that our Constitution should be such that suits our circumstances and conditions, and, secondly, that it should not admit of any political instability under any circumstances. To produce such a Constitution will require a lot of realism and courage and bold departure from clichés and borrowed ideas if need be."

Meanwhile, the president of Pakistan has proclaimed a land reform which sets a ceiling of 1,500 acres on land ownership by an individual, and provides for the confiscation of land above this figure, to be distributed among the landless, in return for compensation. This reform is of particular significance to West Pakistan, where land had been hitherto concentrated in the hands of large landowners, conservative in politics, who have had deep-seated conflicts with the more liberal-minded leaders of East Pakistan with its economy based not only on more modern agriculture but also on industry and trade.

Once the land reform has been carried out, it could serve the same key purpose as that contemplated for the "basic democracies" system by creating a stable middle class in which small agriculturalists, professional men, owners of business enterprises, and others would play an increasingly important role. Such a middle class, literate and, it is assumed, politically articulate, could prepare the way for "true democracy," which, in Ayub Khan's opinion, "is only possible when a literate electorate exists, such as in Britain and America."

Ayub Khan's critics, primarily among the former political leaders whom he has displaced and publicly mocked, do not believe that he sincerely plans to restore "democracy." But like many other influential figures, political and military, in newly emerging nations Ayub Khan is convinced that, without the existence of conditions favorable to the development of democratic practices, attempts merely to imitate the outward forms of Western institutions will prove a failure and a tragic mockery of the ideals they are intended to achieve.

In foreign policy, unlike India, Pakistan aligned itself with the Western bloc led by the United States in 1950, under the impact of the Korean War, and it is a member of the SEATO and CENTO alliances.

## SUKARNO—

## INDONESIA

Sukarno (or Bung Karno, Brother Sukarno, as he is familiarly known), president of Indonesia, one of the largest of the newly emerged nations with a population of 90 million living on three thousand islands, said on May 16, 1956, during his state visit to the United States: "A man's life is unpredictable indeed. I am the son of poor parents. My father was a small teacher who earned 25 guilders a month. This is $10. I am the child of common people."

He was born on June 6, 1901, at Surabaya in East Java, the son of a Javanese father and a Balinese mother. During his childhood he lived with his paternal grandparents, also in East Java. According to Leslie H. Palmier, in his article, "Sukarno, the Nationalist" (*Pacific*

*Affairs,* June, 1957), "it was here that he was steeped in the Javanese culture which has contributed so much to his political success with the Javanese peasantry" and has made him an enthusiastic connoisseur of native art and the native dance.

After an indifferent career in the village school and in the one where his father taught, he entered a Dutch elementary school at the age of twelve, and then began to show an aptitude for study. Two years later he obtained the clerkship diploma which entitled him to enter lower positions in government service. But a friend of his father took him into his home in Senabang and paid for his education in an urban high school, largely reserved for children of Dutchmen and of senior Indonesian officials.

This friend, Umar Said Tjokroaminoto, had formed in 1912 the Muslim Union, which subsequently became one of the most important nationalist organizations in what was then the Dutch East Indies. In the home of this friend Sukarno learned about politics at first hand, and began to write articles and make speeches. He joined the *Jong Java* (Young Java) organization and, on completing high school, entered the Engineering College at Bandung in West Java, where he obtained a degree in civil engineering in 1925.

Modest though his father's job was, Sukarno's family belonged to the nobility who, says Palmier, "both before and under the Dutch, manned the administration, and his education had prepared him for government service." After graduating as engineer, a profession where only subordinate positions were at that time open to non-Dutchmen, Sukarno entered politics. His declared objective, which he unswervingly pursued from that time on, was to free his country from the rule of the Netherlands. He was an ardent nationalist, and contended that nationalism must be based on the common people and achieve its goals through non-co-operation with the government.

Sukarno had expressed his ideas in the General Study Club which he helped to form in Bandung in 1926, and which became the core of the Indonesian National Party (PNI). According to Palmier, this party, aided by the then governor general's liberal policy, gained 10,000 members within two years. A fundamental aspect of Sukarno's doctrine at that time was that the Indonesians had to depend on themselves to win freedom and should not rely on either Muslims or Communists.

As the PNI developed into the most powerful nationalist organization in the Indies the Dutch became alarmed and arrested Sukarno and seven of his associates in 1929. Sukarno was sentenced to three years' imprisonment on September 3, 1930, but was released on December 31, 1931. On his re-emergence on the political scene, Sukarno, who had never been to the Netherlands, found himself in sharp conflict with two new leaders, Hatta and Sjahrir, who had recently returned from that country.

While Sukarno continued to stress non-co-operation with the Dutch through a mass party as a matter of principle, Hatta and Sjahrir believed that their main task was to educate the Indonesian people in politics through a small and politically conscious group. The PNI had split on this issue. Sukarno, failing to heal the rift, in July, 1932, joined the *Partai Indonesia* (Indonesian party, or *Partinado*). "Sukarno's party grew rapidly and by mid-1933 it had 20,000 members, as against only about 1,000 in Hatta's party." The government again arrested Sukarno in August, 1933, and this time exiled him without trial to the island of Flores. Subsequently Sukarno was transferred to Benenlin, and he remained there until he was released in 1942 by the Japanese, who had invaded the Dutch East Indies. His political adversaries, Hatta and Sjahrir, were arrested in February, 1934, and exiled first to Western New Guinea and then to Banda Island until their release by the Japanese in 1942.

Once free, Sukarno returned to Java, and there he and Hatta agreed to co-operate with the Japanese; Sjahrir was to organize an underground resistance movement, while maintaining contact with them. "It is now accepted," says Palmier, "that Sukarno's actions were motivated not by opportunism but by the desire to obtain national independence by any means open to him."

In 1943 the Japanese permitted the establishment of an all-inclusive nationalist organization, Center of People's Power (*Putera*), and promised Sukarno and Hatta independence in the near future. Sukarno and Hatta became chairman and vice chairman, respectively, of the new party and worked to create first of all a pro-Indonesian point of view among the masses, to such good effect that the Japanese dissolved the *Putera* and created another organization under their close control which, however, was used by Sukarno and his associates for their own nationalist objectives.

When the Japanese became aware that the war was not going in their favor, they set up an Investigating Committee for Preparation of Independence, with Sukarno and Hatta as members. In this committee, on June 1, 1945, Sukarno presented the *Pantja-Silá*, or Five Principles—nationalism, representative government, humanitarianism, social justice, and belief in God. On August 7 the Japanese permitted the formation of another committee which was to prepare to take over authority, with Sukarno as chairman and Hatta as vice chairman. The two leaders, however, hesitated to take anti-Japanese action even after Japan's collapse a few days later, fearing a bloody struggle might ensue, in spite of pressure from the underground headed by Soetan Sjahrir, who had them briefly kidnaped "in order to force their hands," says Palmier. Finally, on August 17, 1945, "when it became clear that a bloodless revolution was impossible," Sukarno declared independence only to see the strong united front forged during the war disintegrate into a multiplicity of parties, which he has since found it increasingly difficult to unite for common action.

The country was plunged into confusion as the Dutch sought to regain power by military action. Plots against Sukarno and Hatta multiplied, and students who supported the newly emerged republic demanded that an advisory Central National Committee formed at the time of independence to aid Sukarno and his cabinet be transformed into a parliament, with the cabinet responsible to the Committee.

Sukarno, believing the politicians were not sufficiently representative of the people, appointed new members to the Central National Committee. Among his appointees were "not only members of political parties but also representatives of occupational groups, of regions outside Java, of ethnic minorities, of minor parties, of irregular armed organizations, and some socially prominent persons."

This system presaged the functional parliament which Sukarno formed in 1960 after he had dismissed the elected legislature which had blocked many of his policies. He then attempted to implement what he calls "guided democracy."

For Sukarno "guided democracy" is ruled by a governmental elite which functions without benefit of a representative parliament and seeks, through discussion, to arrive at agreement among different points of view. This concept, according to Richard C. Bone, Jr., in his article "Will Indonesia Disintegrate" (*Foreign Policy Bulletin,* May 1, 1957), is deeply rooted in Indonesia's traditions. "President Sukarno's own Javanese-Balinese cultural heritage consists of a customary law (*adat*) which calls on its members to live together in a state of mutual help (*gotong-royong*) and achieve decisions by a process of discussion until various factions are satisfied with the ultimate conclusions."

Sukarno, in September, 1948, had crushed the revolt of the Communist party on the ground that nationalism and not the rule of this or that party was his goal, and an independent Indonesia was not to be subjected "to any other country whatsoever." In 1949 the Dutch transferred sovereignty over the Indies to the Sukarno government, except for West New Guinea or, as the Indonesians call it, West Irian, whose relinquishment Indonesia continues to demand from the Dutch. Failing to shake the determination of the Dutch to maintain their hold on Irian, Indonesia broke off diplomatic relations with the Netherlands in July, 1960.

Nationalism for Sukarno—as for other Asian leaders, for Nasser, for Castro—means, to use his own words, "the rebuilding of our nation, it means the effort to provide esteem for our people . . . [it] is the love of country and the determination to improve it. . . ." Basically, as Palmier points out, this is a desire to be regarded as an equal by Western nations. During his visit to the United States in 1956 Sukarno said at the state dinner given in his honor in Washington on May 16: ". . . I am a brown man, an Indonesian, an Asiatic. I am the son of poor parents, and the son of a nation only recently emerged into the world of national existence. Yet you accept me as a friend, you accept me as a human being, and perhaps you accept me as a brother. Is that not real democracy?" Addressing the United States Congress he declared: "Democracy, when all is said and done, is the introduction of equal opportunity in human activities among the indigenous peoples themselves. . . ."

The two main principles which have determined Sukarno's policy in Indonesia since independence have been his ardent nationalism and his abiding conviction that politicians do not and cannot adequately represent the people. His nationalist sentiment—his belief in forging a society which truly reflects the ideas of Indonesia—has caused him to oppose the Communist party, which he did successfully in 1948. His distaste for westernization has led him to oppose the predominantly Muslim, pro-Western, Masjumi party and to seek the ouster from Indonesia's economic life of all foreign elements, from the Dutch, former rulers of the Dutch East Indies, to the Chinese, who until 1959 controlled trade in the rural areas. In 1948 Sukarno said that his goal was to have the new country become "an independent Indonesia which is not subjected to any other country whatsoever. . . ."

Sukarno's second principle—his conviction that politicians do not and cannot represent the people—has led him to the concept of "guided democracy." He has been shocked by the multiplicity of political parties in Indonesia, by their continued struggle with each other for prestige and power, by the civil war between some of the islands and Java which broke out in 1957 and is not yet over. He has repeatedly called for national unity, for the elimination of political parties, and for a common front, rejecting parliamentary institutions which, in his opinion, are unsuited to the needs of an underdeveloped country. "Democracy," he has said, "is not merely government by the people; democracy is also government for the people." And on June 1, 1956, during his visit to the United States, he asserted that the Indonesians, in contrast to Americans, "have no time for the slow progress of evolution. . . . We must seek explosive evolution."

In his efforts to establish "guided democracy" Sukarno has obtained support from the Communists, whom he had once opposed because of their international connection with Moscow, but who since 1952 have pursued a "national front" policy and have thus appeared to be in accord with Sukarno's first principle—nationalism. Palmier contends it is not that Sukarno has deserted his nationalism for communism, but that "the Communists have become nationalist." The Communists, however, believing in state control, economic as well as political, find themselves much more in sympathy with Sukarno than does the Masjumi party led by Hatta, which opposes authoritarian government and, having many businessmen and traders in its ranks, particularly opposes state control of the economy. Meanwhile Sukarno, since the outbreak of civil war, has relied on Army Chief of Staff Lieutenant General A. H. Nasution, who opposes the Communists, but having invoked martial law, applies strict regulations of all kinds, economic as well as political, with the avowed aim of restoring order.

The army has been increasingly critical of the Communists, whose strategy, it declared on July 25, 1960, "is not in conformance with our national aspirations." The Communists' tactic, according to the army, "hid an idea that was national in nature," and the nation was urged not to be hoodwinked by "cheap mottoes" and "cheap agitations."

By contrast Sukarno, the following day, declared in a speech before the Nationalist party congress in Central Java that the Communist party need not be feared by the people of Indonesia. The party, he said, had views that were similar to his on some issues, such as anti-colonialism and anti-imperialism.

Students of Indonesian politics believe that Sukarno is not a Communist and has no intention of making Indonesia any more subservient to Moscow or Peiping than to Washington or The Hague. In the low esteem he has for politicians Sukarno resembles Nasser of Egypt and Ayub Khan of Pakistan, whom he also resembles in his ardent desire to forge a united nation capable of fulfilling the aspirations of the people for a better life. In world affairs Sukarno contends that he refuses to enter either the Western or the Soviet bloc. "Our policy," he has said, "is a policy of forming our own personality"—Nasser's phrase in his *Philosophy of the Revolution.*

What is the personality of Indonesia, and of Sukarno? William A. Hanna of the American Universities Field Staff answered this question in 1959 in a series of twenty-five reports issued by the AUFS in a book, *Bung Karno's Indonesia.* "Bung Karno," he says, "is what and where he is precisely because he typifies Indonesians both in their strengths and their weaknesses. He is susceptible not to the planned focusing but to the random convergence of many influences such as make him at once, but to varying degrees at different times, a Marxist, a socialist, a capitalist, a democrat, a dictator, a puppet, a playboy, a prophet, and more than a little of an intellectual anarchist."

Bronzed, handsome, alert, trim-looking in impeccable uniform and fez, with his familiar swagger stick, he looks youthful at sixty and fascinates men as well as women. Here is how Louis Fischer, veteran journalist with a far-ranging experience of Russia and Asia, describes Sukarno in his book, *The Story of Indonesia*:

> I like President Sukarno for his warmth, informality, vivacity, versatility, artistic temperament, love of women, absence of hypocrisy about it, absence of arrogance, absence of color prejudice, wide reading, encouragement to painters and writers, resilience after defeats, dedication to Indonesia, sense of mission and kindness. I do not think he could ever be cruel. I like him despite his faults.
>
> He wanted power. To some, power is the possibility of compelling obedience, of subjecting others to one's will. There must be elements of this in Sukarno's desire for power, but I do not believe that it is the essence. Rather it is the possibility to stage-manage, rearrange, sway masses, express his personality, exert influence, display showmanship. His power is for pleasure, like the pleasure of winning a woman, of driving a good car, the pleasure of demonstrating skill, not the pleasure of crushing, pushing, or dominating. It is power for the joy of a theater producer, of an editor who puts out a newspaper, of an architect who sees a building rise from his blueprint, of a city planner who watches a city grow from his sketches.
>
> Sukarno wanted power without the routine of executive office. He scorned the paper work that accompanies governing. He loved the peak of the pyramid. In youth he climbed the highest trees, and his playmates called him "djago" or rooster. His politics were personal. He took support where he found it. His first criterion was, Are they for me? That, rather than ideological affinity, explains his flirtation with the Communists, that and their making him the object of a copied-from-Moscow cult of personality.
>
> Like Nehru, Sukarno yearned to be loved. Unlike Nehru, he exuded happiness. But his joys, I felt, were not unalloyed.

Sukarno himself, in commenting on the course of events in Indonesia since independence, has said, "We went astray. We went astray in all fields. . . . The democracy we have applied up to now is Western democracy—call it parliamentary democracy, if you like. Because it is not in harmony with the Indonesian atmosphere, excesses are bound to occur . . . excesses such as misuse of the idea of 'opposition' in the political field; violation of discipline and hierarchy in the military field; corruption and other such like offenses in the socio-economic field."

The solution of Indonesia's problems, in Sukarno's opinion as summarized by Hanna, can be found only by "Return to the 1945 Constitution," which harmonizes best with the Indonesian atmosphere and provides for guided democracy, that is "Democracy led by wise guidance in consultation with representatives," and "guided economy," which would eliminate "free-for-all free enterprise economy" of "vulture capitalists . . . subservient to foreign masters." Only thus can Indonesia "retool" to achieve "its own identity . . . its own pure soul and spirit. . . . Let the imperialists abroad roar. Yes, let the imperialists be in an uproar! We will march on. Let the dogs bark, our caravan will go passing by."

To outside observers, both the situation in Indonesia and the statements of Sukarno often seem confused, as Hanna points out. "In talking with one shrewd Indonesian observer and participant in the recent national developments," said Hanna in 1959, "I tried to sum it up this way: 'What is not clear to me is who is leading whom where and how fast. What is clear is that forces build up counterforces, action builds up reaction, and confusion compounds confusion.' He agreed with me. 'Yes,' he said. 'And you know, we prefer it that way.'"

## MAO TSE-TUNG—
## CHINA

The chairman of the Chinese Communist party and former chairman of the central government of the People's Republic of China was born in 1893 in the village of Shao Shan in the northern province of Hunan. His father, Mao Jen-sheng, whose name means "Hair Increase Gentlemanliness" (Mao's name can be translated as "Hair Anoint East"), was a farmer who owned three and a half acres of land and had built up an income by trading in rice, which gave him the status of what was then regarded as a "rich" peasant.

Mao's father was an intemperate and intransigent man, given to outbursts of temper and to quotations of Confucian maxims, who had no understanding of or patience with Mao or his other children. Mao once told Edgar Snow, author of *Red Star Over China*, that he engaged in an increasing "dialectical struggle" with his father. By contrast, Mao's mother, a devout Buddhist, had a significant influence on her son. According to Robert Payne's book, *Mao Tse-tung: Ruler of Red China*, Mao "attended Buddhist ceremonies with his mother, sang Buddhist hymns, and believed that nothing was more criminal than the killing of living things, and nothing more necessary for salvation than the giving of rice offerings to the poor." Students of Mao's writings find indications of his knowledge of both Confucianism and Buddhism not only in his ideas but in the way in which he has expressed them.

While Mao lived a relatively comfortable life at home, he witnessed riots of famine-starved peasants, insurrections in the countryside, and a minor uprising in his own village. He became concerned about the lot of peasants. As he studied the great Chinese novels at school after witnessing an insurrection, he was particularly impressed with one called *All Men Are Brothers,* for it "told the story of bandits who took refuge in the hills," like the nearby rebels, who after months in hiding were caught and publicly executed.

Far from being an average peasant, Mao early showed an ardent desire to pursue the career of a scholar, the most respected career in traditional China. His father, who wanted him to enter the rice trade, was not interested in scholarship, but finally agreed to let Mao go to the middle school at Hsiang-hsiang, fifteen miles from his village, in the hope that study would help his son to earn a good income. "Carrying only some books and a few ragged clothes in two pieces of luggage, which hung from a carrying-pole slung over his shoulders, Mao arrived at the school," where, writes Payne, he had a very unhappy time because of his poverty as compared with his fellow students. "Most of the other students were comparatively rich; they could afford good clothes, good food, and sometimes good servants," and called Mao "the dirty little peasant from Shao Shan." Their contempt made a lasting impression on him.

His teachers, however, recognized his intellectual gifts and urged him to work ever harder at his studies, and particularly to write. One of his classmates, Hsiao Chu-chang, son of a rich farmer, recalled that Mao had been enthralled by a book, *Great Heroes of the World,* translated from an American work, which described the lives of such men as Peter the Great, Napoleon, Washington, and Lincoln. Mao read this book overnight and said, "We need great people like these. We ought to study them and find out how we can make China rich and strong, and so avoid becoming like Annam, Korea, and India." This same friend said that later, when he read Turgenev's *Fathers and Sons,* he was reminded of Mao, who was, like Bazarov, the young hero of the novel, "dedicated to scholarship—particularly history—and the peasants." According to these recollections, "Mao talked continually about social rights and social duties, from the point of view of one who sees hope of peaceful change."

His ideas altered, however, as he watched the rise of rebellion in China and became acquainted with Socialist and, later, Communist ideas. This was a period of great intellectual ferment among Chinese youth. Western thought, particularly the impact of the science and technology of the West, had made a profound impression on Chinese minds. As in Russia during the nineteenth century, Western influence had a twofold result. On the one hand it stimulated the desire to adopt Western ways of thinking and acting, strongly encouraged by scholars like Hu Shih, subsequently China's Ambassador to the United States, who expressed a pragmatic view of the modern world, and deprecated the traditional influences of religion, clan, and family in China. On the other hand, Western influence served to break up the foundations of Chinese society, and was resisted by those who sought to maintain time-honored customs. It was opposed also by the young generation, who wanted not only "reform," through a synthesis of East and West, but the opportunity for making "new people"—in accordance with Confucius' phrase in the *Great Learning* when he pointed with approval "at the famous bath-tub on which were written the words: 'Everything must be made anew.'"

The American scholar, Robert C. North, in his book *Moscow and the Chinese Communists,* has summarized the intellectual ferment of that period as follows:

> Individual leaders under the empire tended to range themselves according to their attitudes toward the foreign impact. Some hoped to resist through rigid preservation of the structure as it was; others wanted to

modify the structure, machinery, and functions to cope with foreign influences and new conditions; still others saw no solution short of tearing down the old framework and rebuilding according to Western models; a few, rejecting the past of China, and of the West, dreamed of something totally new.

The key question was not whether change should come—whether the static world of the Manchus was to be overthrown—but whether change could be made by peaceful means or would have to be carried out by violence, and whether in the process Western influence would be rejected or woven into the new fabric of Chinese society. Here was a society where political instability and civil strife reigned; where monarchy, war lords, landowners, and gentry had begun to be menaced by the encroachments of Western merchants and investors and the rise of a new class of Chinese industrialists and capital-owners; where the great wealth of the few contrasted with the misery and often outright hunger of the vast majority of the peasants; where the old values of Buddhism and Confucianism were being undermined by Western concepts that created not a new order of ideas but intellectual and spiritual chaos; and the proud Chinese, who had regarded other peoples as "barbarians," were treated as "barbarians" by contemptuous Westerners who thought themselves superior. In this troubled society the new generation searched for new beliefs which would give them new goals, new purposes, and would free them from the humiliation they experienced when, in their technological backwardness, they confronted the West. This search was characteristic of all the Chinese leaders of the period, of Sun Yat Sen and Chiang Kai-shek as well as Mao Tse-tung and his associates.

The Bolshevik revolution of November, 1917, in Russia suddenly crystallized the inchoate and often contradictory ideas generated in China by its inner turmoil. Marxism seemed even less adapted in practice to China, still a predominantly agrarian country, than it did to Russia, already in the early stages of industrialization. This time differential was later to have a significant effect in creating divergences between the Communist doctrines of Lenin, Stalin, and Khrushchev, on the one hand, and Mao Tse-tung, Chou En-lai, and their associates on the other.

In spite of such divergences, Marxism, to quote Amaury de Riencourt in *The Soul of China*, "presented a doctrine that would satisfy both the Chinese yearning for unrestricted universalism—for doctrines applicable to all men Under Heaven, *T'ein Hsia*—and also satisfy their deep-rooted inclination toward some form of socialism." For the ideas of communism brought recollections of comparable ideas in China's turbulent history, particularly those of the Taipings, a group founded in 1851 by Hung Hsu-ch'uan following a peasant uprising against tax-gatherers.

The Taipings advocated agrarian reform, with land to be allotted according to the number of mouths in the family, "though," writes Robert Payne, "some preference was given to men above sixteen and under fifty, largely because these were the men who formed the army." An important provision of the Taiping program was that "all shall eat food, all shall have clothes, money shall be shared, and in all things there shall be equality: no man shall be without food or warmth." These reforms "correspond to the age-old desires of the peasantry," and led to the destruction of land titles a hundred years later under the Communists. The Taipings, says Payne, "destroyed private property. They regarded themselves as people with the mission to share the world's wealth equally among the world's inhabitants, and they used the phrase, 'The wealth must be shared,' a phrase which the Chinese Communists were to employ later when they came to name their party *Kung ch'an-tang*, or 'the Sharing Wealth party.'"

On the eve of World War I and of the Bolshevik revolution, Mao had come to the conclusion that he would become a Socialist. According to Hsia San, "He looked around, and saw no Socialist party in China, and thought the time had come to bring one into existence, with himself perhaps as the founder. Later he read three books: the *Communist Manifesto*, Kautsky's *The Class-War*, and a history of socialism by someone whose name I've forgotten. He was completely thunderstruck by these books."

Meanwhile, Mao had attended the Changsha Middle School, which he entered in 1911, had worked at the Hunan Provincial Library, and had studied for five years at the Hunan Normal School. In 1918, following the death of his mother, Mao traveled to Peking University, where he took the post of assistant librarian, intending to pursue his studies. There he came under the influence of the two founders of the Chinese Communist party, Li Ta-chao and Ch'en Tu-hsiu, both professors at the university. It is important to note, as many commentators on Chinese communism have pointed out, that none of the founders of the Communist party were workers or peasants. They were scholars, like Mao Tse-tung; sons of mandarin families, like Chou En-lai; or of well-to-do merchants or landlords. These were the young men—and women—who keenly felt both the chaotic conditions within China with resulting injustices and poverty and the contempt in which the West held the Chinese people during those decades of travail.

At that time Chen Tu-hsiu, dean of the department of Chinese letters at Peking University, appealed to the youth in words which deeply influenced Mao's own books subsequently written in Yenan. "O young men of China!" he said. "Will you be able to understand me? Five out of every ten whom I see are young in age, but old in spirit; nine out of every ten are young in health, but they are also old in spirit. When this happens to a body, the body is dying. When it happens to a society, the society is perishing. Such a sickness cannot be cured by sighing; it can only be cured by those who are young, and in addition to being young are courageous. We must have youth if we are to survive, we must have youth if we are to get rid of corruption. Here lies the only hope for our society."

Mao became absorbed in the ideas of Marx and Lenin, and in June, 1921, went to Shanghai for the founding of the first congress of the Chinese Communist party. On his return to Hunan he became secretary of the provincial party and started to organize labor unions. He soon discovered that the unions were interested not in political struggle but in improvement of their material conditions. From that time on until the Communists established their rule over mainland China in September, 1949, Mao concentrated on uniting the peasants in a revolutionary drive against the ruling Kuomintang party headed by Chiang Kai-shek, who had also studied communism and had Russian Communist advisers.

The Chinese Communist party found itself between two fires. On the one hand the Communist International in Moscow urged the Chinese Communists to develop their own policies; on the other, it was in favor of Communist co-operation with the "bourgeois" government of Chiang Kai-shek during the period of "capitalist" development, which orthodox Marxists expected to be fairly prolonged before the "Socialist" revolution could be effectively carried out. Lenin himself had expected that Russia, too, would pass through a period of "capitalist" development before the consummation of "socialism," but after the brief interval of his New Economic Policy (NEP) Russia moved directly into "the dictatorship of the proletariat." Lenin justified the distinction he drew between Russia and China by arguing that Russia, unlike China, had already acquired a modest degree of industrialization in the Tsarist epoch, and had a semideveloped economy, as compared with the undeveloped economy of China. Moscow's insistence on co-operation with Chiang Kai-shek brought disaster to the Chinese Communists, who found their organization in urban centers shattered in March, 1926, when Chiang Kai-shek seized full control of Kuomintang machinery, removed Communists from all prominent positions and, after his final break with the Communists in April, 1927, instituted a campaign of "white terror" against all those suspected of Marxist sympathies.

The defeat of the Communists was also the defeat of Moscow, which had counseled the dual policy that had resulted in Chiang Kai-shek's successful anti-Communist drive. Mao, rejecting the Communists' previous reliance on the as yet numerically small and ideologically weak urban proletariat, as urged by the Russians on the basis of their own experience in the November, 1917, revolution, deeply believed, to quote de Riencourt, "that the real power of China rested in the hands of its huge rural majority." After studying conditions in his native province of Hunan, Mao "decided to devote himself entirely to agrarian action" and "acquired a passionate, almost mystical faith, in the resilient faith of the Chinese peasant."

Mao's "Report on an Investigation of the Agrarian Movement in Hunan," which ignored the proletariat, was written, as befitted a man who is one of Communist China's distinguished poets as well as its top political leader, in poetic style:

> The force of the peasantry is like that of the raging winds and driving rain. It is rapidly increasing in violence. No force can stand in its way. The peasantry will tear apart all nets which bind it and hasten along the road to liberation. They will bury beneath them all forces of imperialism, militarism, corrupt officialdom, village bosses, and evil gentry. Every revolutionary comrade will be subjected to their scrutiny and be accepted or rejected by them. Shall we stand in the vanguard and lead them, or stand behind them and oppose them?

"To give credits where they are due," he wrote, "if we allot ten points to the accomplishments of the democratic revolution, then the achievements of the urban dwellers and the military units rate only three points, while the remaining seven points should go to the peasants in their rural revolution." Subsequently, under Moscow's influence, Mao eliminated this thesis from official Chinese Communist doctrine. In the United States, American observers who had reported this phase of his career were ridiculed and even denounced for having believed that Mao thought in terms of an "agrarian revolution," but Professor North believes that the concept of a peasant revolution remained "fundamental to Mao's political strategy and tactics between 1927 and 1950." At that time Mao warned that revolution was "not a dinner party, nor literary composition, nor painting, nor embroidering." Improvising on the *Analects* of Confucius, he said, "It cannot be done so delicately, so gentlemanly, and so 'gently, kindly, politely, plainly and modestly.'" Revolution, says North, in analyzing Mao's views, "amounted to insurrection, the violent action of the one class overthrowing the power of another." Mao declared, "If the peasants do not apply great force, the power of the landlords, consolidated over thousands of years, can never be uprooted. There must be a tidal wave over the countryside. . . ." Today, when Communist China is intent on transforming its economy through industrialization, agriculture still remains the major occupation of its people, and the peasants are still the vast majority of the population.

Like a true Marxist, Mao believed in historical determinism and asserted that "the broad masses of the peasantry have arisen to fulfill their historic destiny." He insisted—and in this he challenged even then the efforts of the Russians to mold Chinese communism into their own image, as well as their drive for "wholesale westernization"—that Chinese communism would be, first of all, Chinese.

> So-called "wholesale westernization" is a mistaken viewpoint. China has suffered a great deal in the past from formal adoption of foreign things. Likewise, in applying Marxism to China, the Chinese Communists must fully and properly unite the universal truth of Marxism with the specific practice of the Chinese revolution; that is to say, the truth of Marxism must be integrated with the characteristics of the nation and given a definite national form before it can be useful; it must not be applied subjectively as a mere formula. Formula Marxists are only fooling with Marxism and the Chinese revolution, and there is no place for them in the ranks of the Chinese revolution.

During nine critical years of intense maneuvering between the Communists and the Kuomintang, Mao displayed the qualities of military leadership which he later put to good use in the struggle with the Japanese. While leading Communist forces into the wilderness, on the rugged "Long March" across China and Central Asia into Yenan, where he established a Soviet state, Mao remained determined to build up the agrarian movement, to the exclusion of work with the proletariat of the big cities. This does not mean, as Western critics of Mao have argued, that the Chinese leader had hypocritically held out the promise of land to all peasants, only to create a society of communized peasants and workers when he came to power in 1949. He was aware that the leaders of the party, including himself, were primarily intellectuals of "bourgeois" origin. What he did was to build the power of communism on China's agrarian base.

Then, after the Japanese had invaded China in 1937, Mao, as the undisputed leader of the Communist party he had rebuilt from the nadir it had reached a decade before, could offer co-operation to Chiang Kai-shek in a common national struggle against Japan. In this struggle the military organization and political discipline Mao had created for the Communists proved superior to the forces of the Kuomintang, even though Chiang Kai-shek had at his disposal arms and funds from the United States which were not available to the Communists. Following the defeat of Japan achieved in 1945 by the Chinese, both Nationalists and Communists, with the aid of the military power of the United States, Mao found himself in a strong strategic position to defeat the Kuomintang and eventually drive it off the mainland, with Chiang Kai-shek and the remnants of his troops forced to take refuge on the island of Formosa. This military victory might not have been won had not Mao also placed himself in a strong ideological position by the control and influence he exercised over the peasants, whom Chiang Kai-shek, relying on the landlords, the gentry, and the industrialists and bankers of the port cities, had disregarded in the days when he was in power.

After Mao had proclaimed the People's Republic of China on September 21, 1949, and had become chairman of the Central People's Government on October 1, 1949, he found, as Lenin had done in Russia, that the long period of "capitalism," which both had believed would precede "socialism," was impracticable, and proceeded to integrate not only the peasants but also the workers, intellectuals, landlords, gentry, bankers, and business men into a Communist society. He did so at a far more rapid pace than Lenin and even Stalin had done in the USSR, and, having long ago given up his earlier reliance on peaceful change, used violence to achieve his goals. With a speed and precision which surpassed the experience of the Russians, and with far less violence, Mao collectivized land and initiated industrialization, and in 1958 he went beyond anything contemplated by Moscow when he created the militarized agrarian communes—which were made less rigid in early 1961, following a disastrous harvest. In the course of this vast transformation of China's ancient economy Mao and his associates also sought to transform rapidly the character and the traditional way of life of the Chinese people by methods whose intensity exceeded anything attempted in Russia.

When public resistance made itself felt in spite of totalitarian repression, Mao in 1958 issued the order about letting a hundred flowers bloom. Since this order seemed to presage new freedom for the expression of diverse opinions, it was greeted with particular satisfaction in Poland, which was taking advantage of the post-Stalin "thaw" in Eastern Europe. Differing opinions were promptly expressed, but the dissatisfaction, and even hostility to communism which were thus revealed, alarmed the Communist regime and the blooms were allowed to wither before they had come to full flowering. Instead, the Chinese Communists began increasingly to describe Khrushchev's policies, both at home and abroad, as those of "modern revisionists" of communism, and particularly criticized the Russians for their unfavorable view of the Chinese communes and for Khrushchev's policy of "peaceful coexistence" with "Western imperialism." The Russians, in their opinion, have "exaggerated the consequences of the destructiveness of nuclear war." Utter destruction, they said, awaits the United States if it dares to launch a war "at a time when the east wind has further prevailed over the west wind." They also asserted that the Chinese would triumph in a military showdown, and as victors would build a "beautiful" society on the ruins of defeated capitalism.

The Chinese Communists under Mao have differed with the Russian Communists in the formative years of their movement as to the base on which they should build. Mao insisted on the paramount importance of the peasants, "who are our all," instead of the urban proletariat, whom orthodox Marxists in Russia, as well as in industrialized Western Europe, had previously regarded as spearhead and keystone of communism. Like the Russians, however, the Chinese have been animated by a deep feeling of anti-Westernism, actually more profound than that of the Russians because of their prolonged experience with Western encroachments on their territory at a time when China was disorganized and weak and therefore unable to resist "the foreign devils."

This experience with the West has inspired in the Chinese a xenophobia more bitter and more unrelenting than the anti-Westernism of the Russians, who in part at least have shared some of the experience of the West. The Chinese have found in Communist theory two key concepts of their past, as expressed by Confucius and other philosophers—the concepts of universalism as contrasted with nationalism, and of social and economic equality for all without reference to liberty. And, like the Russians, the Chinese Communists have displayed a messianic spirit in their determination to carry the ideas they have nurtured beyond China's borders into neighboring countries as, before communism, the Chinese had carried their way of life intact into many Asian countries and into Western lands overseas.

Although the Chinese Communists in their early period drew heavily on Russian communism both for ideas and for moral and material support, and at that time recognized the primacy of the USSR in the world Communist hierarchy, they have since developed their own set of concepts, which today can be described as Maoism, just as Yugoslavia's concepts have come to be known as Titoism. Maoism has departed from the Russian doctrine in two important respects: at home, by contending that the phase of agrarian collectivization undergone by Russia can be skipped and a more rapid change-over from private farming to "socialism" made through peasant communes; in world affairs, by viewing the world as divided not between two poles—Russian communism and Western democracy—but in terms of a trinity, with China, the nation with the largest population on the globe, commanding a role of its own, capable of challenging the two former pole-powers and making demands upon both. In its new position of independence from both the USSR and the United States, the Chinese Communists believe, to quote Doak Barnett in *Communist China and Asia,* that "as Asians, they can and should play an especially important role in aligning anti-colonialist and nationalist forces with the Communist bloc." In practice they are taking a more and more active part in developments not only on the Asian mainland, but also in Africa and even in Cuba.

In communism, as Professor H. G. Creel points out in his little book, *Chinese Thought: From Confucius to Mao Tse-Tung,* the Chinese found a welcome antidote to the superiority they had had to endure from the West. "With the advent of Chinese Communism this is changed. For many of them believe that the Communist party 'represents the most brilliant and progressive side of contemporary human society,' and that 'the Chinese Communist party is one of the best Communist parties in the world.'" Moreover, the Communists now feel in a position to preach to the West, instead of being subjected, as in the past, to the West's preachments. "For it is the reactionary capitalist world above all," says Mao Tse-tung, "that constitutes a 'world of darkness'; the Communists will overturn it and transform it 'into a world of light that never existed before.'"

Nor do the Chinese Communists regard their communism as a foreign product. In their opinion, it is rooted in the best traditions of China. Liu Shao-ch'i, next to Mao Tse-tung the principal theoretician of the Chinese Communist party, says in his treatise on *How To Be a Good Communist* that the party is not only "powerfully armed with Marxist-Leninist theory," but is also "the heir of all the splendid traditions of the many progressive men of thought and action who have illumined the pages of Chinese history." Among these Confucius, once denounced by the Communists as a foe of progress representing "the corrupt" past, and for the present replaced by Marx, may someday be included again in the Chinese pantheon.

## RAMON MAGSAYSAY—

## THE PHILIPPINES

The late President of the Philippine Republic, Ramon Magsaysay, was born on August 31, 1907, the second of eight children of Exequiel Magsaysay and his wife, Perfecta del Fierro, at Iba, capital of the province of Zambales, 127 miles from Manila, in a bamboo and cogon grass hut—the Philippine equivalent, as his biographer Carlos P. Romulo has pointed out, of the American "log cabin." When Ramon was six, his father, who had a spirit of independence and honesty inherited by the son, was dismissed from the school where he taught carpentry because he would not pass the son of the school superintendent.

The family then moved to Castillejos and opened a general store. Ramon and his father were hired as a working team with a road construction gang. The future president got up at 3:30 A.M. and earned 17½ cents a day. Eventually he and his father opened a carpentry and blacksmith shop near the store. But there was also politics in the family circle. When Ramon was eleven, his grandfather was elected mayor of Castillejos.

Ramon had had little opportunity to receive a formal education, a point about which his political opponents later often derided him. At the age of thirteen, however, he left home and went to Zambales Academy at San Narciso, where he was noted for his singing. In 1927, at the age of twenty, he enrolled in the College of Liberal Arts at the University of the Philippines, but became ill from overwork, and transferred to José Rizal College, nearer home, from which he was graduated. He then worked as a mechanic for the Try Tran Bus Company in Manila and became proficient at repairing cars, rising to the job of company manager. In 1933 he married Luz Banzon, whom he had courted for two years, and had a happy family life, with two daughters and a son, Ramon, Jr. (A fourth child died.)

When the Japanese invaded the Philippines in World War II, Ramon volunteered as a private, but he was made a captain and put in charge of ten ambulances, while his family went into the hills. In April, 1942, he joined forces with some American officers in a group called the Zambales Guerrillas, and fought in the resistance movement so effectively that the Japanese offered one hundred pesos for Magsaysay, dead or alive. Because of his outstanding guerrilla performance, the American Colonel Gyles Merrill submitted his name to General Douglas MacArthur for military governor of Magsaysay's native province, Zambales, where he took office on February 4, 1945.

This appointment marked the beginning of Magsaysay's political career. He distinguished himself immediately by qualities he showed for the rest of his life. He understood, and had a profound sympathy for the poor, whom he often found ill-treated by the rich and powerful. He was concerned with human welfare, and allowed neither red tape, nor political opposition, nor personal vilification to stand in the way of accomplishing his objectives. He could not abide corruption, and severely treated those who tried to buy his support. He fought for justice to all, but particularly to the little man who was at the mercy of unscrupulous and authoritarian politicians. These qualities endeared him to soldiers as well as to civilians, won him the respect of political opponents, enabled him to defeat the Communist guerrilla movement, the Hukbalahap, and eventually raised him to the highest office in the land.

As military governor of the province of Zambales, Magsaysay labored to pacify the region and to resettle landless war victims. The slogan "Land for the landless" became the keystone of his administration. When he found that a forester whom he had ordered to clear a piece of land for resettlement "was still waiting until mañana," as Romulo put it, "he blazed at the forester with such anger that the man remembers every word to this day. 'I want action!' Magsaysay shouted. 'The people can't wait. I will not pardon indifference and procrastination. If you had told me you could not do it, I would have chopped down those trees myself!' " He ended Negrito pygmies' banditry in Zambales after dicovering that they were raiding the countryside because they were hungry, by promptly arranging to have the pygmy warriors join forces with his own men.

His term as governor was of only two months' duration. But he became widely known, and won strong support when he campaigned as an independent for the Philippine Congress, and on April 23, 1946, was elected by the biggest majority in the history of Zambales. During this campaign he became known for his "inexhaustible handshaking."

[President Quirino (1948-53) called it] "the Magsaysay stroke." Later he would use a stronger descriptive word—"vulgar." Vulgar or not, the people whose hands were shaken remembered the boyish, husky candidate who spoke and dressed so simply, who drove a dilapidated jeep, and who conversed with them in their native dialect. Clearly he was one of them. He had no political group or party behind him. . . . In the jeep, which he had refused to permit his guerrillas to replace, he was hurtling over the worst and loneliest roads in the province, a firm believer in bringing government to the people.

[The new congressman] took over his new duties in a ramshackle office in the ruins of Manila. The legislative building was one of the most spectacular heaps of debris in the city. In the year 1946 the rebuilding of Manila was just starting and the representatives had temporary offices in an old school house. It was in this building rather than on the floor of Congress that Magsaysay made himself known as something new and entirely unorthodox in the political field. At first his more sophisticated colleagues did not know what to think of this congressional Hercules who seemed so determined to clean the Augean stables. There was need for a clean-up crusade in the newly fledged government. The morale of the country was in ruins, as was the beautiful city of Manila, and the wrongs to be righted and the innovations to be made kept Magsaysay hard at work, night and day.

In the Congress chamber Magsaysay kept quiet. He did not indulge in oratory, as did many of his colleagues, some of whom ridiculed him. One of them "complained in the suavest terms that the Zambalese representative was wearing a hole in his Congressional chair with the seat of his pants. Another denied this as gravely, saying that the charge was impossible—Magsaysay's pants could not possibly make a hole in the official chair since the pants themselves were already full of holes." Magsaysay, although deeply upset, "would not apologize for his dress to his enemies. But to friends he explained simply, 'I am a poor man.'" And on another occasion, when he called, in shirt and pants, on a government official with a farmer on whose behalf he was requesting aid, and was made to wait in the anteroom for hours only to be received when the official heard he was a Congressman, Magsaysay shouted, "You and your attitude is what is wrong with our present government. You ignore the common man. You evaluate a person by his clothes."

As he had done when military governor of Zambales, he cut red tape to obtain what he felt his people needed. When he discovered that surplus war material, including Quonset huts, was being bought and sold by politicians and businessmen, he commandeered one hundred huts and had them transported to Zambales by boat, to be installed as schools in the province. When the case was brought to the attention of President Roxas (1946-48), Magsaysay pointed out the illegality of surplus goods sales, and the president not only accepted his view but sent him to Washington as chairman of the Committee on Guerrilla Affairs to secure passage of the Rogers bill giving benefits to Philippine veterans. Magsaysay won many friends in Washington, and obtained $18 million in veterans' aid. "When, some time after this one of his critics sneered that 'Magsaysay could not compose one grammatically correct English sentence,' Magsaysay countered: 'It is a good thing that President Truman could speak Tagalog, otherwise I would not have returned from Washington with eighteen million dollars for our veterans.' "

His continued struggle for justice and honesty in government, against all forms of corruption, notably the stuffing of ballot boxes, brought him a second term in Congress. When President Quirino became a virtual prisoner of the Communist guerrillas, the Huks, Magsaysay offered a plan to outwit the Communists, and Quirino appointed him Secretary of National Defense on September 1, 1950. In this post Magsaysay ruthlessly weeded out officers who were not able and energetic. The Army, he contended, could win over the peasants who had become followers of the Huks if it only understood their problems and worked to rehabilitate them.

He fearlessly met with a Huk leader, whose confidence he won, and who eventually led him to the homes of the top Communist leaders. They were arrested in one swoop, except for one who was killed in the raid. He planted his own men among the Huks in the countryside, and then arranged to have all the Huk commanders killed at a "picnic" to which they had been invited ostensibly to hear news about Communist policy. But he did not only destroy Huk leaders. He built villages for reconstructed Huks, thus fulfilling promises the Communists had made to the peasants but had never kept. One of the Communist leaders often said that communism's worst enemy in the Philippines was the popularity of Magsaysay.

In spite of the brilliant success of his anti-Huk campaign, he eventually came into conflict with Quirino by insisting that voters should be protected in the 1951 elections. Magsaysay sent 40,000 soldiers, 4,500 ROTC cadets, and 5,500 reserves to watch ballot boxes, and in this election many members of Quirino's Liberal party lost.

The final break with Quirino came when Magsaysay challenged the governor of the province of Negros, Rafael Lacson, who was terrorizing all who dared to oppose him in any way. A poor but courageous editor-politician, Moises Padilla, had decided to run for mayor of a small town in Negros. He was not a Lacson man, and was warned to stay out of politics. When Padilla refused to be cowed, Lacson's men seized him at home, beat him, dragged him through the town as a warning to others, then brought him back to his house and shot him in cold blood. When Padilla lay dying, his last words to his mother were, "Tell Magsaysay." The mother sent a telegram to Manila. Magsaysay immediately flew to Negros airport, then drove a car himself through the night over lonely roads to Padilla's town. To Padilla's mother he said, "I swear to you that your son's death shall not go unavenged. He will not have died in vain. I promise."

He took the body of Padilla to Manila and the newspapers spread the Padilla story throughout the Philippines. Then for six days Magsaysay pleaded with Quirino to dismiss Lacson, a leader of the president's party. He finally won when he told Quirino, "The people are so outraged by the death of Padilla that they are ready to stone Malacañang" (the presidential palace). Quirino ousted Lacson, who was brought to trial and sentenced to death.

Quirino, however, no longer wanted Magsaysay in office and Magsaysay resigned on February 28, 1953. A movement to elect Magsaysay for President, called MPM, promptly developed. People from all over the Philippines gathered to campaign for their hero, even leaving their jobs to work for him. Magsaysay ran on the Nationalist party ticket, and on November 10, 1953, he was elected president by the greatest majority in the history of the Philippines. He assumed office on December 30, 1953.

In the office of president Magsaysay remained as simple, unaffected, and hard-working as he had been throughout his life. He wanted to be in close touch with the people and insisted on receiving all those who asked to see him, until the pressure of public affairs made it impossible. He enjoyed showing visitors from the countryside through Malacañang Palace, remembering the modest huts from which many of them came.

His objectives in internal affairs were, as in the past, honesty in politics, economic and social improvement of the people through education, development of agriculture, and construction of small village industries. He opposed not only the Communists but also the extreme nationalists who spoke of "Asia for the Asians," who wanted to nationalize all foreign properties in the Philippines, and who constantly found fault with Americans. He firmly believed in the need of cooperation with the United States. He avoided political retaliation against those who denounced his policies, and abstained from electioneering on behalf of his party's candidates in the November, 1955, elections on the ground that he had to do his "home work." His confidence in the people was justified when he won his greatest triumph in these elections, and all his candidates gained seats in the Senate.

He was still in the early stages of carrying out his plans for political, economic, and social reform when early in the morning of March 17, 1957, his plane, en route to Manila, crashed into a mountainside on the island of Cebu, and he was killed. "Some died from the shock of the news," says Romulo. When Magsaysay lay in state in the Palace grounds, hundreds of thousands of persons poured in and a million lined the road to the cemetery.

But even after his death the memory of what he had undertaken, and had hoped to achieve, lingered on, affecting the expectations that Filipinos have had of subsequent political leaders. His best-remembered phrase is the one with which he concluded a speech in the Plaza Miranda in Manila the night before the presidential election of 1953, after the Quirino administration had called him an ignoramus, incapable of making himself understood, of running a government, or of representing a nation. Speaking in Tagalog, Magsaysay retold the story of his flight to Negros to bring back the body of Moises Padilla. To quote Romulo, "He described the tears on the face of Padilla's mother when she recognized him as a friend," and exclaimed, "Do you think she felt I was too ignorant to serve the people?" His brother Jesus said in 1953, "Ramon will always be one of us. He is a man of the people."

# 4

# Africa

FOR a newcomer to Africa the most dramatic first impression is the sense of hearing many clocks ticking away the hours of historic decisions—historic not only for the Africans, but also for the Europeans, Asians, and Arabs who for better or worse have linked their destinies to those of the native peoples.

In north and south, in east and west and center, the clocks are registering different hours: the hours of independence achieved by Ghana in 1958, and shortly after by Guinea; the rapidly struck hours for one French territory in Africa after another, from the Federation of Mali (split in 1960 between the Senegal and Sudan) to the Ivory Coast; from the Republic of the Congo to Madagascar; for the former Belgian Congo on June 30, 1960; for Nigeria in October of that year. Will the clock strike for Tanganyika in 1965? And when will it strike—amid peace or civil strife—for Kenya and Uganda, for Algeria? Success or failure in synchronizing Africa's many clocks will determine the future of the continent and the role its leaders hope to play in the world community, which is itself torn by conflict between the West and the Communist bloc.

What, if anything, can one foresee in Africa? "Nothing in Africa is unpredictable," said a thoughtful and sensitive Belgian administrator in 1959. Yet in spite of ample warnings on the spot, in spite of the West's postwar experience in Asia and the Middle East, the British, French, and, most of all, the Belgians—except for some outstanding individuals, among them Sir Andrew Cohen, former governor of Uganda, General Charles de Gaulle, and former Governor Léon Pétillon of the Belgian Congo—were slow to sense the explosive forces of nationalism gathering momentum in Africa. And even today Spain and Portugal, both ruled by authoritarian governments, remain unmoved by changing times in their African colonies—as do the Portuguese in their colony of Goa, a small enclave on the territory of otherwise independent India.

In those areas of Africa where the hot, humid climate made European settlement impractical, from Dakar to Lagos, Westerners have found it possible to accept, if not with enthusiasm at least with friendly resignation, the surge of African peoples toward autonomy or independence. In north, east, and south, where the cooler climate favored European immigration, and the returns on investment in agriculture and/or the extraction of raw materials—copper, gold, uranium— brought rich rewards, Westerners are still struggling to keep time back: by armed force in Algeria, by repression in the Rhodesias, by harsh segregation in South Africa, and by delaying policies based on a variety of motives in East Africa. Yet everywhere European men and women who have the courage to face realities are aware that sooner or later, in one form or another, political independence is the goal Africans seek and will achieve.

The French manager of an airline in Dakar has another answer about the future. *"En Afrique,"* he says, *"tout s'arrange"* ("In Africa everything takes care of itself"). In situations which were not predicted soon enough, and which in Asia and the Middle East and Eastern Europe produced bloody revolutions, military *coups d'état*, or totalitarian dictatorships, Africa's vast process of change-over from colonialism to nationalism is going ahead, on the whole, with remarkable self-control and lack of mutual recrimination on the part of all concerned, except for the tragic events in the Congo. The grievous exceptions—the Congo, the six-year war in Algeria and the unremitting apartheid in the Union of South Africa, an independent country, not a colony—only point up the generally orderly liquidation of colonial rule ("decolonization," as the French call it) and the West's acceptance of revolutionary changes—economic and social, as well as political—in its relations with the Africans. Those who talk about politics in Africa do not brood on the past. "Life is not yesterday, it is today," said a Ghanian neswpaperman to A. N. Rosenthal of *The New York Times* in October, 1960.

The degree and temper of this acceptance seem to depend on the attitude each colonial power displayed when confronted with comparable problems in Asia and the Middle East during the past forty years. The British, who made a timely exit from the Indian subcontinent, although they did not avert the tragedy of partition between India and Pakistan, have proved sensitive to the need for readjustment in Africa. The French, after suffering a disastrous defeat in Indochina, have been profoundly torn between two sentiments: their realization, made explicit by de Gaulle as early as 1944 in his famous speech at Brazzaville, that their relationship with their African colonies had to be altered if the *présence française* was to continue in Africa; and their reluctance to recognize that the Algerians would not accept terms less generous than those France had accorded to Tunisia and Morocco and, in 1958, had promised to grant to those African territories which, having joined the Community, might eventually seek independence.

Meanwhile Belgium, whose colonial experience had been limited to Africa, did not wake up to the problems posed by fast-moving events in British and French colonies—and particularly in Brazzaville, capital of the former French Congo, now a republic, a ferry ride across the Congo from Léopoldville—until the riots of January 4, 1959. These riots, although apparently accidental in nature, made Brussels aware, as one Belgian put it, that the hour of decision had struck—but struck five minutes after midnight. Then the Belgians, shocked by the riots and fearful of becoming involved in a prolonged bloody war such as the French had been waging in Algeria, decided to relinquish their African colony, rich in copper and diamonds, without the orderly preparations made by Britain and France.

If the Western colonial powers, in dealing with Africa, are to draw on their experience in Asia and the Middle East, what comparisons, and what contrasts, can be found between the various areas where colonialism flourished until World War II?

In Africa the Westerner experiences an acute sense of the lack of history; of that heritage of other ancient and glorious civilizations in which we have a share, if not through their absorption into Western ideas and beliefs, at least through familiarity with their religions, their monuments, their contributions to art and philosophy. One of the characters in Elspeth Huxley's novel about East Africa, *The Flame Trees of Thika,* vividly expresses this feeling when she says, "Doesn't it strike you as strange that nothing people have created here has survived? Not even a few traces? No ruins of cities or temples—no ancient overgrown roads—no legends of past empires—no statues hidden in the ground—no tombs or burial mounds? No sign that generations of people have lived here, lived and died?"

This sense of historical void, of lack of contact between the past of the West and that of Africa, has two simultaneous results. It makes the Westerner feel remote from African experience, causing him to say, as many do, that "it is impossible to understand Africans." And it makes him assume that the Western heritage—in terms of Christianity, as well as of administrative talent and technological skill—is superior, and for many years to come will remain superior to that of the Africans.

Is it true that Westerners cannot understand Africans? An American Negro educator who has worked in India and the Caribbean as well as in Africa contends that the difficulty of understanding is mutual and is due to the fact that neither Westerners nor Africans "hear," literally, concepts which are unfamiliar to them. For example, many Africans say in all honesty that they do not hear Western classical music even when they listen to it. Both sides need to become tuned in to the same wave length, so that the words exchanged may have the same meaning for both. To do this, the Westerner must come to realize that the traditional values of African tribes, strange and in some instances even repugnant as they seem to us—like the ritual murders still performed by fishermen near Abidjan, capital of the Ivory Coast, a few paces from the sumptuous villas of Western bankers and industrialists—constitute a historical heritage which Western anthropologists and sociologists have only begun to piece together. Unless we can understand these values, we shall be unable to engage in a dialogue of ideas with the Africans; and Western influence will remain limited to the superficial acquisition by Africans of our methods of producing and distributing material goods.

The Reverend Father Placide Tempels, a Belgian missionary in the Congo, points this out in his eloquent study of Bantu philosophy when he says: "If one has not penetrated the depth of their personality, if one does not know against what background their actions take place, it is not possible to understand the Bantus. One does not enter into spiritual contact with them. One does not make oneself heard by them, especially when one broaches the great spiritual verities. On the contrary, when thinking to 'civilize' the 'man,' one risks striking at him instead, working to increase the number of the uprooted and becoming the artisan of revolts."

Basically, and quite aside from errors of administration or economic development which may be charged to the colonial powers, Westerners have made the mistake of trying to change Africans into their own image—to make them Christians, to make them French or British —on the theory that they were thus conferring on Africans the greatest boon at their command. The Westerners thus set up for the Africans a standard of attainment which not only was impossible of achievement within a century by peoples still living in large part at the level of Europe's premedieval period, but which in effect downgraded those achievements of which Africans could be proud. The Africans have not yet had an opportunity to choose freely, as the Japanese did in the Meiji era and the Indians are doing today, those values of the West they want to accept and those they may prefer to reject.

Having thus deprecated Africa's past, the Westerners tended to use the deficiencies of Africans—as measured by European standards of the nineteenth and twentieth centuries—as justification for the continuance of colonial rule.

As the French sociologist, Georges Balandier, points out, the Western nations resorted to a series of rationalizations to explain why they had to remain in Africa. Among them were the superiority of the white race—in terms of historical advancement, military power, technology, and Christian religion (as compared with fetishism, paganism, and Islam); the incapacity of the Africans to rule themselves; the despotism of traditional chiefs (the alternative, it was feared, was that the stability maintained by these chiefs as representatives of the Western rulers might be destroyed by their disappearance and the rise of modern political leaders who might become a "dictatorial clique"); the inability of Africans to make effective use of the raw materials of their territories; and the meager financial resources of the colonial areas, which would hamper their future development once they had become independent.

How true are these "rationalizations"? To what extent will the prophets of doom be proved right in their predictions that Africa "will return to chaos" once the liquidation of colonialism has been completed?

It would be a grave error—and an error which responsible Africans endeavor to avoid—not to recognize the great contribution which Europe has made to the development of the African continent in the past century. Sir Philip Mitchell, a former governor of Kenya, in his book, *African Afterthoughts,* has summed up the conditions the Europeans found in East Africa as follows:

These people had certainly reached a remarkable level of culture in many respects, but even they were totally ignorant of writing or ciphering; they had no alphabet or hieroglyphics, no numerals, no calendar, or division of time, no wheel, plough, nor machine of any kind. Nor had they any respect for human life, especially the lives of the common people, who were killed in wars, raids, or mere palace ceremonies with much less compunction than cattle. If, then, they had come far from the Stone Age, they had halted surprisingly short of the time at which suddenly, in a few short years, the curtains of the ages were torn aside and showed the world at large African man and woman plainly to be seen for the first time on the contemporary stage, at the turn of the 19th century.

Giving full recognition to the contributions the West has made over periods of rule varying from three hundred years by the French in Senegal to sixty years by the French in Guinea and the British in Kenya, what are the assets, and what the liabilities, which the Africans possess today as they move into a new era of relations with their former, or still present, colonial rulers?

On the asset side of the ledger both West and East Africa, in sharp contrast to Asia and the Middle East, with their vast populations (in India, China, Japan, Egypt) pressing increasingly on limited food resources, at present enjoy a favorable ratio of food to population—except when catastrophe strikes, as in the Congo. No one goes hungry, for the tribal community or the family clan takes care of the poor, the feeble, the aged. By comparison with the often emaciated and listless villagers of India, subsisting in one-room mud huts, the Africans look healthy, strong, gay, and full of vitality, and are often decently housed. There is, however, a great deal of undernourishment due to lack of proteins, and this is one of the causes of widespread blindness, with an estimated 500,000 blind people, for example, in Nigeria.

In the future, however, as the population grows with improvement in public-health measures (Nigeria's 37 million population is expected to double by the year 2000, and that of France's African territories to increase by 60 per cent in thirty years), more food must be produced at home if famines are to be averted and foreign currency now spent on food imports (rice, canned meat, and other products increasingly sought as living standards rise) is to be conserved for the development and diversification of each country's economy. Yet the local meat supply cannot be increased in Ghana, Nigeria, and other areas in the tsetse-fly belt until the deadly germ the fly carries (the trypanosome) has been eliminated, and cattle have been made safe from infection. The West African Institute for Trypanosomiasis Research (WAITR) at Kaduna, Nigeria, and its counterpart in East Africa are hard at work on this problem, with remarkable success. Through the joint efforts of WAITR for West Africa as a whole and of the medical authorities in Nigeria, that country's human sleeping-sickness cases have been reduced within a decade from 100,000 a year to 5,000.

The central economic problem of the Africans who have already achieved independence or seek to achieve it in the near future is, first, to modernize their agriculture so that it can provide increased sustenance for their people and compete successfully in world markets with similar products from newly developing countries of other continents (particularly Latin America, in coffee, cocoa, bananas, sugar); and, second, to create consumer industries (bicycle tires, glassware, textiles, bottling plants, and so on) which could replace goods now imported and offer employment to farmers who leave the land. Otherwise the African countries, with their now mutually competitive economies, vulnerable to sharp fluctuations in the prices of primary commodities, might find that political independence had only increased their economic dependence on the technologically advanced nations outside Africa. This is what Felix Houphouet-Boigny, premier of the Ivory Coast, means when he says, "Independence is a fiction."

In the task of economic reorganization the Africans have a psychological asset. This is their common-sense, hardheaded attitude toward their own future, which, again, is in sharp contrast to the often highly emotional attitude of Asians and Middle Easterners during their struggle for independence from the West.

The Africans are determined to have a voice in their own affairs, if not immediately, then within the next five, or at most, ten years. But they recognize the benefits brought by the Western powers in terms of opportunities for education, health, economic improvements, and financial investment. They know that once they have achieved independence they will continue to need outside aid, both capital and technical, and hope to obtain it from London, Paris, and Brussels as well as from West Germany, Italy, the United States, the USSR, and new sources such as Israel and Japan.

They have a sober sense of the limitations of their economic resources, and are not inclined to think in terms of grandiose plans for industrialization, as Yugoslavia and several Asian and Middle Eastern countries did in the early postwar years. True, Ghana hopes to build the Volta River project whose maximum cost is estimated at $300 million, and to harness the resulting power for the development of an aluminum plant, using local bauxite; and Guinea, where an alumina plant was being constructed by the French firm of Fria, looks forward to the construction of the Konkouré dam.

But African leaders, however great their desire to achieve prestige by industrial expansion, are aware that alumina or other plants would provide relatively little relief for the unemployment created by the drift of villagers to urban areas. (In Brazzaville, for example, three quarters of the population are unemployed and subsist on the wages earned by the few who have found work.) Improvement of agriculture by modern methods, however, might be made to appear at least as important and respectable as industrialization, and the amenities of city life might be brought to village areas—as the British in Kenya are trying to do through their land-consolidation and village-building programs in the once-turbulent Kikuyu areas aroused by the Mau Mau. Then the African countries might be able to achieve at least a modest rise in living standards without the political convulsions experienced in other underdeveloped continents.

Nor is this sober realism of the Africans contradicted by the emotional "messianism" which is rife in the Belgian Congo and which has from time to time also emerged in other areas of Africa. The various "messianic" movements, springing from neo-Christian sources, often with the full complement of organized churches and "saviors" who proclaim their readiness to die for the redemption of their peoples, represented an attempt to escape from the rule of colonial governments which had shown themselves unready to prepare the way for ultimate independence. Forged through appeal to faith and emotion under conditions of crisis, such African organizations can play a powerful political role. This has been particularly true in the former Belgian Congo, where Joseph Kasavubu, leader of the nationalist movement Abako, which has strong religious overtones, called before independence for the creation of an independent Bakongo state, and succeeded in organizing a political boycott of the Belgian administration. Kasavubu, devoted to his tribe, became president of the Congo on the eve of Belgium's departure in 1960, with the late Patrice Lumumba, who urged a unitary Congo state, as premier.

In the midst of the subsequent chaos, the UN, under the statesman-like leadership of Secretary-General Dag Hammarskjold, acted to prevent attempts by Belgian mining interests to break up the Congo's territory through the secession of copper and diamond-rich Katanga and other areas, to bar intervention by the USSR, and to restore some semblance of political order and economic organization. Before Lumumba's death early in 1961, some observers believed that, in spite of his mercurial temper, his theatrical exhibitionism, his outspoken sympathy for communism, and his seeming irresponsibility (displayed in some degrees by other Congolese leaders) Lumumba was in a better position to command the enthusiasm and support of the Congolese than any of his rivals.

Still another asset for the future is the passionate desire of the Africans for education. This is true not only among those who have been exposed to Christian teaching by Protestants or Catholics, but also among Muslims, especially in northern Nigeria, who because of their resistance to non-Islamic ideas had previously lagged in educational development.

The colonial powers have found it increasingly difficult to finance education for Africans on the scale required for the development of a modern society. Some (for example Belgium) had provided facilities for primary education, but until recently had done little about secondary education, and practically nothing at the university level, leaving behind them about twenty college-trained Congolese. They thus created a large pool of Africans with a modicum of literacy, but no elite to lead them—millions of privates, but no generals or even officers. Others (for example Britain in Kenya) have only now realized the need for universal education, but they have offered to a still very small elite opportunities for study at English universities, and they had established Makerere University College in Kampala, the capital of Uganda in East Africa. Many Africans regard education primarily as a tool for material advancement in modern society, whether as employees of European business firms, civil servants, or technicians. Others see education as the key to genuine political independence.

But, many Westerners ask, are the Africans ready for independence? Or should independence, which all but the diehards in areas of European settlement—particularly Algeria and Kenya—admit to be inevitable, come only gradually, by stages, anywhere from five to fifty years, depending on conditions in a given area? Gradualism, in the opinion of those who urge it, is required by the "backwardness" of the Africans, who are not yet "ripe" for freedom. A staged withdrawal, gradualists believe, would permit the Europeans, many of whom have a guilty conscience about what they regard as a failure to prepare "their" Africans more rapidly for political, economic, and social change-over, to train them for the tasks of self-rule. Yet, given the small number of educated Africans today, would European plans for further training mean postponement of independence for another generation, as many Africans fear?

This emphasis on the need for further preparation has been given fresh impetus by the West's disappointment with the experience of Ghana. There, President and Prime Minister Kwame Nkrumah, in the three years since his country achieved independence, has challenged the authority of hereditary chieftains in the northern region of Ashanti and has made the existence of a parliamentary opposition increasingly difficult, although not yet impossible. Critics of Ghana in Britain, the United States, and even some Asian countries have deplored the authoritarian character of its government; and some have asked whether independence should be granted to regimes which do not practice democracy. But is democracy possible in Africa?

In making their legitimate defense of democratic institutions, these critics appear to regard self-rule as necessarily identical with democracy. Desirable as this identity would be, it is difficult to see how a colonial power could insist on withholding independence until a country had demonstrated its capacity to operate democratically. For colonial rule, by its very nature, is a contradiction of democracy, and even with the best of intentions a technologically backward non-Western country cannot begin to develop on democratic lines until it has ceased to be subject to colonial authority. Nor can the Western nations, when they look back on their own political institutions at a stage of economic growth comparable to that of Ghana or Guinea today, truthfully claim that twentieth-century democracy was flourishing in England or France in the premedieval period, or even by 1900.

Many of Africa's new political leaders—notably in Ghana—are first-generation literates. They are proud of having spanned the gulf between their tribal illiterate society and the responsible posts they occupy as administrators and diplomats, but have not had an opportunity to acquire the experience in public affairs which Western democracies have accumulated over centuries. Nor does time, in a period of jetspeed changes, permit them to develop new institutions at leisure. The process of political telescoping, characteristic of many non-Western nations, is particularly rapid in Africa. Tribal chiefs who resist change are being shorn of authority by modern-minded politicians, who, in turn, before they have had time to develop into nineteenth-century liberals on the Western model, find themselves already being crowded off the stage by trade-union leaders like Sékou Touré and Tom Mboya.

Moreover, the tasks of economic development on which the colonial powers had made a successful start, but a start largely limited to their own commercial and security needs—such as ports, railways, and roads which service European-owned plantations, farms, and mines—require intervention by governments for many years to come, as Professor W. W. Rostow of the Massachusetts Institute of Technology has pointed out in his study on economic growth. It is the state, not individual entrepreneurs, foreign or domestic, which will have to build the infrastructure—roads, bridges, dams, additional communications facilities—that will be needed before a soundly based program for a country's economic "take-off" toward maturity can be effectively started with internal and/or foreign financial resources.

Under these circumstances, regrettable as this may seem to those who had hoped independence would automatically bring about democracy, the African states may be expected, at least in the early stages, to live under one-man or one-party rule. This has been made clear by the experience to date of African countries with a wide variety of colonial backgrounds. Liberia with William V. S. Tubman, Guinea with Sékou Touré, Ghana with Nkrumah, Tunisia with Habib Bourguiba, the Ivory Coast with Houphouet-Boigny—much as they differ in historical development, religions, and cultural heritage from their own experience or from the contributions of foreign cultures—have one common denominator. Each is ruled by an able and successful leader who, subject to a few qualifications, is in effect an authoritarian head of state, even though not a totalitarian ruler on the Communist model; and each, when questioned about the existence of an opposition, usually refers to dissenters as "young hotheads" or as "malcontents without a following."

Each has used pressures of all kinds, implicitly or explicitly, to reduce the power of the tribal chiefs—hereditary or elected rulers—on whom the colonial governments had usually relied to carry out their commands in "the bush." Sékou Touré, with his experience as a trade-union organizer, built a network of local units across Guinea, through which he succeeded in isolating and circumventing the chiefs by peaceful means. Nkrumah, less well prepared for the resistance of the Ashanti chiefs (who rightly feared that the new independent government would end their domination), resorted to strong-arm methods, with the result that at the outset dangerous tensions between the new and the old order threatened Ghana. Experience, however, brought an easing of tensions in 1959, and unless fresh difficulties flare up Nkrumah may succeed in integrating the old chiefs into a modern state. Thus gradually throughout Africa, in areas under the direction of more or less authoritarian politicians, the transfer of power from the *ancien régime* of tribal institutions to twentieth-century governments, which in other areas of the world involved bloody conflict, is being effected by relatively peaceful means—again with the exception of Algeria and the Congo.

Nigeria, which achieved independence in October, 1960, may prove an exception to this one-man, one-party trend, because of three important factors: (1) the need to create within the Nigerian Federation a balance between the country's three regions with their three main tribal groups—the Yorubas in the west, led by Chief Obafemi Awolowo, head of the Action party; the Ibos in the east, led by Nnamdi Azikiwe, head of the National Council of Nigeria and the Cameroons (NCNC); and the Muslims in the north, the Hausa and Fulani, whose premier is Sir Alhaji Ahmadu; (2) the democratic ideas and experience of the Yoruba tribe of the western region, whose capital, Ibadan, the most populous city in Africa, is the seat of Nigeria's university; and (3) the newly emerging desire of the Muslims for education and social reforms, and their respect for British methods of administration. The first prime minister of the federation, Alhaji Sir Abubakar Tafawa Balewa, a northerner, is noted for his moderation, his dedication to public service, and his gift as reconciler of conflicting factions in Lagos, which is now the federal capital. The Nigerians have also proved more skillful than other Africans in integrating traditional chiefs into the framework of their emerging parliamentary government through the creation of a House of Chiefs. This House, somewhat comparable to the British House of Lords, will give the country the benefit of the views of its elder statesmen who, in turn, will have the satisfaction of participating in the new state's affairs.

Most of the African political leaders, irrespective of their origins and training, were at one time or another exposed to Communist ideas and influence—whether in the United States, Paris, London or Moscow. This was true of Nkrumah, son of an artisan, who studied at Lincoln University, Pennsylvania, and in London, and plied many trades to earn a living in the United States; of Sékou Touré, grandson of the famous chief Somary, foe of the French, who did not finish grammar school in Guinea but successfully organized a trade union in the railway administration where he worked, and went on to become a labor leader in 1956, and a member of the French Chamber of Deputies before the creation of the Community; of Houphouet-Boigny, a Catholic, a prosperous physician and planter, now prime minister of the Ivory Coast; and of Tom Mboya, who rose from sanitary inspector in the service of Nairobi's City Council to general secretary of the Kenya Federation of Labor and leader of the Independence Movement party formed in August, 1959, and who hopes to be Kenya's first prime minister.

Nor was this widespread interest in communism either fortuitous or surprising. In the depression years of the 1930's and again after World War II, when the Communists, particularly in France, exercised a significant influence, communism seemed the most promising ally of those seeking independence from colonial rule in Africa. This does not mean, however, that African leaders became either blind followers or tools of communism, as their political opponents often assert. Their passionate desire for independence means independence from Communist intervention as well as from Western colonialism, as Nkrumah proved when he turned in the first instance to Israel, not to the USSR, for economic aid to counterbalance aid from Britain.

Other African leaders, trained for the priesthood in Catholic seminaries, which at one time offered the best opportunity for higher education, were defrocked when they abandoned their vocation (notably Abbé Fulbert Youlou, premier of the Congo Republic and the late Barthélemy Boganda, the able premier of the Central African Republic, killed in an airplane accident in 1959). Such men, even if not suspected of past Communist sympathies, share some of the social ideas of their Marxist-inspired contemporaries.

The real test of the intentions of the African leaders will be not their predilection for or opposition to communism, but the direction they take on two major issues: (1) racialism; will they seek an Africa for Africans, to the exclusion of Europeans and Asians?; and (2) orientation in world affairs; will they retain links with the French Community, the British Commonwealth, a Belgian-Congolese Community of the future; drift into the Soviet orbit; or adopt a policy of neutralism?

To paraphrase a statement Sir Andrew Cohen, a former governor of Uganda, made about Ruanda-Urundi in 1959 before the Trusteeship Council, where he represents Britain: Those who have had the privilege of visiting Africa are invariably struck by its great beauty. No one, I think, now would call this continent a sleeping beauty, but some of us might call it a waking beauty.

Africa is indeed awake, and its relations with the rest of the world are changing at breath-taking pace. Until World War II, which precipitated the breakup of Western colonialism throughout the non-Western world, the position of each African territory in world affairs was determined by the Western nation which administered it. The Africans had no voice of their own, and even their contacts with one another were limited by lack of communications over the continent's vast distances and by the cultural as well as political and economic orientation of each colonial area toward its respective metropolitan country—Britain or France, Belgium or Spain or Portugal.

With the spread of movements for independence, the map of Africa is astir with changes in nomenclature and in relationships between African territories and their colonial rulers, as well as between the various newly formed African units. The multiracial and multinational Commonwealth, with Britain at its core, welcomed Ghana to its membership in 1957 and Nigeria in 1960, in spite of the violently anti-African policy of one of its members, South Africa. The Community, established by President Charles de Gaulle under the 1958 constitution of the Fifth Republic, offers a framework for the co-operation of France with its African territories, from Senegal to Madagascar, all of which, under Article 87, were granted the right to choose independence if they wished; and one after another made use of this right. Today the Belgians, in spite of the shock they suffered in 1960, hope that a Belgian-Congolese Community may emerge by peaceful means from the current turmoil in their former colony.

Three major questions dominate discussions in Africa about the future shape of its relations with the world. First, will some territories be satisfied with autonomy within an organization established, in the first instance, by the colonial power, or will all demand independence? Second, if all achieve independence, will Africa run the danger of being "Balkanized" or will the new states avert this danger by creating one or more federations? And, third, will independent African states, whether federated or not, retain strong ties with the West, drift into the Communist orbit, or follow the example of India and Egypt and adopt a policy of nonalignment?

The debate about autonomy and independence has been unequivocally answered by Britain in favor of independence within the Commonwealth. In the French Community, however, the issue was at first undecided. Guinea's abrupt decision in October, 1958, to proclaim its independence from the Community, in spite of de Gaulle's warning that it would do so at its peril, caught France unprepared; and the hostility promptly shown by Paris toward Sékou Touré was not lost on the other African territories. The French feared—and rightly—that Guinea's decision might set an example for its neighbors. If those who voted "no" were treated as well as those who voted "yes," the Community would break up before it had had time to become consolidated.

For a few months after Guinea's withdrawal it looked as if the other French territories would follow the advice of Felix Houphouet-Boigny, premier of the Ivory Coast, and remain satisfied with autonomy within the Community and the prospect of continued financial aid from France. In the hope of winning the support of other territories to his policy, Houphouet-Boigny in 1959 organized a loose Council of the Entente with three neighboring areas, Dahomey, Niger, and Upper Volta.

But signs of unrest soon became visible in the Senegal and the Sudan, which had formed the Federation of Mali. Léopold Senghor of Senegal, noted for his French poetry as well as for his political talents, spoke in July, 1959, of independence as the ultimate goal. Younger men among his supporters demanded that Senegal should have its own spokesmen in international bodies, such as the United Nations and the International Labor Organization. Leaders of the Sudan urged independence. At the September, 1959, meeting of the Executive Council of the Community in Paris, Modibo Keita, the Sudanese premier who was also president of the Federation of Mali, declared that the Federation would seek independence by peaceful means, within the framework of the Community. The other members of the Community promptly followed suit, including those which had formed the Council of the Entente. Thus by 1961 France's African territories had become independent one after another. Meanwhile, Sengal had seceded from the Mali Federation, in spite of protests by the Sudan. The question now is whether the French Community can prove as successful as the British Commonwealth in reconciling the interests of the metropolitan country with those of its former colonies. The answer will depend on the extent to which France, with its traditionally centralized government, can develop the flexibility of Britain's unwritten constitutional system.

If and when the African territories all achieve independence, will Africa become a new Balkans, constantly subject to eruptions of conflicts between neighboring states, and thus a temptation to great-power intervention? Or will the independent states stabilize the continent through one or more federations?

In 1960 two general patterns for combining the new states into larger groups were under discussion. The first pattern was a loose union, proposed by Houphouet-Boigny, and illustrated under his leadership in the Council of the Entente (the Ivory Coast, Upper Volta, Niger, and Dahomey), whose members retained their own political institutions but undertook to co-operate with respect to customs, trade, communications, and other technical matters. The second pattern was a strong federation, for West Africa to start with, but later for Africa as a whole, urged by Sékou Touré and Kwame Nkrumah, who formed the Guinea-Ghana union in 1958, and had hoped to win the support of the Congo's Patrice Lumumba.

This union, however, has so far remained on paper. Meanwhile, President William S. Tubman of Liberia, at the Sanoquelli conference of July, 1959, attended by Liberia, Ghana, and Guinea, urged a loose West African union for the time being. It is doubtful that any decision on federation will be taken until after Nigeria, the West African country which has the largest population—and thus a strong voice in world affairs—decides on the course it will follow.

Moreover, the question of who would lead a West Africa Federation may raise delicate problems of national prestige. Nkrumah of Ghana seemed to be a front-running contender until Sékou Touré took power in Guinea. Then some observers thought that the Guinea leader, with his greater sophistication, might win out; others pointed out that Ghana's cocoa-produced wealth would give it a head start in the race. And Africa waits to see which leader will assume paramount influence in independent Nigeria.

In 1959 President Tubman emerged as a conciliator between the contending aspirants, Ghana and Guinea. Subsequently, however, the ruthless and dynamic Premier Lumumba of the Congo boldly called for a united Africa with Léopoldville as its capital. Now will the latest entry, Julius Nyerere, win out as an all-African leader when Tanganyika achieves independence in 1965?

As one looks out of the Ghanian Foreign Ministry at the nearby race track, one cannot help speculating about the identity of the ultimate winner at the goal post. Few, however, believe that even if a West Africa federation is achieved, it will attract East Africa, whose problems differ in many important respects. There, under auspicious circumstances, another federation might be formed by Kenya, Uganda, and Tanganyika, for which many joint technical services are already operated by the High Commission for East Africa with its headquarters in Nairobi.

But whether the new African states federate or not, will they remain linked to the West, will they turn to the USSR and Communist China, or will they remain on the side lines of the East-West struggle?

If the Western nations are patient and wise there is good reason to believe that the Africans, freed from Western political overlordship, will retain close economic and cultural ties with the West. The Africans, as has already been pointed out, are sober-minded and realistic. They are aware of cultural ties—language, education, contacts through literature, art, and music—which link them to the former metropolitan countries. If the Western colonial powers forbear making political use of past cultural attachments, the Africans may well request increased cultural give and take, import additional teachers from France and Britain, as well as from the United States, and seek to develop bilingual education in French and English as proposed by Ghana and Guinea.

The Africans are also keenly aware of the economic advantages they can derive from maintaining relations with the metropolitan countries. Former French and British colonies are accustomed to dealing with French and British merchants and bankers, in francs and pounds sterling. They welcome the prospect of selling their mutually competitive goods—bananas, coffee, cotton—in new markets. For example, Guinea since independence has been selling bananas and coffee to Russia and Eastern Europe, a decision applauded by French planters and merchants. But the former colonies hope to obtain continuing and —wishfully—increased financial aid from Paris and London through the French Fund for Assistance and Cooperation with the states of the Community (FAC) and the British Colonial Development Fund.

The alternatives to such aid often look attractive. But hopes for aid from the six European countries joined in the Common Market, from international institutions, from the Communist bloc, have not yet been realized on a significant scale. Guinea's expectations of prompt assistance from the UN following the departure of the French administration were dashed by the customary investigations and delays which seem inordinately long to impatient peoples. As seen from Africa, the mills of international financial agencies grind slowly and they grind exceeding small. The UN Technical Assistance Board allocated $5.3 million for countries and territories in Africa for 1960. For 1961-62, however, the Board contemplated the allocation of $21.7 million. The World Bank in 1960 granted a total of $132.7 million for African projects. The United States, under the Mutual Security Act for economic and technical assistance assigned $123 million to Africa in 1960.

What can be done to improve this situation? One French economist, Pierre Moussa, has proposed a "cosmic tax" which would be collected throughout the developed areas for the development of all Africa. Others—among them President de Gaulle and President Eisenhower —have urged a pool to which Western nations would contribute for the development of the underdeveloped. Still others contend that the Colombo Plan, in which both donors and recipients, meeting together, allocate funds to the projects regarded by both groups as most worthy of support, would prove a useful precedent for Africa.

Whatever scheme or combination of schemes may be adopted in the future, it already seems clear that, with a multiplicity of new countries in Africa, it will be necessary to assign grants on a pooled basis if each territory is to obtain aid without having to enter into a dangerous contest for the favors of either the Western or Communist powers. As Paul G. Hoffman, managing director of the UN Special Fund established in 1958, has said, what is most needed for Africa as well as other underdeveloped areas is an international development association with substantial funds at its disposal. President Eisenhower, in his September 22, 1960, address to the UN General Assembly, proposed that aid to Africa be channeled through the UN.

Meanwhile, the Africans, even though they may be indifferent to or opposed to communism, are interested in the methods of economic development used by Russia and, even more, by Communist China. Failure to obtain timely and adequate aid from the West may encourage economic ties with the Communist bloc, as in Guinea, or bring about disappointed aloofness from the West.

Africa is a continent of infinite sadness, the corroding sadness of man's maltreatment of other men because of color, religion, or social status. This kind of sadness is just as destructive in Little Rock, in English cities where West Indians are roughly handled, or in Paris where Algerians live in *bidonvilles* (shacks built out of gasoline cans), as it is in Johannesburg or Léopoldville. This sadness, however, is beginning to lift in those areas of Africa where independence is creating a new relationship between black and white.

But Africa is also a continent of infinite promise, the unquenchable promise that men of all races will one day learn to treat one another not in terms of color, race, or religion but on their merits as human beings. This promise is already being fulfilled in those areas where the absence of white settlers makes African self-rule and voluntary co-operation with non-Africans readily practicable. Will the white settlers in East and South Africa and in Algeria, in turn, find the moral fortitude to fulfill the promise of equality of opportunity which is at the very heart of the democracy that the West offers as a challenge to communism?

In those areas of Africa where Europeans and/or Asians have acquired an important economic stake—Algeria, Kenya, the Federation of Rhodesia, Nyasaland, and the Union of South Africa—the non-Africans have two fears: first, that African leaders will insist on a policy of "Africa for the Africans"; and, second, that a hasty transfer of governmental responsibility to the Africans will produce political and economic chaos, which would play into the hands of the Communists.

To avert both dangers, non-Africans urge a policy of "gradualism." Even those Europeans who can be described as liberals (for example, Michael Blundell, former minister of agriculture in Kenya, who resigned in 1959 to become the leader of a political party, the New Kenya Group) contend that democracy must grow slowly, with the evolution and maturing of a country. They argue that consciousness of nationhood must supersede sectional and racial considerations.

They recognize that since the majority of the population in East Africa is African and will remain so Africans must ultimately hold the levers of political power. (In Kenya, according to 1960 figures, there are 6,000,000 Africans, 64,700 Europeans, 165,000 Asians, and 35,500 Arabs.) But they believe the time has not come for the "one-man one-vote" concept of democracy demanded by African leaders. This should come to pass, in their opinion, only after the Africans have acquired various educational and economic qualifications entitling them to vote, which only few of them now possess. Meanwhile, it is argued, the Europeans and Asians, who are better educated and who make a major contribution to Kenya's economy through agriculture and commerce, should have a specified number of seats reserved for them in the legislature. Even the Capricorn Society, which was first in urging a multiracial society (its emblem is the zebra because each of the zebra's stripes—black, brown, or white—is vulnerable to any shot), favors a weighted vote for some time to come, subject to a wide range of qualifications which would give the non-Africans political power out of proportion to their number.

But, ask the Africans, is this the democracy preached by the West? And does "gradualism" simply mean postponement of independence for twenty-five, or even fifty years, until another generation or two have acquired the education and economic status considered necessary to give Africans the vote? Kenyan leaders like Tom Mboya and Dr. J. Kiano demand independence not in some indefinite future, but "now." They regard Europeans, Asians, and Arabs as "immigrants," who should be decently treated, but should not claim special rights. They want "Africa for the Africans."

In their opinion, Kenya's next constitution should introduce a common voters' roll based on universal adult suffrage and replace all communal seats by geographic one-member constituencies. Reserved seats for minority groups—Europeans, Indians, Arabs—should disappear at the general election following that of 1961, when a degree of responsible government should be introduced. The date of independence should be fixed now, and the period between 1961 and independence should be used in active and practical preparation for Kenya's assumption of "self-government responsibilities."

When Mboya and his supporters are accused of racialism by Europeans and Asians, their answer is that they are neither "racial" nor motivated by ill-will or hate of "the immigrant communities." Non-racialism, they contend, will not succeed unless the Europeans and Asians first win the full confidence of the Africans.

The far-ranging debate about Kenya's future rose to a crescendo before the constitutional conference held in London early in 1960. There the full spectrum of the many political groups which had emerged in 1959 was represented. The government for the first time since "the Emergency" created by the Mau Mau disorders had permitted the formation of parties provided they were nationwide and multiracial. The spectrum included the United party formed by Group Captain L. R. Briggs and Major Roberts, which represents the views of the older "settlers" and favors a form of apartheid; the New Kenya Group of Michael Blundell, liberal-minded but gradualistic, which seeks to build a nonracial society but has so far attracted little African support; the Kenya party, which is led by Asians and moderate Africans, elected members of the Legislative Council, who resent what they regard as the "authoritarianism" and "bullying" of Mboya and his followers, but so far has recruited few Europeans; and the Independence Movement party led by Mboya, Kiano and Oginga Odinga, all elected members of the Legislative Council.

Moderate-minded Kenyans—Europeans as well as Africans and Asians—think that the Kenya party, if it can gather sufficient support among all racial groups, has the best prospect of creating a basis for a multiracial society. Its program of partnership between the races, with independence as the goal, is close to the views of one of Kenya's most active and effective leaders, Sir Ernest Vasey, who resigned in the autumn of 1959 as minister of finance and economic development so as to be free to participate in politics.

Some Europeans believe that the phase of extreme racialism is over in Kenya. This is the view of W. B. Havelock, minister for local government, health, and town planning, who said in 1959 that people are coming to the only conclusion: "to struggle for permanent domination by any one race over another is impracticable and unethical." He urged all groups to concentrate, instead, on teamwork and public service without expectation of reward.

This is a high ideal. But it is important for Europeans to realize that even advanced peoples are only beginning to put this ideal into practice. Can the Europeans expect from Africans a forbearance they themselves did not show when they held unchallenged power? And is it possible for Africans, who are incontestably in a majority, to feel such forbearance until they have achieved power through independence?

To these questions it is difficult to find precise answers. But an African leader in what only yesterday was the French Congo may have provided a clue when he said, on returning from Paris where he had participated in the newly elected Senate of the Community, "As I talked to Africans from many other areas of Africa, as well as to Europeans, on a basis of equality, I suddenly felt aware for the first time that I was no longer conscious of my color."

Racial consciousness about non-Africans was not initiated by the Africans. It was brought to their attention by race-conscious Europeans. This consciousness can be ended—as is so vividly demonstrated by the relaxed multiracial society of Nigeria—but the Europeans must set the example for the conduct they would like Africans to observe toward them.

It is in this respect that time is running out. As Garfield Todd, former premier of Rhodesia, has said, "It is too late for gradualism." Spectacular measures, he contends, must be taken by colonial governments to demonstrate right now, not tomorrow, that the whites really mean what they say when they urge Africans to develop a multiracial society. Whether or not Europeans, Africans, and Asians can find a way to build such a society, many believe, will be decided in Kenya within the next year. And Kenya's success or failure will set the tone for the federation and—who knows?—might even affect South Africa.

The main thing is not to miss the moment when an ounce of generosity might bring untold returns in terms of improved human relations. The psychological importance of timing can be well expressed in the words Samuel Johnson addressed to Lord Chesterfield, who had belatedly recognized his talents: "Seven years, my Lord, have now past, since I waited in your outward room, was repulsed from your door. ... Is not a Patron, my Lord, one who looks with unconcern on a man struggling for life in the water, and when he has reached ground, encumbers him with help? The notice which you have been pleased to take of my labours, had it been early, had been kind; but it has been delayed till I am indifferent and cannot enjoy it. ...."

It is the danger of such indifference that the West must avoid if it is to avert the spread of Communist influence and win the respect and co-operation of Africa's new leaders.

Here is how Julius Nyerere of Tanganyika, the African leader who has shown the greatest awareness of the need for peaceful coexistence among Africa's many races, described the future role of Africa at the symposium on Africa held at Wellesley College in 1960: ". . . Africa's strength is a moral strength. I suggest that the world today needs a champion for democracy and personal freedom, a champion who must be free from ties of history, or ties of alliances, which might embarrass her stand. Today it seems that Africa is in the best position to take that role—to speak to the world from moral strength, in fact, to continue in the world the moral struggle in which she has already engaged herself on the African continent."

The great diversity of Africa is matched by the diversity of its leaders, from Habib Bourguiba to Tom Mboya.

## HABIB BOURGUIBA—
## TUNISIA

The president of Tunisia, former protectorate of France which achieved independence in 1957, was born on August 3, 1903, in the small fishing village of Monastir to a family long known for its opposition to French rule. Both his father and his grandfather had been jailed for political activities before the French protectorate was set up in 1881. His father, an officer in the army of the Bey of Tunisia, had resigned his commission in protest against French control.

In spite of this spirit of opposition, Bourguiba was educated in French-run schools in Tunis and at the University of Paris, where he studied law. During his sojourn in Paris he married a French girl, Mathilda Lorrain, whom he met when he was a student. (Their only son became Tunisia's Ambassador to Italy in 1957, and is now Ambassador to the United States.) In Paris, Bourguiba also developed a great admiration, which he has never abandoned, for French ideas as distinguished from practices and policies he deplored.

On his return to Tunis in 1928 he was admitted to the bar. He joined the moderate Destour party, but broke with it in 1934 and, with a group of French-educated intellectuals, led in the formation of the more activist Neo-Destour party, through which he started a campaign for independence under the slogan of "human dignity." The French outlawed the party, and in September, 1934, Bourguiba was thrown into jail—an experience with which he was to become familiar over the next twenty years.

In spite of this, when he was released in 1943 from a French prison by the Nazis, who had invaded North Africa, he refused to co-operate with them against the Allies. However, he continued his fight for Tunisia's independence, spending much time in Cairo—which since 1945 has served as the headquarters of North African independence movements—and was once more jailed by the French in 1952.

On his return to Tunisia in June, 1955, he was enthusiastically welcomed. A year later, in 1956, when Tunisia became autonomous, Bourguiba was named premier, and acted also as minister of defense and foreign minister. In July, 1957, when Tunisia, having won independence, was proclaimed a republic, he became president and patterned his government on the presidential system of the United States.

Dressed in Western garb but wearing the traditional black-tasseled red fez, Bourguiba is noted for his fiery eloquence, yet urges moderation. He has always been pro-Western in his views and has ousted all known Communists from his government. However, he has argued that Tunisia might benefit by the economic lessons of what the Communists have achieved in Russia, and in 1959, at the height of Tunisia's tensions with France over the Algerian crisis, he said that he would go to any source, even the devil himself, to obtain arms refused by the West, whatever the cost.

Bourguiba has been firm in his support of neighboring Algeria's demand for independence. In co-operation with the late Mohammed V, king of Morocco, he supported the Algerian National Government with advice and has given asylum on Tunisian soil to Algerian refugees and rebel forces, thereby incurring the wrath of the French, who threatened to pursue the rebels into Tunisia. Bourguiba, for his part, criticized the use by the French of arms and planes obtained from the United States through France's membership in NATO.

He persisted, however, in his faith that two French leaders—Pierre Mendés-France, leader of the Radical party and premier (June 18, 1954, to February 1955), and General Charles de Gaulle, who became president of France in 1958—were sincerely determined to solve the Algerian problem by peaceful means. Although shaken in this faith by what seemed unnecessary delays and by de Gaulle's concessions to the French army and to French extremists in Algeria, Bourguiba, along with Mohammed V and Marshal Tito, counseled the leader of the Algerian rebels, Ferhat Abbas, to accept de Gaulle's invitation of June 14, 1960, to open negotiations in Paris for a settlement of the six-year-old Algerian war. Bourguiba took this position despite the belligerent advice of Communist China, which expressed sharp mistrust of French "imperialism."

Even after the disappointment caused in North Africa by the failure of the negotiations started between the French government and spokesmen of Ferhat Abbas in July, 1960, Bourguiba reiterated his desire to find a peaceful solution of the Algerian problem. He hoped to avoid internationalization of this problem through its submission to the UN, which France firmly opposed, or through the intervention of "foreign troops," which according to Tunisians might be a "foreign legion" that would include Arabs and Chinese—an eventuality dreaded by Tunisia.

Once the Algerian problem, on whose solution he worked hard with de Gaulle, has been removed, Bourguiba believes that new vistas might open for co-operation between French-speaking African countries and France. According to Charles F. Gallagher of the American Universities Field Staff, the elite in Tunisia favor anchoring the country's policy to Africa, "although at times one senses a certain amount of well-meaning paternalism" toward the new African states. By contrast, the masses, still deeply affected by Islam, remain attached to their traditional ties with Arab Muslims. Bourguiba himself favors a role of intermediary between the Mediterranean culture acquired from France and the newly emerging nations of Africa, combined with aloofness from the Arabs of the Middle East.

In an interview with Jean Daniel published in *L'Express,* September 1, 1960, Bourguiba spoke about the prospects for the success of the Community, which he described as "an enthralling enterprise." The Community, he said, "could render immense services!" To solve the Algerian problem, to establish a Maghreb federation composed of Tunisia, Morocco, and Algeria, and a Franco-Maghreb confederation which would maintain for "white Africa its Western vocation, its Euro-African orientation and which would be for Black Africans a relay point of Western values," he declared that he was ready to enter the

French-led Community. "Why not? I am not afraid of words! Why the Commonwealth and not the Community, if all the states are really independent and linked together only by free economic and cultural conventions?"

Bourguiba explained his point of view by saying to M. Daniel, "You understand revolts are not made essentially in the name of nationalism but in the name of an immense thirst for dignity. When those who revolt can slake this thirst in [political] structures minutely prepared by their leaders, then it's a success. When there are no structures, then it's chaos." This description could be well applied to the Congo, where Bourguiba, after a long talk with Patrice Lumumba in Tunis, staunchly supported the action of the UN, in spite of the late Congo leader's attacks on Hammarskjold.

Having struggled to free Tunisia from France's colonial rule and supported the anticolonial demands of Morocco and Algeria, Bourguiba is not afraid of being criticized by his enemies, at home or abroad, for lukewarmness in anticolonialism. He was not afraid to challenge Lumumba any more than he was afraid to challenge Nasser, when the Cairo radio denounced Bourguiba as "a valet of French and American imperialists," an accusation which made Tunisians laugh. Like Nasser, Bourguiba is a Muslim who believes in the modernization of Islam. In 1960 he even went so far as to urge the Tunisians to forego the traditional long fast of Ramadan which, in his opinion, is unsuited to the conditions of a modern economy. But, in contrast to Nasser, Bourguiba has been cool to the idea of an Arab League, particularly if it is to be dominated by Egypt, and in 1958 he accused Nasser of plotting to assassinate him. He thinks of Tunisia not as an Arab country but as both a Mediterranean and an African land, with economic and intellectual attachments to France. Nevertheless, in January 1961, Tunisia, after boycotting the Arab League since 1958, decided to rejoin it, on assurance that Cairo would no longer meddle in its internal affairs.

In his administration of Tunisia, and in his relations with France, with Africa, with the Arab countries, Bourguiba practices what he preaches: a policy of moderation which in a period of turmoil, as he said to Daniel, is a policy of "heroism." What he feared was that France, by failing to solve the Algerian problem, would put him in a position where there would no longer be room for moderation. In that case Tunisia would have no choice but to oppose France and plunge into a bloody conflict. This conflict he has done everything in his power to avert.

## FELIX HOUPHOUET-BOIGNY—
## IVORY COAST

The president of the Republic of the Ivory Coast in West Africa was born on October 18, 1905, in Yamoussonkro. Unlike Nkrumah of Ghana, Mboya of Kenya, and Nyerere of Tanganyika, he came not of a poor and illiterate family, but of a family of chiefs, and is the owner of large and rich cocoa plantations. His background, which the French describe as that of a "noble," resembles that of Sékou Touré, president of Guinea and one of the many grandsons of the famous chief, Somary, who in the nineteenth century bitterly fought French occupation of his country.

But in contrast to Sékou Touré, who did not get beyond grammar school and became a political figure through his work as a trade-union leader and his capacity to organize labor for political purposes, Houphouet, although he could have enjoyed a life of wealth and leisure, chose to study and practice medicine. Active also in the economic field, he founded, in 1944, the African Agricultural Syndicate of the Ivory Coast, which represented African planters in their revindications against the French. Yet in spite of his economic position, which the Communists would describe as that of a "capitalist," Houphouet, before World War II, showed a lively interest in Marxism and was at one time suspected by the French of pro-Communist sentiments.

It was not until after the war that Houphouet entered politics, and then he immediately won a large following by his eloquence, his authoritative and calm demeanor, and his political skill. For his people he promptly became a charismatic personality. According to a September, 1956, article in the French publication *Marchés Tropicaux du Monde,* he "was the object of impassioned manifestations. His photograph was in all the huts, on the lapels of coats, on the corsages of thousands of African women and even on the handlebars of bicycles."

In 1946, Houphouet led in the founding, at Bamako in the French Sudan, of the *Rassemblement démocratique africain* (RDA), a political movement which started out with "very progressive" (*trés progressistes*) ideas, to quote the above article—that is, a movement which voiced demands for radical changes in France's treatment of its African colonies. At that time the West African leaders believed that their best chance of obtaining fulfillment of their demands was to have some of their members affiliated with each of the major parties in the French National Assembly which had shown sympathy for African aspirations—the Socialists, the Catholic Mouvement Républicain Populaire (MRP), and the Communists. It was agreed that, of the group, the only two representatives of the bourgeoisie and the *chefferie* (chiefs) —one of whom was Houphouet—could most easily work with the Communist party "without being accused of communism," as the Ivory Coast leader stated in a July 19, 1955, interview given to the magazine *Afrique Nouvelle.* "I, a bourgeois landowner, I would preach the class struggle? That is why we aligned ourselves with the Communist party, without joining it." Shortly after, however, the Africans who supported the Socialist party, then the most powerful in France (notably Léopold Senghor, now president of Senegal), withdrew from the RDA, which thus came to be dominated by the leaders who were working with the Communists in France.

From the start this movement appealed not to the intellectual elite or to the conservative chiefs, but to the masses of villagers and industrial workers, and attracted wide popular support. From the Communist party it learned methods of organization and propaganda far superior to those of other political groups in West Africa. The RDA, moreover, took credit for colonial reforms adopted by the French National Assembly in 1945-46, especially the abolition of forced labor, the suppression of requisitions, improvement of penal justice, and others. "One can thus understand," said R. Fleury in his article, "*Les Partis Politiques en A.O.F. (1945-1958),*" in *Marchés Tropicaux du Monde* of September 6, 1958, "that it encountered from the start a delirious enthusiasm on the part of many of the Africans, at the same time that it obtained a certain number of important successes."

Meanwhile, however, the more conservative elements in French

West Africa, disappointed by the inefficacy of their collaboration with the French Socialist party, began to oppose the RDA and to seek the formation of an African group of their own. Under the leadership of Senghor they founded the *Indépendants d'outre-mer* (IOM) in 1943. Meanwhile the RDA, which in some territories, particularly the Ivory Coast and Guinea, had passed from political activities to acts of violence, had lost some of its prestige in the period 1948-50. When the Communists in France were barred from participation in the cabinet and thus lost the power to aid the RDA through governmental action, the RDA decided in 1950 to dissociate itself from the Communists. Houphouet explained this decision in 1955 at Conakry in Guinea by declaring that the association with the French Communists had been a means for the African deputies in the French National Assembly to advance progress in Africa, but that by 1950 this association had become an obstacle to African development. "One dies for a goal, for an ideal," he said, "but not for a means."

While the IOM gained support among conservatives and some intellectuals, the RDA, once it had broken with the French Communists, regained the ground it had previously lost. It remains the most active and influential political group in French West Africa. As Fleury pointed out, the IOM has suffered from the fact that it chose theory where the RDA chose practice, ideology where the RDA chose action. The RDA, having become widely accepted, consolidated its positions and became more moderate. Only in Guinea, where Sékou Touré was busy organizing labor unions for political action through his *Parti démocratique* affiliated with RDA, did the latter continue the activist policy which Houphouet had encouraged in 1948-49.

The RDA won Houphouet many supporters not only in the Ivory Coast, but also in other French territories of West Africa. As a result he enjoyed a growing reputation for leadership among French-speaking West Africans. Through the RDA Houphouet came to have close relations with Sékou Touré, who led the party in Guinea.

This intraterritorial influence served him in good stead in the postwar years. It was then that France, at the urging of General de Gaulle (who in 1944, at Brazzaville, had proclaimed the need to revise France's policy toward its African colonies) initiated a series of readjustments. These culminated, after de Gaulle's return to power in 1958, in the creation of the French Community. In the new situation thus created, Houphouet discarded his prewar Marxism and became an increasingly devoted supporter of France. In 1945 he was elected a member of the French National Assembly, and also served as president of the Territorial Assembly of the Ivory Coast. By the time the concept of the Community was incorporated in the constitution of the Fifth Republic, headed by De Gaulle, Houphouet was a member of the French cabinet.

The new constitution, offering France's West African territories the choice of either becoming independent or achieving autonomy within the Community led by France, was put to a referendum on September 28, 1958. Guinea, choosing independence under the guidance of Sékou Touré, was the only territory which said *"Non"* to the Community. Houphouet-Boigny took the opposite position of insisting on the closest possible ties with France. Soon after, as it became increasingly clear that other African territories would follow Guinea's example and seek independence, although retaining ties with France through the Community from which De Gaulle, in an angry response to Sékou Touré's action, had excluded Guinea, Houphouet sought to hold the line against independence. He sponsored the creation of a Council of the Entente, in which the Ivory Coast and its neighbors—Upper Volta, Niger, and Dahomey—while retaining political autonomy, agreed to have common institutions for communications as well as for economic and cultural purposes.

The tide of independence, however, proved too strong even for Houphouet. By mid-1960 the Ivory Coast and its Council of Entente neighbors followed the example of the Mali Federation, formed in 1959 by Senegal and Sudan, which after first accepting autonomy asked for independence in November of that year. Thus started a movement which by 1961 brought independence to the African members of the Community with the full approval of de Gaulle.

Houphouet, still dedicated to the Community, then emerged in a larger role, as the man who might become the leader of a federation of the French-speaking countries of West Africa. When Modibo Keita, president of the Sudan, attempted to take over the leadership of the Mali Federation in July, 1960, and Senegal sharply rejected this, proclaiming the federation's dissolution, the Sudan, more radical in its political views than Senegal, gave the impression that it might seek a new relationship with Guinea, hitherto isolated from the Community. In this crisis, Houphouet quietly arranged to hold a conference with Sékou Touré, whom he regards as a "younger brother"—even though

Touré seemed to him to have gone astray in 1958. Houphouet tried with Touré's co-operation to find a peaceful solution for the clash between Senegal and Sudan, with the possibility of eventually drawing the separated states, as well as Guinea, into a larger French-speaking West African federation, loosely organized on the model of the Council of the Entente.

## KWAME NKRUMAH–
## GHANA

As president and prime minister of Ghana, Kwame Nkrumah, has said in his autobiography, *Ghana,* the only certain facts about his origin appear to be that he was born "in the village of Nkroful in Nzima around midday on a Saturday in mid-September." In the outlying areas of what was then known as the Gold Coast, a colony of Britain, "nobody bothered to record the dates of births, marriages, and deaths, as is the custom of the Western world." But a priest who later baptized Nkrumah into the Roman Catholic Church recorded his birth date, with a fair degree of accuracy, as September 21, 1909.

By Nkrumah's own account, his was a happy childhood, lived out of doors among children and animals. Family life was peaceful and affectionate. His strong-minded mother, of whom he speaks with great warmth, had no education herself but she insisted on having Nkrumah sent to school. In his youth he felt that his religion stifled him. Commenting in 1957 on that period, he described himself as "a nondenominational Christian and a Marxist socialist and I have not found any contradiction between the two."

On completing his schoolwork he went in 1927 to Achimota College near Accra, where he trained to be a teacher, graduating in 1927. He then served as primary school teacher at Roman Catholic schools in Elmina, Axim, and Amissano from 1931 to 1934. He came under the influence of the Nigerian leader, Nnamdi Azikiwe (who in 1960 took office as Governor General of independent Nigeria) and in 1935 visited Lagos. Following the example of Azikiwe, who had studied in the United States, Nkrumah left in 1935 for the United States, via Britain. He went first to Lincoln University, a Negro institution in Pennsylvania, where he majored in economics and sociology, graduating in 1942, then to the University of Pennsylvania, where he studied theology and education, receiving M.A. and M.Sc. degrees in 1943. In 1951, when he was already prime minister, he received an honorary doctorate from Lincoln. Like many American students, Nkrumah worked his way through college by doing a variety of jobs, among other things going to sea as an ordinary seaman, working in shipyards and in a soap factory.

He became president of the African Students' Association of North America, and his thoughts began to turn to politics. During his stay in the United States he collaborated with a fellow-student from Ghana, Ako Adjei, now his Foreign Minister, in publishing the *African Interpreter,* organ of African students. In 1945, at the end of World War II, he decided to go to London. There, too, he worked with African students and political organizations, while studying law at London University, and following lectures by Professor Harold Laski. Even at that time he thought in terms of larger political units than the Gold Coast and of the need for some form of united African action. In London he served as secretary general of the West African National Secretariat and joint secretary of the Pan African Congress, and from 1945 to 1947 was editor of a monthly, *The New African,* whose motto was "For Unity and Absolute Independence."

Nkrumah recalls in his autobiographies that he and other Gold Coast students clashed with Nigerians in London who claimed "that there was no question of considering African or West African unity at the existing stage of colonial dependency and insisted that we should leave these colonial territories to struggle for themselves, each one working out its own salvation as best it could, without any link or co-operation with the other territories." The Gold Coast students, by contrast, "felt strongly that the question of territorial solidarity—that is to say, each territory mapping out and planning its own liberation—could not hope for ultimate success until it was linked up with the other movements in West Africa. We believed that unless territorial freedom was ultimately linked up with the Pan-African movement for the liberation of the whole African continent, there would be no hope of freedom and equality for the African and for people of African descent in any part of the world." Nkrumah has undeviatingly acted on this belief since Ghana achieved its independence in 1957.

After he had become prime minister his political opponents in Ghana, Dr. J. B. Danquah and Joe Appiah, claimed that Nkrumah, during his studies in the United States and Britain, had associated with Communists. He did attend Communist meetings, but no evidence has been produced that he was a Communist himself. And it was at the suggestion of Dr. Danquah, a distinguished lawyer and one of the Gold Coast's most prominent political leaders, communicated by Ako Adjei, who was by then in Accra, that Nkrumah returned to his country in 1948 and became general secretary of the United Gold Coast Convention Party (UGCC). The main task assigned to him was to create a link between the professional men and intellectuals who had formed the party, on the one hand, and the masses on the other. At that time, he recalls, he traveled light: "my worldly goods—two suits, two pairs of shoes and a few underclothes—could be easily stored in one small suitcase."

In June, 1949, after arrest and detention the previous year, he left the UGCC and formed his own party, the Convention People's Party (CPP), which became the leading political party in the country, attracting members from the UGCC. In January, 1950, the CPP called a general strike and spearheaded a boycott of British goods. Nkrumah insisted on a policy of nonviolence, but rioting and disorder broke out. The future president was arrested, charged with sedition, and sent to jail for twelve months. When he was released he wore a cap with PG (prison graduate) written on it. His enemies later contended that he had purposely sought imprisonment because, having studied the experience of Indian leaders, he thought it would give him a special standing with the people.

Nkrumah had set forth his views about colonialism in a pamphlet "Towards Colonial Freedom," which he had written in the United States and had published during his stay in London. In the preface he summarized his point of view as "an uncompromising opposition to all colonial policies." He argued:

Existence for the colonial peoples under imperialist rule means their economic and political exploitation. The imperialist powers need the raw materials and cheap native labor of the colonies for their own capitalist industries. Through their system of monopolist control they eliminate native competition, and use the colonies as dumping grounds for their surplus mass-produced goods. In attempting to legitimize their presence they claim to be improving the welfare of the native population. Such claims are merely a camouflage for their real purpose of exploitation to which they are driven by economic necessity. It is from this that the African peoples must constantly strive to free themselves.

The whole policy of the colonizer is to keep the native in his primitive state and make him economically dependent. . . . Whether the dependent territory is administered as a colony, protectorate, or mandate, it is all part of an imperialist plan to perpetuate its economic exploitation. . . . Britain may claim that she holds the colonies under trusteeship until they are capable of self-government, but it is not in her interests to relinquish her strangle-hold. The African, however, was perfectly capable of governing himself before the advent of the white man and should be allowed to do so again. . . .

The national liberation movement in the African colonies has arisen because of the continuous economic and political exploitation by foreign oppressors. The aim of the movement is to win freedom and independence. This can only be achieved by the political education and organization of the colonial masses. Hence workers and professional classes alike must unite on a common front to further the economic progress and indigenous enterprise of the people which is at present being stifled.

In the meantime, during Nkrumah's stay in jail, Britain had announced the terms of a constitution for the Gold Coast. Elections were held under this constitution in February, 1951. The CPP won twenty-nine out of thirty-three country seats and all town seats. Nkrumah was elected municipal member for Accra and was released from prison. In spite of his opposition to colonial rule Nkrumah worked well with the governor of the Gold Coast, Sir Charles Arden-Clarke, and became Leader of Government Business in the Assembly. In March, 1952, the British decided that the leader should be renamed prime minister and the executive council become the cabinet. Nkrumah thus became prime minister. However, he was disturbed by the strength of the opposition against him as revealed in the 1952 elections, and in 1953 asked the British for constitutional changes designed to strengthen the powers of the prime minister. He obtained these changes in the new constitution adopted in April, 1954, which gave the Gold Coast complete self-government in its internal affairs.

But a new political party had emerged—the National Liberation Movement (NLM) with headquarters in the north, the home of the powerful Ashanti tribe which controls the principal source of Ghana's wealth, cocoa. Nkrumah refused on two grounds to regard the members of this party as being in a true sense an Opposition. First, he argued that the NLM was not capable of forming an alternative government. Second, he contended that the NLM was not a national but a tribal group restricted to a region of the country and that its existence threatened the unity of a colonial people struggling to achieve national independence. "In colonial countries," he wrote in his autobiography, "where imperialism has succeeded in dividing the nationalist movement along tribal lines, the anti-imperialist struggle is invariably weakened and the main objectives of the nationalist movement—namely, unity and independence—are sacrificed on the altar of tribalism." Members of the Opposition, however, took the view that Nkrumah was seeking to establish a dictatorship, that he was suppressing political liberty, and that he was ready to use force in order to achieve his ends. In the July, 1956, elections, the CPP won 72 out of 104 seats in the Legislative Assembly, a victory which, Nkrumah asserted, was conclusive evidence that the NLM was not a national party and that the majority of the country's voters were on his side.

In the new Assembly, Nkrumah on August 3 proposed a motion for independence which was passed "by a reasonable majority," although the Opposition, then headed by Dr. Busia (who is now in exile in the Netherlands), failed to support it. On August 23 Nkrumah formally requested the governor to forward to the British government his request that it set a date for attainment of independence by the Gold Coast. On September 17, Sir Charles Arden-Clarke telephoned Nkrumah, saying, "I just wanted to tell you that I had received some good news for you," and asked him to come to see him at Government House.

When Nkrumah arrived, Sir Charles handed him a despatch from the Secretary of State, the fifth paragraph of which set the date for independence—March 6, 1957, the anniversary of the Bond concluded by Britain and the Gold Coast in 1844. When Nkrumah reached this paragraph, he recalls,

> . . . the tears of joy that I had difficulty in hiding blurred the rest of the document. After a few minutes I raised my eyes to meet those of the

Governor. For some moments there was nothing either of us could say. Perhaps we were both looking back over the seven years of our association, beginning with doubts, suspicions and misunderstandings, then acknowledging the growth of trust, sincerity and friendship, and now, finally, this moment of victory for us both, a moment beyond description and a moment that could never be entirely recaptured.

"Prime minister," the governor said, as he extended his hand to me, "this is a great day for you. It is the end of what you have struggled for."

"It is the end of what we have been struggling for, Sir Charles," I corrected him. "You have contributed a great deal towards this—in fact I might not have succeeded without your help and cooperation. This is a very happy day for us both."

After a sleepless night, during which he recapitulated his years of struggle and repeated over and over, "The 6th of March, the 6th of March, *the 6th of March . . .*," Nkrumah, a day or two before his forty-seventh birthday, announced the great news to the Assembly. "The whole of the Assembly was for a few seconds dumbfounded. Then all at once the almost sacred silence was broken by an earsplitting cheer, cheers that must have been unprecedented in the Assembly. Some were too deeply moved to control the tears, among them some of my closest associates, those who had really felt the brunt of the battle and who perhaps realized more forcibly the true meaning of the word, 'Victory.' "

On March 6, 1957, the Gold Coast, renamed Ghana, achieved independence in impressive ceremonies at which Queen Elizabeth II was represented by the Duchess of Kent. Ghana promptly joined the Commonwealth, and in June, 1957, Nkrumah attended the Commonwealth prime ministers' conference in London, the first African prime minister to do so. In 1960 Ghana requested and received permission from the Commonwealth to become a republic, the title earlier adopted by the Republic of India, and Nkrumah thereupon became his country's president.

Nkrumah had expressed his own views about the meaning of self-government in the Independence Motion—later called "The Motion of Destiny"—he presented in the Assembly on June 10, 1953.

> Our demand for self-government [he said] is a just demand. It is a demand admitting of no compromise. The right of a people to govern themselves is a fundamental principle, and to compromise on this principle is to betray it. . . .
>
> The right of a people to decide their own destiny, to make their way in freedom, is not to be measured by the yardstick of color or degree of social development. It is an inalienable right of peoples which they are

powerless to exercise when forces, stronger than they themselves, by whatever means, for whatever reasons, take this right away from them. If there is to be a criterion of a people's preparedness for self-government, then I say it is their readiness to assume the responsibilities of ruling themselves. For who but a people themselves can say when they are prepared? How can others judge when that moment has arrived in the destiny of a subject people? What other gauge can there be? . . .

The self-government which we demand . . . is the means by which we shall create the climate in which our people can develop their attributes and express their potentialities to the full. As long as we remain subject to an alien power, too much of our energies is diverted from constructive enterprise. Oppressive forces breed frustration. Imperialism and colonialism are a twofold evil. This theme is expressed in the truism that "no nation which oppresses another can itself be free." Thus we see that this evil not only wounds the people which is subject, but the dominant nations pay the price in a warping of their finer sensibilities through arrogance and greed. Imperialism and colonialism are a barrier to true friendship. For the short time since we Africans have had a bigger say in our affairs, the improved relations between us and the British have been most remarkable. . . .

The strands of history have brought our two countries together. We have provided much material benefit to the British people, and they in turn have taught us many good things. We want to continue to learn from them the best they can give us and we hope that they will find in us qualities worthy of emulation. In our daily lives, we may lack those material comforts regarded as essential by the standards of the modern world, because so much of our wealth is still locked up in our land; but we have the gifts of laughter and joy, a love of music, a lack of malice, an absence of the desire for vengeance for our wrongs—all things of intrinsic worth in a world sick of injustice, revenge, fear and want.

We feel that there is much the world can learn from those of us who belong to what we might term the pretechnological societies. These are values which we must not sacrifice unheedingly in pursuit of material progress. That is why we say that self-government is not an end in itself.

We have to work hard to evolve new patterns, new social customs, new attitudes to life, so that while we seek the material, cultural and economic advancement of our people, while we raise their standards of life, we shall not sacrifice their fundamental happiness. That, I should say . . . has been the greatest tragedy of Western society since the industrial revolution.

In harnessing the forces of nature, man has become the slave of the machine, and of his own greed. If we repeat these mistakes and suffer the consequences which have overtaken those that made them, we shall have no excuse. This is a field of exploration for the young men and women now in our schools and colleges, for our sociologists and economists, for our doctors and our social welfare workers, for our engineers and town planners, for our scientists and our philosophers.

Nkrumah, who according to friends of his early days used to be gay and informal, remains in maturity a man of great charm, with a quick mind and gracious manner. But the multitude of problems which he faces now that he is in power, as well as the tendency of his close associates to keep him away from contacts with the general public, in a position of aloofness which he sometimes resents, have combined to make him a more remote figure than he might have wished to be when he was engaged in the struggle for independence. His marriage to a young girl from Egypt, who has borne him a son, brought him the warmth of family life which he had lacked. But he looks beyond his home, and even beyond his country, where he has been given the title of "Deliverer," to the possibility of playing a role in the larger setting of a West African, or even all-African, federation. He sought to play such a role during the 1960 UN General Assembly, particularly during the debates on the Congo, and subsequently, after his return to Ghana, vigorously supported Patrice Lumumba. After the military regime of Colonel Mobutu had forced the departure of Ghana's Ambassador from Leopoldville, Nkrumah withdrew Ghanian soldiers from the UN force in the Congo, and urged the creation of an all-African army.

## TOM MBOYA—
### KENYA

Kenya's most outstanding leader, the man who is expected to be its first prime minister when this British colony achieves independence sometime before 1970, was born on August 15, 1930, on a sisal estate in the White Highlands, the land area reserved for ownership and cultivation by white settlers until 1959, when it was opened to "competent" African and Asian farmers.

His father, a member of the Luo tribe, who was first a laborer, then an overseer, earning wages which rose from $2.80 to $6 a month, was illiterate, as was his mother. Both of Mboya's parents were converted to Catholicism, and their son, the eldest of five children, was christened Thomas in church, but also given the tribal name of Ohiambo which, according to tradition, signifies the time of his birth—the evening.

Like the father in the moving novel, *The African*, by William Conton (born in Sierra Leone but now principal of a high school in

Ghana), Mboya's father sent him to school. First, at the age of nine, he attended the Catholic Mission School in Kabaa where he wrote in sand, under a tree. At twelve he went off to the Catholic Boarding School at Yala, in Nyanza Province, and during vacations he sometimes walked the distance of seventy-two miles to visit Rusinga, where his tribe lived. After studying in secondary schools for three years (he worked during the holidays to help pay his fees) and obtaining the Kenya African Primary School Certificate, he was admitted at the age of sixteen to the Holy Ghost College at Mangu, near Nairobi. He achieved his Secondary School Certificate the following year with enough points to go on for the Cambridge School Certificate, but had to forego it for lack of funds.

In 1948 he went to the Royal Sanitary Institute's Medical Training School for Sanitary Inspectors in Nairobi, and later to the Jeanes School, becoming president of the School Council. In 1950 he started his career in the modest job of sanitary inspector. The next year he was appointed to the staff of the Nairobi City Council, where he received one fifth of the pay of a European employee. Mboya decided to form an association of the African staff in the council, became its president, and planned to develop it into a trade union.

When, following the Mau Mau uprising led by Jomo Kenyatta, the Emergency was declared in 1953, Mboya, who comes from a tribe opposed by the Kikuyu, joined the Kenya African Union and became director of its Information Service. The following year the medical officer of health on whose staff he served warned him against his political activities, and he was soon fired from his job. By that time, at twenty-three, he had founded the Kenya Local Government Workers'

Union and registered it as a trade union, becoming its first national general secretary.

Having lost his job, Mboya became a full-time trade-union official, but had to live on donations from fellow trade unionists. When in that same year his union became affiliated with the Kenya Federation of Labor, he was elected secretary general, a post he still holds.

The next year, 1954, was one of both sharp crisis and mounting success for Mboya. The finances of his union improved, but when the British, stepping up their campaign against the Mau Mau, initiated Operation Anvil, 35,000 workers were arrested in Nairobi, throwing the trade unionists into confusion. Mboya went abroad, first to Geneva, Brussels, and London, presenting a memorandum on the Kenya Emergency to the British Trade Union Council and to the International Council of the Federation of Trade Unions (ICFTU), and then visited Pakistan and India, where he attended an ICFTU seminar. Back in Kenya, Mboya took a leading role in the Mombasa Dock strike, and won a 33⅓ per cent wage increase for the workers, the first such victory by an African in Kenya's history. With two others, he represented Kenya at the Inter-Africa Labor Conference in Portuguese East Africa, and became acting ICFTU representative for East Africa. But he also continued his activities in Kenya affairs, as a member of the government-sponsored Labor and Wages Advisory Boards and Agricultural Wages Commission. However, he did not cut his ties with his tribe, which made him secretary of the Nairobi Branch of the Luo Union.

In 1956, Mboya returned to school, this time at Ruskin College in Britain, where he studied industrial relations and political institutions on a scholarship. During that year he also visited the United States and Canada under the auspices of the American Committee on Africa.

By 1957 he was ready to step into a political role. On March 10 he was the first African elected to the Kenya legislature, where he proclaimed the slogan "Africa for Africans" as against "democratic equality for all," the slogan used by more moderate spokesmen, and in July he went to London to plead with the British government for a new constitution.

By 1958 Mboya moved from the Kenya scene to that of Africa as a whole. In March he was the guest of Nkrumah at Ghana's first anniversary celebration of its independence, and in October visited Emperor Haile Selassie of Ethiopia. Elected in July as chairman of the ICFTU's Eastern, Central, and Southern African Sub-Regional organization, he attended the ICFTU board meetings in Brussels, and in London met British Colonial Secretary Alan Lennox-Boyd. The climax came in December when Mboya was elected chairman of the first All-African Peoples' Conference at Accra, and emerged as a contender, with Nkrumah of Ghana and Sékou Touré, president of Guinea, for leadership of a future Pan-African Federation.

Tom Mboya, the youngest of Africa's new leaders, is also, in outward appearance, the most hard-boiled and toughest-spoken. When, in his modest office on one of the business thoroughfares of Nairobi, he calmly but firmly asserts, "Africa for the Africans," one can understand that he causes alarm among British settlers and Indian traders who believe that, once in power, he might well force the departure of non-Africans from Kenya. When his supporters, also hard-boiled and tough-spoken, march at his side, chanting, "Free-dom! Free-dom!" or disrupt public meetings of opposition African groups, one can understand that the leaders of these groups see in him a potential dictator, intransigent and ruthless, who would not hesitate to use any means at his disposal to enforce his decisions.

He has neither the sense of humor nor the breadth of views of Nyerere of Tanganyika, nor the flexibility of Houphouet-Boigny of the Ivory Coast, nor the governmental experience of Nkrumah of Ghana. Yet in the 1961 elections for a new African-controlled Parliament he won a resounding victory in his Nairobi constituency as leader of the Kenya African National Union (KANU). He knows where he is going, he has the poise and self-confidence of a man who believes he can and will reach his goal. But he also conveys the impression that, given a measure of understanding on the part of the British in Kenya, no less than in London, he could ultimately come to terms with non-Africans, provided they, for their part, agree to stay in Kenya not as privileged foreigners but as citizens of the new state.

## JULIUS K. NYERERE—
## TANGANYIKA

In all speculations about the leader who may prove most successful in rallying the many peoples of Africa into a federation, the man who is voted most likely to succeed in this admittedly gigantic task is Julius Nyerere of Tanganyika, the territory ruled by Germany before World War I. After the Kaiser's defeat it became a League of Nations mandate to be administered by Britain, which since 1945 has ruled it as a trust territory under the UN.

Nyerere was born not far from beautiful Lake Tanganyika to a family of the Zenaki, one of Tanganyika's 113 tribes. The year of his birth is variously given as 1921, 1922, or 1923. His father was a tribal chief with numerous wives who bore him twenty-six children, and Nyerere was a son of the fourth wife.

Brought up as a Catholic, Nyerere, after completing his secondary school training at Tabora, received his B.A. at Makerere University College in Kampala, Uganda, the center for higher education in East Africa, and his M.A. in history and economics at the University of Edinburgh, where he completed his studies in 1952. He then taught at St. Francis College in Dar-es-Salaam, the capital of Tanganyika, until 1955.

On his return to Tanganyika, he had become president of the Tanganyika African Association, which in July, 1954, through his efforts was transformed into the Tanganyika African National Union (TANU). In 1958 he was chosen to head the Tanganyika Elected Members Organization and rapidly became the unofficial leader of the Opposition in the Legislative Council.

Nyerere soon displayed a talent for reconciling the interests of the white and Indian settlers in Tanganyika with those of the Africans, and it has been said that he has proved more successful in winning the support of the multiracial Opposition than of the exclusively African TANU. In 1955 and 1956 Nyerere came to the United States as representative of TANU to the UN. Tall, slender, the father of five children, a tireless worker who chain-smokes and likes gin and tonic, Nyerere has a rare gift, not possessed by some of his African fellow leaders—the gift of humor, with a capacity to laugh at himself and at his own people. He is reported to have said that he favored militancy, but "militancy with a smile."

This sense of humor should serve him well in the task he has assumed with a spirit of profound dedication, the task of creating a multiracial nation in Africa. In accordance with an announcement made on December 15, 1959, simultaneously by British officials in London and by Governor Richard Turnbull in Dar-es-Salaam, Nyerere and his followers assumed control of the Legislative Council and key ministerial posts in late 1960, subject for the time being to the governor's veto. This announcement, in the words of the London *Economist*, was a "watershed" in the development of the African continent, marking the first occasion in British Africa that a community of white settlers were to accept the authority of a primarily African government. While no date has been fixed for Tanganyika's independence, it is expected that the territory will become free of British rule not later than 1965.

The peaceful transfer of authority from whites to Africans was due to the political wisdom and moderation displayed by Nyerere throughout his brief but remarkably successful career. Unlike Tom Mboya, he does not proclaim "Africa for the Africans." He has shown a sympathetic understanding for the fear of the whites and Asians that independence would spell not only the end of their political domination but also the end of their presence in Tanganyika. He has ceaselessly pressed for independence, which to him is a matter of justice for the Africans. He has well expressed his views in a statement, "We Cannot Afford to Fail" published in *Africa Special Report* in December, 1959. "There can be no tampering with a principle," he said then, "and the principle here is the right of a people to govern themselves. No colonial power, however benevolent, has the slightest right to impose its rule on another people against their will; nor may such a self-appointed ruler claim praise or credit when it 'grants' independence to its former colonial territories: neither more nor less credit is due than would be due to any other reformed wrongdoer."

But while insisting on independence as the African's right, Nyerere contends that

> . . . we, the Africans of today, can afford to be generous, for we know that we speak from strength. We have suffered bitter humiliation under the imperialism of the past, but our suffering has taught us patience and it has taught us to understand the fears and prejudices of our former

"rulers" better perhaps than they understand themselves. A child robbed of a treasured possession by an elder brother will scream and kick out at the oppressor, and will try to snatch back his property by force; we are not children. We can use courtesy in our methods of gaining what is rightfully ours; and we in Tanganyika are prepared to go even further—we have asked for, and we are getting, responsible government and complete independence to demonstrate to the diehards and the reactionaries that democracy is possible in countries with immigrant minorities, the so-called "plural societies."

In countries like ours, where human relations have been so long bedeviled by mistrust and resentment between the three races, where these races have lived for generations side by side in the same land and yet remained isolated from each other behind artificial barriers of racial prejudice, and where the minority races have enjoyed privileges far beyond the reach of the majority, it is only natural that the immigrants should fear retaliation under majority rule. I have said that we understand those fears, and that we want to remove them. We know that the only effective way to do that is to prove our sincerity by our actions, for it is hard to reassure a frightened man by words and promises alone. . . .

We have fought our battle here against the injustice of a colonial system which qualified the "rights" of an individual according to the color of his skin. Are we now to turn around and deny that principle ourselves, by discriminating against those whose skins are *not* black?

I have been asked by visitors to Tanganyika, and especially by those who come from the Central African Federation, from Kenya or from South Africa: "How have you people achieved unity? Why is Tanganyika so different from other mixed territories?" There is one great difference: in Tanganyika the Asians and the Europeans have decided to trust us; in other territories nationalist leaders have said exactly what I have said and they have been locked up.

Nyerere recognizes that the most critical years will be the early years of independence, and has urged TANU to change its slogan from *uhuru!* (Freedom) to *uhuru na kazi* (Freedom and Toil). Then the paramount task will be to close the gap between the rich and the poor—and this means between the whites and the Africans.

In this country [he says], as in most other colonial or excolonial "plural societies" of Africa, the economic divisions between rich and poor coincide almost exactly with the divisions between the races. Wherever extreme poverty exists beside a visibly high standard of living there is the rush of bitterness; when the problem is linked with racial differences it is even more potentially dangerous than in a monoracial society. . . .

Tanganyika has demonstrated that the "race" problem in itself can be overcome by teaching the immigrant minorities to trust in the good will of the majority. Our success or failure to overcome the parallel economic problem within the next few years may well decide the pattern of the future for the whole of East, Central, and Southern Africa.

# 5

# Latin America

*T*O A WESTERNER, Latin America at first glance appears to belong to the Western world; and indeed there is no denying that geographically it forms a part of the Western Hemisphere. But we shall not be able to understand the revolutions which again and again convulse Latin-American nations, the emotions which, seemingly without reason, suddenly erupt into anti-Yankeeism from Cuba to Bolivia, from Brazil to Guatemala, unless we understand that politically, socially, and economically these nations share many of the problems and feel many of the aspirations we find in Asia, the Middle East, and Africa; and that, because of these similarities, they are also attracted by the successes as well as repelled by the cruelties of communism in the USSR and Communist China.

Like the peoples of Asia, the Middle East, and Africa, until recently the Latin Americans have been little affected by the forces that shaped Western civilization—with the notable exception of the Catholic Church. But even the Catholic Church, coming into contact with paganism among the Indians, found it necessary to adapt itself to circumstances unknown to Western Europe in modern history. Yet in other respects, Latin America is confronted by the major factors which affect non-Western areas: population explosion, economic backwardness, authoritarian governments overthrown in frequent revolutions (often led by military men), the harsh experience of the early stages of industrialization, the need for land reform, and the growing demand for greater political freedom side by side with improvements in human welfare.

Summing up the momentous events of the year 1959 in Latin America—the year which saw the overthrow of President Fulgencio Batista by Fidel Castro—*The New York Times* in an editorial on December 31, 1959, said, "A revulsion against dictatorship, the demand for social reform, especially agrarian reform, the threat of communism, extreme nationalism with its corollary of anti-Yankeeism, the effort to industrialize and diversify economies, the redistribution of wealth, the raising of living standards, greater educational opportunities, more independent foreign policies—these are the threads that make a lurid pattern in Cuba because of the revolution, but which can be traced more or less clearly in every one of the Latin-American countries."

In a continent composed of twenty independent nations, significant differences, of course, exist. Some of these differences are due to accidents of geography, with the rugged Andes mountain range separating East Coast from West Coast; steamy jungles blocking exploration and settlement of a region of Brazil; long coastlines which have not encouraged communication by sea; and in various areas difficulties of terrain which have kept neighboring peoples isolated from each other for lack of railways and good roads, except where the use of the airplane has bridged vast distances.

There are differences, too, resulting from the uneven distribution of natural resources. Some nations are richly endowed, like Venezuela with oil, Brazil with rubber and coffee, Argentina with its cattle-raising pampas. Others are poor, like Bolivia, which relies primarily on tin; and Cuba, whose national economy depends on the price of sugar in world markets.

Some of the differences are due to accidents of history, with Spaniards conquering, occupying, and ruling many of the lands of Central and South America, and Portugal establishing its domination over Brazil. There are consequent differences in the make-up of populations. Some nations were settled predominantly by white immigrants from Spain, Italy, Germany. Others had Indian inhabitants at the time when Spanish conquistadors discovered them—Mexico, Peru, Guatemala. Some, like the South of the United States, imported from Africa slaves who now live side by side with Indians and whites, as well as Japanese immigrants, as in Brazil. The multiracial societies, in turn, have produced mixed populations—mestizos born of unions between whites and Indians, mulattoes born of unions between whites and Negroes.

This diversified continent, however, has many common factors which link the twenty Latin-American nations. All of them at one time or another were subject to the colonial rule of Western powers (Spain, Portugal, France, Britain, the Netherlands); some still are colonies (British Honduras, British Guiana, Dutch Guiana, and, in the Caribbean, the British West Indies.) All of the Latin-American nations came under the influence of the Catholic Church. This influence has had beneficial results in two important respects: the Church, recognizing that all men are born equal and are made in the image of God, draws no color line, and has encouraged intermarriage between races, notably in Brazil; and, in recent years, the Church has understood the need for land reform and has encouraged efforts to achieve it. However, the predominance of the Church and its long-time association with the colonial rule of Spain and Portugal and the landed aristocracy have aroused anticlericalism on the part of those Latin Americans who favor political and social change. And anticlericalism has led to separation of church and state in Chile, Brazil, and Mexico.

The determination of the United States to bar European intervention in the Western Hemisphere through the proclamation of the Monroe Doctrine in 1821 created a common situation for the twenty Latin-American nations. At one and the same time they found themselves safeguarded from further colonization by their great neighbor to the north, united with it in creating the Organization of American States, and increasingly dependent on the United States for economic and, more recently, military aid. These nations, moreover, between 1810 and 1825, followed the example of the United States by throwing off the rule of European colonial power through revolutions and establishing republican governments.

But the Latin-American peoples, unlike North Americans, had not yet developed a strong middle class, which would have served as a foundation for stable political democracy. Instead, they had inherited a tradition of authoritarianism from the rule of Spain and Portugal, neither of which had achieved democracy as late as 1961. In their political life, ties between rich and influential families have played a far more important role in the formation of governments than votes of citizens, and the strong man, the *caudillo,* has been familiar as head of state, whether he be a political boss like Rafael Trujillo of the Dominican Republic, or a military leader like Perón of Argentina, Odría of Peru or Batista of Cuba. Oligarchy, civilian or military, has until recently often triumphed over efforts to establish Western-type democracy.

Meanwhile, the economy of Latin America, like its politics, has until recently remained static, retaining its colonial character of heavy dependence on the production and export of one or two commodities, whether foodstuffs (sugar, meat, coffee, cocoa, bananas) or raw materials (rubber, copper, tin, lead, oil). Industrialization is still in its early stages, and the emphasis, as in other underdeveloped countries, is on light industries (textiles, cement, sugar refining) and handicrafts.

This economic situation holds two dangers for Latin America. First, continued dependence on the export of one or two commodities whose prices in world markets fluctuate sharply according to crop conditions and availability of the same product from other sources (for example, coffee and cocoa from West Africa) means that the Latin-American countries may discover from one year to the next that what seemed a source of wealth has abruptly lost much of its value. Second, the Latin-American countries find that their foreign currency earnings from exports may not be adequate to pay for imports of the manufactured goods they need to accelerate their industrialization and to fulfill at least a modicum of their peoples' demands for a higher standard of living.

These interconnected problems tend to arouse in Latin America resentment against the wealth of the United States and criticism—ill-founded though it may be—that "the Colossus of the North" does not provide its neighbors to the south with sufficient funds and technical assistance for their economic development. Then, if demands for more, and still more, financial assistance to stave off inflation do not bring the expected results some Latin Americans threaten to turn for aid to the Soviet bloc, as Castro did by selling sugar to the USSR and obtaining Soviet oil, which he then unsuccessfully ordered American companies in Cuba to refine.

The difficult task of carrying out the Industrial Revolution in Latin America is further complicated by the rapid growth of population, which in 1960 was slightly less than that of the United States (187 million), but which is growing more rapidly than ours, at the rate of 2½ per cent a year—the highest rate in the world—and is expected to reach 303 million in 1975, and 572 million (or approximately Communist China's 1960 total) by the year 2000. This growth is due to the same factors which have brought about the "population explosion" in Japan, India, and Egypt: a sharp decline in mortality due to public-health measures and improved medical care, unaccompanied by a comparable decline in the birth rate. And the population explosion has had the same economic and political results in Latin America as in non-Western areas: a growing pressure on available land resources, which results in demand for land reform; and growing political unrest when the state, as yet insufficiently industrialized to offer factory employment to peasants driven off the land, finds it increasingly difficult to supply employment opportunities, education, housing and other amenities which have become standard items in the list of "the revolution of rising expectations."

Of all the demands for change, the one which stirs the deepest emotions in Latin America is for land reform. When the Spanish and Portuguese arrived in the sixteenth to eighteenth centuries they transplanted to Latin America their feudal landowning institutions of that period, which survived the overthrow of colonial rule and have remained by and large unaltered in our own times. Today 1½ per cent of the people, holding 15,000 or more acres each, own half of the agricultural land in Latin America. In Venezuela 3 per cent of the population own nine tenths of the country's land. Meanwhile, as Chester Bowles has pointed out in his article, "Cry for Land in Latin America" (*The New York Times Magazine*, November 22, 1959), "a heavy proportion of all Latin Americans are impoverished tenant farmers, deeply in debt to their landlords." What is worse, the rural system, devoted primarily to the output of cash crops (coffee and sugar), does not produce adequate food for the population of Latin America, which continues "to suffer from diet deficiencies."

The demand for land reform which would assure full permanent ownership of the land to those who till it comes not only, as often believed in the United States, from Leftists, as in the case of Fidel Castro in Cuba, but also from the Roman Catholic Church. In April, 1957, the Fourth International Catholic Congress on Rural Life Problems in Santiago, Chile, concluded that "the establishment of small, independently owned farms was the key to freedom, to stability and progress of Latin America and of most of the underdeveloped world." The charter adopted by the congress stated: "All men have a right to live lives worthy of human beings. God does not will that some shall enjoy extravagant riches while others . . . lack even the barest necessities." The charter also "observed that the necessary changes in the old pattern of society cannot be achieved merely by exhortation. 'A certain measure of intervention by the state is necessary.'"

Far-reaching changes in the land-tenure systems of Latin America are regarded as inevitable. As Chester Bowles says: "Only one question remains to be answered: How will these changes come? By bloody revolution or by long-range democratic planning?" Mexico was the first country in Latin America to carry out a land reform, and it did so by violent means. Between 1916 and 1934 about 25 million acres of feudal land were expropriated and assigned to peasants. More than 900,000 people received their own small farms during that period. Then President Cardeñas, who took office in 1934, arranged for the expropriation of an additional 50 million acres, which were reassigned to 5 million landless. The Mexican experience demonstrated that land redistribution is not enough unless it is accompanied by measures to provide the landless, who have no financial resources of their own, with good seeds, farm animals, and tools. This was eventually done by the Mexican government, with United States private and public assistance.

Following Mexico's example, President Romulo Betancourt of Venezuela in July, 1959, submitted to his Congress a bill providing for liberal government credit for the purchase of equipment, seeds, and fertilizer, and for an agricultural extension service to advise new land-owners "what, where, and how to plant." In Bolivia the revolutionary government in 1952 planned to give each farmer between 25 and 2,000 acres of land, depending on estimated soil productivity, but persisting political instability has prevented fulfillment of its land reform. A major difficulty in Latin America—as in India since its independence in 1947—is the problem of compensation for land expropriated by governments already short of capital. Compensation regarded as reasonable has been paid only in Mexico and Puerto Rico. In the latter case the United States Congress passed legislation in 1900 limiting land ownership by corporations to 500 acres.

Given this prevailing concern with land reform in Latin America, it is not surprising that one of the first acts of Fidel Castro was to proclaim the expropriation of land above 1,000 acres, in return for compensation which was to be fixed on the basis of the land's value—usually very low—given by the owners, Cubans and North Americans, for tax purposes. Payment was to be made over a period of twenty years in the form of 4½ per cent bonds, with interest and principal payable in Cuban currency. Future purchase of land was to be limited to Cubans. Castro has compared this compensation with that given by Japan after World War II, when on the advice of the American occupation authorities, it expropriated land for redistribution to farmers in return for 3½ per cent agrarian bonds payable in annual installments over twenty-five years. The United States, however, pointed out that Japan had expropriated the land of its own citizens, whereas Castro was expropriating the land not only of Cubans but also of American corporations which owned thousands of acres devoted to sugar production. Actually no arrangements have as yet been made for compensation.

In spite of mounting conflicts between Cuba and the United States, Castro admitted in 1959 that the United States government has always been "consistent and unequivocal" in its support of rural land reform "in countries where it was long overdue." The question in Cuba, as in other Latin-American countries, is whether land reform will be carried out by democratic means, with reasonable compensation, or whether land will be confiscated outright, as in Communist countries. Castro has emphasized that he is seeking not only political but also social revolution. To this Cuban Catholics have answered by declaring, "Social justice, yes. Communism, no."

Today, the main trends in Latin America are revulsion against dictatorship; demand for social reform, particularly for redistribution of land; an effort to industrialize backward economies and diversify agricultural output now dependent on one or two crops; a drive for greater educational opportunities and better living standards; and a tendency, under economic pressures, toward extreme nationalism, with an emphasis on anti-Yankeeism. The questions which still await answers are whether the overthrow of dictatorships (only four now exist in Latin America, counting Castro's rule in Cuba) means the creation of stable Western-type democracies; whether the capital necessary for industrialization can be obtained through domestic savings or through increased financial aid by the United States and other industrial nations, or both; and, above all, whether democratic methods of change will come soon enough and achieve tangible results with sufficient rapidity to avert resort to the violent methods of communism, backed by offers of trade and aid by the USSR and Communist China.

In mapping out a policy for the United States under these fast-moving conditions, Chester Bowles, talking particularly about land reform, suggests:

> We can adjust ourselves in advance to the certainties that reason will not always prevail, that injustices will almost surely occur, and that the short-term price paid for long-term stability will often appear exorbitant.
> Above all, let us not lose sight of the essential issue. The real choice in Latin America, as in Asia and Africa, is citizenship or serfdom, hope

or despair, orderly political growth or bloody upheaval. Our failure to understand this choice, or to support the vital new elements which are striving to assert leadership, would be catastrophic.

The difficulty of arriving at an understanding between Latin Americans and the United States was illustrated by the letter which the Federation of Chilean students, controlled by Christian Democratic—not Communist—leaders submitted to President Eisenhower during his 1960 tour of Latin America outlining a set of grievances against American policy. The students wrote:

> The majority of us are Christians. And almost all of us, Christians and free thinkers, are firm supporters of democracy. . . .
> Then, if our capitalization . . . cannot be based on the unmerciful exploitation of our own people as the Communist alternative demands, the moral solution demands that it be the product of just prices and adequate remuneration for the raw materials which we sell to the industrial nations.
> We understand that the substitution of an ethical notion of a just price, and one in accordance with the needs of the producing country, for the false concept of "market mechanism," offers many practical problems. . . .
> If trees are known by their fruit, it is a mockery to pretend that this situation reflects the Christian or the democratic order for which the immense mass of starved, illiterate and uncultured people, as well as those lacking rights, freedom and property, populating the majority of Latin America, could hope. It is a crime against the spirit. If the injustices of today are all that Christianity or democracy can offer this continent, no one should be surprised if the best children of these nations turn toward communism, seeking those elementary needs which they lack and which are the essentials to morality and civilization: food, shelter, and education.

What is most significant for the future of relations between the United States and Latin America is the conclusion the Chilean students reach about Castro when they say:

> . . . But it seems to us that it is plainly immoral to classify the Cuban revolution, its government or its social fulfillments, especially the agricultural reform, as "Communist." . . .
> In the United States, and in Western Europe, it makes sense to fight to defend the "prevailing order," because their social order represents values which are shared by everybody. . . . In Latin America to "defend the prevailing order" means maintaining the privilege of a thin layer of the population which controls the power and the wealth, surrounded by an ocean of poor people for whom the "social order" means little or literally nothing. . . .

Commenting on this letter, K. H. Silvert of the American Universities Field Staff wrote in a May 16, 1960, report:

> These Chileans are doing no less than asking the United States to:
>   a. destroy the effectiveness of the Latin American armed forces so that government can be clearly and decisively civilist;
>   b. use the full weight of American foreign policy to support democratically nationalist governments and overthrow personalistic, authoritarian ones; and,
>   c. make possible an economic integration of Latin America and a general economic development "in a way more compatible (than the present situation) with the elementary necessities of civilization."
>   The United States may have the naked power to do these things. Is there any possibility that American decision makers would agree to these requests? Have we the will and the techniques necessary to the task? Has the United States enough internal conviction of the right and the wrong to accomplish these objectives? Should the United States play God and remake other countries? Would doing so demand a significant cultural shift, a different self-conception in the United States?
>   But I doubt that the Chileans really mean these things. Perhaps they merely want the United States to run their revolutions for them, guarantee their economies and then let them inherit their rebuilt homelands. If this is the case, what makes them think the United States is willing to manage these social revolutions and the implantation of a kind of economy most American leaders deem highly undesirable?

Some of the many difficulties the United States faces in Latin America are illustrated by Cuba's challenge to this country. Few foreign policy issues since World War II have created as much anxiety in the United States.

This is understandable for at least six major reasons. First, Cuba is situated geographically in close proximity to the United States, 90 miles from the Florida coast. Second, Cuba, like the other 19 republics of Latin America, comes within the purview of the Monroe Doctrine; and it is a member of the Organization of American States (OAS), to which the United States also belongs. Third, American citizens have had substantial properties in Cuba, in the form of land for the raising of sugar, tobacco and cattle, and sizable investments in various enterprises. Fourth, the United States, under a treaty with Cuba signed in 1903 and renewed in 1934, maintains a naval base at Guantanamo Bay, which has a $70 million installation and a complement of 1,550 sailors and Marines with 3,200 dependents. Fifth, the government of Fidel Castro, established on January 1, 1959, has not only sought trade with, as well as economic and technical aid from, Moscow and Peiping, but has also declared that it relies on the Communist powers for military assistance against any "invasion" from American soil. The establishment of a national base for international communism in the Western Hemisphere so close to our own shores is of most important concern to the United States. And, sixth, the Castro government has been engaged in widespread activities in Latin America, fostering revolutionary movements and encouraging hostility to the United States.

When Castro, for three years, was struggling to overthrow the dictatorship of General Fulgencio Batista, many Americans were aware that the Batista dictatorship had used harsh methods incompatible with our concepts of democracy and had done little to solve the grave problems which Cuba, like many other of the Latin American republics, had long faced. Among these were the problems of land reform; of diversifying the country's economy so that Cuba would not be so heavily dependent on sugar, which in the past has constituted 80 percent of its exports; and of providing at least a modest improvement in the low living standards of the island's 6.7 million population. The United States government had taken no action to bring about the overthrow of the Batista dictatorship. Such action would have represented intervention in the internal affairs of Cuba, and even if welcomed at the time by Castro and his followers, would have been resented in Cuba as well as in other Latin American republics, all of which are jealous of their sovereignty.

Meanwhile many private individuals in the United States sympathized with Castro's proclaimed intentions to carry out a far-reaching program of political, economic and social changes, and welcomed his victory. Nor did Washington oppose the new government at Havana, as it had earlier opposed other new Latin American governments when they were created as a result of revolutions. On the contrary, the United States promptly recognized the Castro regime on January 7 in a note which said that "the government of the United States expresses the sincere good will of the government and people of the United States toward the new government and the people of Cuba."

Since then, many of the measures taken by Castro in Cuba during the two years he has been in power have caused increasing concern in the United States. The mass public trials of former Batista supporters and subsequent mass executions created a revulsion among Americans. The failure of Castro to prepare for free elections, and the imposition of political controls similar to those of Communist countries and some non-Communist dictatorships, alarmed Americans who had hoped that Castro's victory would bring about democracy in Cuba. The expropriation of a wide range of enterprises, from oil refineries to banks, with a total investment estimated at over $1 billion, shocked the United States.

Castro's land reform, which involved expropriation of holdings over 3,330 acres if the crop be sugar, cattle or rice, and over 1,000 acres for all other crops, and plans for redistribution of expropriated land to 200,000 landless, also raised many questions here. The United States has favored land reform in other countries, and did not oppose Cuba's land reform which is an internal matter.

American observers, however, have pointed out that the Cuban peasants, formerly tenants on the estates of landowners, Cubans as well as North Americans, would not be able to own land outright, but would in effect be under the control of the National Agrarian Reform Institute which directs expropriation and redistribution. Henceforth no foreigner may own or inherit land. The question was also asked how the Castro government would compensate dispossessed American owners of land, who held 1,666,000 acres of caneland worth millions of dollars and 36 out of 161 sugar mills, accounting for 37 percent of the island's sugar production. Although Castro announced that former owners would receive 20-year government bonds bearing 4.5 percent interest, the bonds have not as yet been issued; and even if they should be issued, payment could not be made in currency convertible into dollars. Other underdeveloped countries which have carried out substantial land reforms, notably India and Mexico, have found that with the best will in the world it was difficult to marshal funds for payment to expropriated native landowners in local currency.

Looking toward the future, American experts have expressed serious doubts that Castro can succeed in maintaining a viable agrarian economy in Cuba at the modest level where it was in 1959, let alone carry out his program for diversification of the country's production. Among other things, Castro has had to face a crisis not of his own making created by the fall of the world price of sugar to a 20-year low at the very time he came to power. As a result Cuba started out under his regime with a dangerous trade deficit, which has been further increased by the discontinuance of United States purchases of Cuban sugar in 1960, the decline in foreign investments and the stoppage of tourism. In an effort to find markets for sugar, as well as sources of economic and technical aid, and of arms, on the basis of barter trade, Castro has increasingly turned to Moscow and Peiping to an extent which, according to most observers, has transformed Cuba into a satellite of th Soviet bloc.

Still more alarming for the United States has been the increasing reliance of the Castro regime on the Soviet bloc for arms. Some observers do not regard Castro himself as a Communist, although he had associated with Communists in Cuba as well as in other Latin American countries before he undertook his campaign against Batista. But, unlike President Gamal Abdel Nasser of Egypt or Premier Abdul Karim Kassim of Iraq, Castro has not created a national party of his own. Instead he has supported or acquiesced in the activities of his closest associates who are either Communist sympathizers or Communists, among them his brother Raul Castro, the Argentine Ernesto (Che) Guevara, tsar of Cuba's industrialization, who has made extended visits to Moscow and Peiping, and Foreign Minister Raul Roa.

Moreover, Castro himself made a series of verbal attacks on the United States, which rose to a crescendo of vehemence and vilification, and ordered measures against this country which reached a climax on January 2 when he charged that this country was plotting an "imminent invasion" of Cuba and demanded that Washington cut its embassy staff in Havana to 11 within 48 hours. As a result of these various attacks, the United States on January 3, two years after its recognition of the Castro regime, broke diplomatic relations with Cuba, stating that "there is a limit to what the United States in self respect can endure. That limit has now been reached." This break came after the United States had patiently endured many actions by Castro against American citizens and repeated denunciations of this country. It raised many new problems for the United States.

In Latin America, perhaps more than in any other non-Western area, the United States is forced to ask itself more questions than it can yet find answers for. To the Latin Americans' own questions, two divergent answers have been offered—those of Cuba's Fidel Castro and of Venezuela's Romulo Betancourt.

### FIDEL CASTRO—
### CUBA

The man who became president of Cuba in 1959, at the age of thirty-three, was born on August 13, 1926, on a farm in Biran. His father, Angelo Castro y Argiz, had been born in Spain and had married as his second wife, Lina Ruz Gonzales, who belonged to Cuba's old established gentry. Fidel Castro was the third of five children by this second marriage. His younger brother, Raul, was to be his constant companion-in-arms in the July 26 Movement against Batista and one of his closest associates in the task of implementing the revolution.

In addition to operating his sugar farm Castro's father hauled timber from the hills with a tractor, and through its sale acquired a modest but comfortable fortune.

Castro attended Catholic schools, and in the Jesuit colleges of Santiago de Cuba and Havana he received the equivalent of M.A. and LL.B. degrees. Over six feet tall, lean and wiry, he starred in baseball and basketball and made a name for himself in track.

When he entered the University of Havana he became active in student affairs and soon was involved in politics and international intrigues, for which he early showed a strong flair. The Communists supported him for the vice presidency of the student government body. After winning this office, Castro campaigned against the Communists, who denounced him. Later he became student government president. At the age of twenty-one he joined an expeditionary force in an unsuccessful coup against the government of Generalissimo Rafael Trujillo, dictator of the Dominican Republic.

Castro married a fellow student at the University of Havana in 1948, and their son, Fidel, Jr., was born on September 1, 1949. Meanwhile Castro had gone to Bogotá, Colombia, to attend a student congress, and had participated in the "Bogotázo" riots of April 9, 1948, during the ninth conference of the Organization of American States, which, it was claimed at the time, had been inspired by Communists.

After obtaining his law degree from the University of Havana in 1950 he became a member of a Havana law firm, devoting most of his time to defending the poor, often without fee.

Castro was convinced that the regime of Colonel Fulgencio Batista, who had risen to political power from the rank of sergeant, was corrupt and ruthless and should be brought to an end. On March 15, 1952, he wrote Batista saying that graft and corruption would lead to overthrow of the dictator's rule. Nine days later he filed before the Court of Constitutional Guarantees in Havana a brief requesting that the assumption of power by Batista be declared unconstitutional; and another with the Urgency Court in which he advocated prison terms up to one hundred years for violations of the Code of Social Defense. The Court of Constitutional Guarantees ruled that "the revolution is the source of the law." Castro then decided to organize a revolution himself.

Under his leadership revolutionary cells were formed. One of his followers set up business as a chicken farmer on the outskirts of Santiago de Cuba in April, 1953, obtained weapons and ammunition, and provided a gathering place on his farm for the revolutionaries.

During his trial after his unsuccessful military revolt when questioned by the prosecutor about people who had given money to his movement, Castro replied, "Among those of us who are alive and those who are dead, the following persons gave money." Then he read the following list:

> Jesus Montane, who is present, gave the sum of $4,000 which he collected as severance pay from General Motors when it liquidated its business in Cuba. Ernesto Tizol, owner of a chicken farm, placed his property at the disposition of the revolution. Oscar Alcade mortgaged his laboratory for the sum of $3,600 and liquidated an accounting office which he owned, thus making another contribution. Renato Guitart gave $1,000. Pedro Marrero sold the dining room set of his house, the refrigerator and the living room set—he didn't sell the bedroom set be-

cause I forbade him to do so. Moreover he borrowed $200 from a money-lender to increase his contribution to the cause; and he didn't seem to mind losing his job in the Tropical Brewery, where he earned $250 a month.

Fernando Chenart pawned his personal belongings, including his camera. He was the photographer who took the picture for the magazine *Bohemia* of the studio of the sculptor Fidalgo when it was raided by the state. His only crime, you remember, was having sculptured a statue of Marti that was called: "For Cuba that Suffers." Chenart gave $1,000. Elpido Sosa sold his job as treasurer of an important company. Abel Santamaria mortgaged his automobile, but that was not his only contribution. He gave much more and, if it seemed little, he gave his life. Thus I could go on amplifying the list, but it appears to me that it would be better if I deliver it in writing to this court.

The revolt, staged on July 26, 1953, the centenary of the birth of Cuba's apostle of liberty, José Marti, when Castro attacked the Moncada barracks at Santiago de Cuba, failed. Castro escaped, but the soldiers were ordered to take him alive. He was eventually caught and tried at the Moncada Prison, where he acted as his own counsel. The government sought to keep him from court, but he managed to send a letter to the Court in which he eloquently denounced the Batista regime, and voiced his own aspirations for Cuba's future. He was locked up for seventy-six days in solitary confinement. When he was finally brought before the Court he was sentenced to fifteen years in the penitentiary on the Isle of Pines; so was his brother Raul. Some of his devoted followers had been killed in the unsuccessful raid or brutally tortured to death in its aftermath.

At the penitentiary Castro organized a school and taught his fellow prisoners history and philosophy until he was placed in isolation. He was released under an amnesty bill signed by Batista on May 13, 1955, and left in July for Mexico, where without delay he began to prepare for an invasion of Cuba. Shortly after, his wife divorced him.

In October, 1955, Castro flew to Miami, and then went to New York, in an effort to obtain funds for his group. In Mexico he hired Colonel Alberto Bayo, a former colonel of the Spanish army, who was both anti-Franco and anti-Communist, to train his fighters. Castro had previously belonged to the Orthodox party, but by March, 1956, he had become disillusioned with what he regarded as its conservatism, and formed the 26th of July Movement. He called it "the revolutionary organization of the humble, for the humble, by the humble."

In November, 1955, Mexican police captured Castro's entire arsenal, but he managed to obtain a ship and sailed for Cuba in late December. His plans for a quick successful coup failed, however, and for days he and his followers lived on sugar cane. They took refuge in the rugged mountains of Sierra Maestra, and began to seize food from the rich and give it to the poor.

Arms kept trickling in to Castro from Cubans in other countries. The 26th of July Movement had established sixty-two branches of the organization throughout the Americas, including Puerto Rico. Undeterred by the difficulties of waging guerrilla warfare against the well-armed and well-financed army and police force of Batista, Castro, on March 12, 1958, issued a manifesto to the people of Cuba, announcing a plan for the start of what he called "total war" against Batista. Men, women, and youths of all classes—peasants, townspeople, professional men, business leaders—began to rally to Castro's cause, and to defy Batista, who, for his part, resorted to increasingly ruthless measures—imprisonment, executions, and torture. On July 20, Major José Quevedo, whom Castro had known as a law student at the University of Havana, surrendered his troops to Castro in the first major military defection. On October 10, Castro issued two important rebel measures: a comprehensive law for agrarian reform, and an order instructing all voters to remain away from the polls on November 3, the date Batista had set for presidential elections.

As unrest spread and more and more supporters rallied to Castro, Batista signed a statement resigning the presidency and took a plane for the Dominican Republic. The army, however, went on fighting against Castro. The rebel leader made a radio appeal to the people not to take justice into their own hands and promised that every "war criminal" would be arrested, tried, and punished. As the remnants of the Batista administration began to disintegrate, Fidel Castro, who had grown a legendary beard in the Sierra Maestra, led a triumphal march of his followers, "the bearded ones," into Havana on January 3, 1959. On February 11, under tremendous pressure from the families and friends of the thousands who had been tortured and executed by Batista, and whose bodies had been discovered in mass graves, Castro ordered the convicted "war criminals"—about 600 military personnel accused of tortures and killings—to be executed by firing squads after perfunctory spectacular mass trials.

In the calendar of the Cuban revolution, 1959 became known as the "Year of Liberation." Describing the situation in Cuba a little over a year later, Tad Szulo wrote in an article, "Cuba: Profile of a Revolution" (*The New York Times Magazine* of April 26, 1960):

> No man, woman or child—Cuban or foreign—can ignore the march of revolution: it has pervaded every field of activity, it has penetrated the privacy of homes, minds and hearts, the days and the nights, the work days and the holidays. It is present in the rich sugar cane fields, in the factories, in Cuban towns and cities, on the air waves, in the newspapers, in the schools and in the homes of the poor and of those who still are wealthy. It takes so many forms that the bedazzled spectator imagines himself watching a circus of twenty rings, each with its own fascinating show.
>
> [The Castro revolution, said Szulc,] has taken giant strides to uproot Cuba's *ancien régime,* and no matter what the future brings these changes cannot be undone. The nation simply is not prepared to go back to the old days. A Havana businessman who is threatened with the loss of all his property summed up the feeling one evening when he said, "You know, I hate this guy Castro, but in a funny way I'm proud of being Cuban."

The revolution has brought about the establishment of the National Institute of Agrarian Reform (INRA), which carries out the agrarian reform law providing for seizures and expropriations of "sugar and cattle estates, of tobacco farms, of sugar mills, of rice fields and potato patches," owned by foreigners as well as Cubans, in return for compensation whose payment has not yet been arranged. It has brought to the peasants liberation from "their virtual serfdom on vast estates," and "the excitement of the new deal, of the schools and decent homes that are beginning to rise on many of the new co-operatives." The peasants, however, become not small landowners, but employees of INRA co-operatives, "often earning less than they did, and some times not being paid at all for weeks." The revolution has brought "the progressive regimentation of the urban laborer through government-controlled unions, the increasing difficulty of changing jobs without an official permit, the virtual impossibility of working at all unless one is enrolled in the nationwide labor census." It has brought "the sacrifice of wage deductions to help pay for land reform, industrialization and the purchase of aircraft and weapons." But it has also brought new housing, financed by the national lottery and social-security funds. It has brought "the enthusiasm of the young men and women in the ministries and government agencies as they plan Cuba's metamorphosis from the old misery and neglect to a new justice and happiness."

What worries many Cubans, however, and most of all many of Castro's devoted early supporters, is that they believe "the revolution is being betrayed, that the promise of restoring democracy has been violated and that communism is taking over Cuba." They also fear that the USSR and Communist China will gain more and more influence in Cuba and that this rise in foreign Communist influence will further alienate the United States, already alarmed by Castro's expropriations of American landholdings, his seizure of many American business enterprises, his violent diatribes against the American government and American property-owners in Cuba, and his unremitting efforts to rouse Cubans against the United States.

Castro had outlined his political, social, and economic blueprint for a free Cuba in his impassioned defense to the Court before which he was tried in 1953. In that document he had written:

> We call on the people, the seven hundred thousand Cubans who are without work but who desire to earn their bread honestly without fear of having to emigrate from their country in search of sustenance; the five hundred thousand camp workers who dwell in miserable shacks, who work four months of the year and are hungry the rest, sharing the misery with their sons, who do not have an inch of land to plant and whose existence should move more to compassion if there were not so many hearts of stone; the four hundred thousand industrial workers and stevedores whose retirement funds all have been embezzled, whose conquests are being taken away, whose homes are infernal habitations of the rustlers, whose salaries pass from the hands of the boss to the hands of the usurer, whose future is a pay reduction and dismissal, whose life is perennial work and whose rest is the tomb. We call on the one hundred thousand small farmers who live and die working a land that is not theirs, always sadly contemplating it like Moses and the promised land, only to die without possessing it; who have to pay for their parcels, like feudal slaves with a part of their products; who cannot love it, nor improve it, nor plant a cedar or an orange tree to beautify it because they do not know the day when a sheriff or a rural guard will come to tell them that they have to go; on the thirty thousand teachers and professors so devoted, sacrificed and necessary to the better destiny of future generations and who are so badly treated and paid; on the twenty thousand small businessmen overwhelmed with debts, ruined by the crisis and harangued by a plague of filibusters and venal officials; on the ten thousand young professionals: medicos, engineers, lawyers, veterinarians, pedagogues, dentists, pharmacists, newspapermen, painters, sculptors, etc., who leave the classrooms with their degrees, desirous of working and full of hope, only to find themselves in a dead end street, all the doors closed, deaf to clamor and supplication.

These are the people who suffer all the unhappiness and are therefore capable of fighting with all courage! To the people whose roads of anguish are stony with deceit and false promises we were not going to say: "We are going to give you," but: "Here you have it. Fight now with all your forces so that liberty and happiness may be yours!"

Castro ended his statement with a ringing summons to the Court: "Condemn me! It doesn't matter! History will absolve me!"

As of early 1961 the image of Castro varied widely, depending on the personal reactions of those who viewed "the bearded one." Some, particularly in the United States, which understandably resented the anti-American actions and statements of Castro and his associates, were convinced that he was either, at best, a foolish man who had unwittingly become a stooge of the Communists or, at worst, a willing and conscious adherent of Moscow and Peiping. This view was shared by a considerable number of Cubans, among them some of Castro's early admirers and supporters, who believed that he had betrayed the cause for which they had fought at his side and perhaps had been a Communist all along.

Others, however—in Cuba, in the United States, and in Latin America—disagreed sharply with this appraisal. They believed that Castro, in spite of his ruthlessness, his inexperience, his mannerisms, and his flamboyant oratory, genuinely reflects the aspirations of a majority of his people as well as of the peoples of other Latin-American countries, particularly with respect to the need for drastic social change and most of all for land reforms. At the Costa Rica conference of the Organization of American States (OAS) in August, 1960, the foreign ministers of Venezuela and Peru, two countries which have followed policies of moderate reform, indicated sympathy for Castro and disapproval of their governments' agreement with United States criticisms of Cuba's actions; and the Peruvian foreign minister subsequently resigned his post on this issue. In Mexico, too, a good deal of enthusiasm had been expressed for Castro's policies, not only among students and intellectuals but also in government circles. And some Latin-American leaders stated after the Bogotá economic conference of September, 1960, at which the United States offered new aid to Latin America for the purpose of speeding social and economic reform, that "for this aid we owe thanks to Castro." "The bearded one," they thought, had frightened Washington into doing more for Latin America than it had done in the past in order to avert other Cuban-type revolutions.

In retort to Cuba's charges of United States aggression and discrimination, made by Castro during the fifteenth session of the UN General Assembly, the United States, on October 14, 1960, issued a ten-thousand-word indictment of Cuba, charging the Castro government with deliberate sabotage of long-standing good relations between the two countries, and with an extensive list of misdeeds, including wholesale expropriation of American properties in Cuba. Many Americans expressed the hope that Castro's opponents—whether his own former supporters, now disenchanted by what they call his police-state methods, or Batista's followers—would overthrow Cuba's new dictator and create conditions propitious to democracy. But Irving P. Pflaum of the American Universities Field Staff, in "A Note on Cuba," September, 1960, was less certain that the future would necessarily improve on the present. "Cuba's *reforma agraria*," he said, "is deteriorating into an archaic transfer of ownership and control from individual capitalists to state capitalists. Thus a return to individualism would not be too difficult. But Cuba's *reforma moral* and *reforma social* may not be so easily stopped; indeed, they must be kept alive if today's inequities are not to be exceeded by tomorrow's as were yesterday's by today's."

So the verdict of history must still be awaited. But meanwhile a policy which differs markedly from that of Castro is being developed in Venezuela by Romulo Betancourt.

## ROMULO BETANCOURT—
## VENEZUELA

Romulo Betancourt, an economist, who took office as president of Venezuela on February 13, 1959, after winning an impressive victory the previous December in his country's second free election, was born on February 22, 1908, to the family of a wholesale grocer in the village of Guatira, twenty-five miles from Caracas. He was educated at Liceo Caracas, where he met Don Romulo Gallegos, Venezuela's distinguished writer, who at that time was a professor at the Liceo. Betancourt has said that Gallegos influenced him more than anyone else in his life, and Gallegos has declared that Betancourt profited more from his teachings than any other student he has taught.

The future president started on a career of antidictatorial agitation, imprisonment, exile, and political triumphs when, as a third-year law student at Central University, he demonstrated against the then dictator, Juan Vicente Gómez, was jailed, and had to take refuge first in Costa Rica and then in Colombia. He sought to overthrow Gómez in unsuccessful revolts staged from Santo Domingo, Curaçao, and Trinidad. For a brief period, during his stay in Costa Rica, he joined a Communist-front group, from which he subsequently withdrew. He married a young schoolteacher, Carmen Valverde, and their daughter, Virginia, has done graduate work at the University of Chicago with her husband, José Lorenzo Pérez.

After the death of Gómez, Betancourt returned to Venezuela and organized a revolutionary underground party. Seized by the police, he was again sent into exile in 1938, this time in Chile. Four years later he returned to Caracas and founded the National Democratic party, a Leftist but not Communist group which subsequently became the Democratic Action party. In 1943 he supported Gallegos for the presidency, but his candidate lost. Two years later Betancourt participated in a revolt against the president, General Isaías Medina Angarita, and headed the junta which then took power until the election of Gallegos as president in 1947. Betancourt's critics say that at that time he made the mistake of trying to cram decades of reform into three turbulent years.

When Gallegos was ousted in November, 1948, following his arrest by the military junta headed by Pérez Jiménez, who became dictator, Betancourt left Venezuela, lived for ten years in Washington, Havana, and New York, and visited Puerto Rico. John Molleson of the New York *Herald Tribune,* has written that Betancourt "had plenty of time to ponder his past errors and to mellow his political philosophy through conversations with men like Puerto Rico's Luis Muñoz Marin."

During this period in the political wilderness, Betancourt wrote an impressive volume of over seven hundred pages, *Venezuela: Política y Petróleo* (Venezuela: Politics and Petroleum). In this book Betancourt contended that Venezuela's situation "was not different from that of whole continents: Africa, a great part of Asia, and Latin America," because of the dependence of its economy on a single product—oil— whose output, he argued, should be greatly increased, so as to provide a growing source of income for the country. He did not favor whole-sale nationalization of resources, but he strongly believed in government direction of economic production, particularly with respect to oil. This point of view he expressed again in August, 1960, when, in responding to a poll about President Dwight D. Eisenhower's plan for additional United States aid to Latin-American countries, Betancourt expressed approval, but added, "The United States must abandon the deification of 'free enterprise.'"

At the same time Betancourt said in his book that the Democratic Action party

> . . . has always followed a thoughtful and responsible line in reference to what concerns the United States. . . . We consider that the inter-American relationship in Spanish, Portuguese, and French-speaking areas [of Latin America] should not be colored by either colonialist submission or provocative verbal aggressiveness. . . . Parties called upon by unavoidable responsibilities to exercise a guiding influence on the direction a country takes cannot be nor should be, in Latin America, either anti-Yankee or Yankeefied. . . . We have never been pro-Soviet and Democratic Action criticized the brutal methods of Stalin's dictatorship at least fourteen years before Nikita Khrushchev presented his hard condemnation at the 20th Congress of the Russian Bolshevik party. . . . The directing organs of Democratic Action have not included either folly, irresponsibility or flirtation with the Russian government in its political plans; neither permanent nor transitory alliances with Communist groups in the country.

On January 24, 1958, Betancourt, by that time head of the Democratic Action party, formed a group with two other Venezuelan exiles in New York, Dr. Rafael Caldera, chief of the Christian Social party, and Dr. Jovita Villalba, leader of the Republican Democratic Union. This group, known as the Great Civic Front, pledged itself to avoid civic strife until democratic processes had been restored in Venezuela. That same month the dictatorship of Pérez Jiménez was overthrown, and Betancourt returned to his country. On October 12, 1958, the Democratic Action party nominated him for the presidency and on

December 7 he was elected to a five-year term, taking office on February 13, 1959.

Described by Molleson as "a stocky, serious, pipe-smoking man," Betancourt, at fifty-three, hopes to carry out political, economic, and social reforms which would modernize Venezuela and develop its rich resources without resort to nondemocratic methods and with constant regard for the welfare of the people. His emphasis on political democracy, on reforms which respect the claim of private owners to compensation for expropriated property, and his insistence on friendly relations with the United States are in sharp contrast with the policies of Cuba's Fidel Castro. At the same time, Betancourt, like many other Latin-American leaders of varied opinions, believes in limited nationalization of natural resources and in effective land reform.

He explained his ideas in an interview with *U.S. News & World Report,* published on February 15, 1960. Venezuela, he said, does not seek to expropriate American or other foreign investments. "What we are after is an adequate and equitable participation in the revenue from oil. Oil and mineral ores are public property under our law—and under the law of all Latin-American republics, all of whom inherited that concept from Spain. Under that law, there may be no private ownership of subsoil wealth; it belongs to the state." * This point of view had been presented by the Latin-American countries before the Economic and Social Council of the United Nations in 1956. Venezuela, second in production of oil in the world and first in export, wants to establish a national oil agency both in production and refining. "But," Betancourt added, "it is not our intention to take over the fields now exploited by the foreign companies or to displace these companies in any way." He called attention to the situation in Iran "where, along with private enterprise, there exists the national Iranian company, with its own oil fields and refineries."

As for private investment, Betancourt stated that his government encourages investment from the United States, as well as from Europe, Japan, or any other country of the free world. "We need foreign capital because, if we relied exclusively on our national savings, we could not develop our marvelous—I should say spectacular—potentialities, especially in the mining field. We have in the southeastern area of our

* Reprinted from *U.S. News & World Report,* an independent weekly news magazine published at Washington, D.C., "Venezuela's Plan to Get Ahead," February 15, 1960.

country enormous deposits of iron ore and of almost all other minerals extensively used in industry." The best form of relationship between foreign capital and Venezuela, in his opinion, would be an association of foreign with Venezuelan capital.

Betancourt, leader of a coalition government which consists of the country's three major parties—the Democratic Action party, the Social Christian party, and the Republican Democratic Union, with the Communists excluded—believes that the principal problem of the country is not political, but economic. Many of the current economic troubles, he contends, are due to mismanagement by the dictator Pérez Jiménez, who was overthrown in 1958.

Betancourt has tackled the economic situation in three ways. First, he has sought to balance the budget by cutting expenditures, but his plans for budget-balancing, he asserts, cannot succeed without a loan of $200 million to bridge the current gap between expenses and revenue. Second, his government has adopted a program of public works "and numerous economic, industrial, and social activities" designed to diversify the economy of Venezuela, hitherto dependent on the output and export of oil, and to provide additional opportunities for employment.

Third, he has introduced a land-reform program to meet an acute problem in the rural areas, where out of 635,000 families only about 17 per cent, or 108,000, own land, and 83 per cent are landless peasants who feel increasingly discontented with their lot. Eighty per cent of rural families have an annual income of less than $250 (actually about four times the current income of India's peasant) and a quarter of these families have a monthly per capita income of $3.50. Housing is pitifully inadequate. "Scattered through the country are 700,000 shacks, very primitive dwellings," said Betancourt. "They are no better than the dwellings that were found here in the fifteenth century by the Spanish conquerors. Only there are more of them now—with earth floors, thatched roofs, and no sanitary facilities to speak of. They are the source of great health risks. In these areas we have a powder keg that may explode one day." To Betancourt, Venezuela's peasants and workers are not merely workers but "human capital."

Betancourt does not plan at present to expropriate land in the hands of private owners if it is being cultivated. "We will, however, purchase or expropriate holdings of absentee landlords whose land is not cultivated." The land-reform program will be managed by the National

Agrarian Institute, which "will pay part of the purchase price in cash and part in agrarian bonds. These bonds will be very well guaranteed because our government is in a very solvent position. For us, the bonds will constitute a comparatively small debt. Remember that our annual government revenue is around $2 billion." Venezuela's land-reform will affect only a few Americans, because most Americans in Venezuela own oil fields, not land for cultivation; those who do, cultivate their land. This situation is in contrast with that of most Americans in Cuba, who have owned vast tracts of land for the production of sugar cane not as individuals but through large corporations.

The government plans to do more than redistribute land. It will also "give credit, without which agrarian reform is meaningless. This credit is already being given, principally through the agricultural bank, which is state-owned. Credit was not given to any large extent during the dictatorship. . . . In 1957, credits to peasants amounted to about $16.5 million. In 1959, the first year of this government, we have extended $90 million in such credits." The government is also energetically developing livestock and building irrigation projects.

Betancourt believes that the Communists, who received only 4 per cent of the vote in the presidential and legislative elections of 1958, do not represent a danger for Venezuela as long as the country has a democratic, reform-minded government. The Communists, he contends, "developed their strength under the dictatorship. One can say that despotism generates communism. Now, under the democratic regime, they are being reduced to isolation and to an inability to influence public opinion at large." He has faith that "we can defeat them with democracy and social justice. This is the view that is held by almost all chiefs of state in Europe and Latin America." His faith appeared to be justified by the events of November, 1960, when his government, with the loyal support of the Army, defeated the attempt of left-wing students inspired by Castroist influence to create disorder. When one has a headache, says Betancourt, "one doesn't cut one's head off. One rather looks for the causes of the disease and deals with it by adequate means. Democracy and social justice are moral vaccines against communism, while despotism and carelessness provide a good atmosphere for the growth of all sorts of totalitarian philosophies."

Opposition to communism, however, does not prevent Betancourt from frankly discussing what he considers the mistakes of the United States in Latin America. "It would be like trying to conceal the sun with one finger," he said, "to pretend that there has been no deterioration in the sentiments of some Latin-American people toward the U.S." The main reason for this deterioration, in his opinion, "has been the U.S. official attitude during that time, an attitude of unnecessarily friendly relations toward the dictators in Latin America." Washington has even decorated dictators with medals, Betancourt exclaimed, referring specifically to the medal bestowed on his dictator-enemy, Pérez Jiménez, who after his downfall found refuge in the United States.

Washington, moreover, has in the past shown little interest in the economic problems of Latin America as compared with its interest in Europe and Asia. "However, a change has been noticeable recently. Signs are emerging that the U.S. is becoming less friendly toward dictators and, conversely, is developing a more sympathetic attitude toward democratic governments; and it is also more active in giving aid to Latin America." Betancourt, however, urges "stabilization of prices of raw materials and elimination of the threat of restrictions in the U.S. market against Latin-American products such as minerals and foodstuffs." But he states emphatically that "we in Latin America are not looking for alms or gifts to be given at the expense of the U.S. taxpayer. What we need most of all and what we want is long-term financing for projects which do not normally come within the scope of private initiative—such projects as irrigation, electrification, housing, and agrarian reform."

# 2

# The Ideas

# 1

# Authoritarianism: With or Without Totalitarianism?

THE BUILDERS of the emerging nations, however much they may differ among themselves in political concepts, have one significant thing in common: they all believe in "democracy," or assert they do.

If the ubiquitous rose is deemed sweet by any other name, so in our times is democracy. In the society of twentieth-century nations it is simply not the thing to use such harsh words as "autocracy," "tyranny," or "dictatorship"; even the "dictatorship of the proletariat," once so widely proclaimed by Communist pundits, is falling into desuetude. The Russians, instead, refer to the USSR, to Communist China, and to the countries of Eastern Europe as "people's democracies." As C. L. Sulzberger pointed out in his *New York Times* column, March 14, 1960, Pakistan's Marshal Ayub Khan speaks of "controlled democracy," Indonesia's President Sukarno of "guided democracy," and Nasser of "popular democracy." Castro of Cuba, by-passing governmental institutions, listens to and seeks to interpret "the voice of the people," reminding one of Rousseau's faith in "the general will." This new terminology is dismissed by Sulzberger as "murkophrenia." A less skeptical interpreter might describe it as the tribute nondemocratic vice pays to the concept, if not the practice, of democratic virtue.

In essence, this world-wide tribute indicates the desire of new nations to set for themselves a goal they respect, a goal which may be unattainable today but is a badge of respectability which every people should strive to win tomorrow. This reminds one of a family which regards a piano in the living room as a sign of respectability, even if no one in the home can play it. But who knows, perhaps someone will, someday.

Yet it is important that all concerned—the West, the new nations, and the Communists—should not confuse the word with the deed. Otherwise the possibility of creating political as well as economic and social conditions that would eventually set the stage for democracy could be undermined by false semantics. And, at the same time, the Western nations, accepting the currency of "democracy" of one denomination or another at face value, might subsequently recoil with revulsion and disappointment from countries like Korea and Turkey, described as part of "the free world," whose governments have maintained the outer façade of parliamentary institutions, only to collapse under popular pressure for a genuine attempt to create democracy.

The key difficulty in all discussions about democracy, or the lack thereof, in the non-Western world is that we often fail to agree as to what constitutes democracy. And the preconditions usually regarded by Westerners as essential for the successful operation of a democratic society make up a formidable list.

Among them are: (1) A homogeneous population (here Britain is always adduced as a shining example, in spite of occasional tensions between English and Scots, and English and Welsh—not to mention the Irish—yet democracy flourishes in multilingual and multinational countries such as Belgium and Switzerland). (2) A workable ratio between population and resources (Russia has this factor at its disposal without having as yet developed democratic methods, while India, in spite of shortages of important foods and raw materials, is acknowledged to be a democracy). (3) Universal literacy (yet India, with a population 80 per cent illiterate and fourteen major languages, has held two successful general elections since achieving independence in 1947, while highly literate Germany produced Hitler). (4) A degree of industrialization that fosters the growth of a middle class which, in turn, insures political stability (yet France, in spite of its strong bourgeoisie, experienced prolonged post-World-War-II political instability, ended only in 1958 when General Charles de Gaulle took over supreme power for the second time). And (5) either a high degree of security from external attack (the British and the Japanese in their island homes, or the United States, safeguarded until the advent of nuclear weapons by its east and west ocean frontages and the absence of more powerful neighbors to north and south) or, if geography is unfavorable, then capacity to achieve security by superiority in manpower (Russia) and/or contemporary weapons (yet Japan did not become a democracy until it had been occupied by the United States in 1945, and Russia's superiority in manpower has not yet assured democracy).

If we apply any or all of these tests, non-Western nations have not reached the point at which they can achieve genuine democratic institutions. We in the West can, of course, encourage these nations to adopt the outward trappings of democracy even though we know these may be a false front for a seething power struggle such as we have witnessed in Korea and Turkey. But all we then achieve is what the Indian historian and diplomat, K. M. Pannikar, in his perceptive little volume, *The Afro-Asian States and Their Problems,* calls "textbook democracy."

If we do this, it will not be long before we discover our self-deception about parliamentary government, as we did in the case of Japan after Pearl Harbor; and as we may do again and again in some of the countries we number among our allies. Instead, it would be wise for us to look at the non-Western nations with all the realism we can muster. Above all we must see them as they see themselves.

The reality is that most non-Western countries (with the exception of insular Japan) have populations composed of widely diverse racial and linguistic groups, often at varied stages of political, economic, and social development. A number of them—India, Indonesia's island of Java, Ceylon, Egypt, some of the countries of Latin America—suffer from a population explosion brought about by the sharp decline of the death rate with no commensurate decline in the birth rate. They do not possess or have not yet developed their resources to the point where they can adequately feed themselves, let alone provide a modicum of consumer goods within the income range of the majority of the people. There is still, in these countries, a wide gap between the few who are very rich and the many who remain very poor. In most cases the small, newly emerging group of business and professional men and women and intellectuals have been deeply involved in the struggle for independence against a Western colonial power or against a native authoritarian ruler. These men and women have had little or no time to focus their thoughts on the development of postindependence or postrevolution political institutions, and are still too limited in numbers and influence to act as a stabilizing force in the midst of a rapidly changing society in full spate of transformation.

To this broad generalization India constitutes a striking exception, due first to its own millennial tradition under both Hindu and Muslim rulers of responsibility by the ruler to the ruled and his concern for their welfare; and second to the affinity, unique in history, between Indian concepts of good government and sound administration and those of the Western colonial power, Britain, which was present in India for over three hundred years. The unique combination of these two factors has made it possible for India to emerge from colonialism into independence and from a premedieval peasant economy into a technological society by nonviolent means through the voluntary cooperation of its citizens. India's experience is in sharp contrast with that of Japan, which after it had opened its island empire to Westerners in 1854 remained psychologically divided between Western and Japanese ideas and ways of life, using authoritarian methods to modernize its economy on the Western model, but at the same time retaining its own traditions.

Thus today, although aspiring to "democracy," most non-Western peoples are either still in the throes of internal revolution and/or struggle for independence, or have barely emerged from the turmoil of adjustment to twentieth-century conditions. In the midst of the turmoil and confusion created by this change-over, it would be not only unrealistic, but actually unfair to the non-Western peoples, should the West continue to insist on the planting of democratic institutions in a soil not prepared to nurture them, or to show disappointment when these institutions wither away. Lee Kuan Yew, Prime Minister of Singapore, thirty-eight-year-old Cambridge-educated lawyer and leader of the militantly Leftist People's Action party, who advocates not democracy but "democratic socialism," summed up the problem faced by Asia, the Middle East, Africa, and Latin America when he told Bernard Kalb of *The New York Times* on May 24, 1960: "We have stated that Western democracy in its complete undiluted form is unworkable in a revolutionary situation in Southeast Asia, where loyalties are more to persons and personalities than to institutions of state. It is, therefore, essential that the government in power must be equipped to govern and govern effectively while it is the government."

The basic problem of the emerging nations, as Lee Kuan Yew and other leaders have pointed out, is to devise political institutions which can be effectively used to bring these nations abreast of Western technological and, hence, political and social development, and to make these institutions work with maximum efficiency and minimum coercion without total subordination of the individual to an impersonal Moloch-state. Solution of this problem is the top priority for the non-West. At this particular moment in its history nothing else is of comparable importance, not even the problem of abolishing war. For if the new nations are to wait for mankind's apocalyptic decision to beat nuclear weapons into plowshares before they start to transform their societies, they risk perishing from internal upheavals rather than from nuclear attack.

But the creation of new political institutions requires a profound readjustment in human relationships, constituting nothing less than a revolution. To assume—as some Western critics do when they talk apprehensively about the tremors that shake Eastern Europe, Asia, the Middle East, Africa, and Latin America—that those who spearhead change err by engaging in revolution is to blame a long-gathering storm for wreaking havoc wherever it strikes. As Albert Camus has said in a collection of essays, *The Rebel,* it is impossible to do away with rebellion, for this would mean giving up the means of striking at injustice. "Art and rebellion," he wrote, "will die only with the last man." The important thing is to keep rebellion within reasonable limits, so that the process of historical change will not in and of itself destroy man or revolution, Saturn-like, devour its own children. But since the impetus to revolt comes usually when all reasonable avenues of change have been blocked, it is as impossible to enjoin reason upon rebels as it is to enjoin restraint upon lovers. The most we can hope for is that the emerging nations will achieve authoritarianism without totalitarianism.

It is difficult enough to make orderly changes in organized Western societies which have already traversed the arduous road from the Stone Age or feudalism to the age of democracy and the atom, and through the experience of the Renaissance, the Reformation, the English, French, and American revolutions, have learned the necessity, dignity, and effectiveness of dissent from an established order. How much more difficult this task becomes in societies where the absolute rule of hereditary prince or chief, the spiritual domination of priest or holy man, is not a matter of dusty history but a living contemporary experience.

What are the features of democracy as it has developed in the West which the non-Western peoples find inapplicable to their present conditions? And by what methods have they rejected these features?

Experience has so far revealed two major aspects of democracy which appear to be inoperable in non-Western countries at their present stage of development.

1. *Gradual Change Impossible.* The Western peoples had the good fortune—some would call it the great skill—to undergo their transformation from the rule of authoritarian monarchs like Louis XIV and Henry VIII to a continuously broadening democratic society over a span of two or three centuries. Even so, this transformation was punctuated by three great revolutions—English, French, and American, all not only political but also economic and social in character—by the upheavals of 1848 in France, Central and Eastern Europe, and Italy, and by the Civil War in the United States.

Today, the non-Western peoples who are determined, to quote Stalin's phrase, "to catch up with" if not, as Russia hopes, to surpass the West cannot afford gradualism. For they fear that then the wide gap which separates them from the West will grow ever wider, and that failure to reduce it in the lifetime of the present generation will create such profound disappointment as to bring about the overthrow of existing governments and, eventually, chaos and destruction of the goals for which independence had been sought. The new leaders, even if they might be inclined by philosophy or temperament to favor moderation, are thus under tremendous pressure to avert possible extremist revolution by taking revolutionary measures themselves. Otherwise theirs might be the fate of Chiang Kai-shek or Syngman Rhee—who, no matter how devoted they have been to the interests of their people, were too slow, too cautious, too ambitious, or too unimaginative to respond in time to the revolution of rising expectations—and, like them, they might have to spend the rest of their lives in exile. They are thus forced to telescope into a few decades, and often even a few years, changes which in the West had been absorbed slowly in small doses.

The urgency for rapid change has been acknowledged by all the leaders of emerging nations, but only a few—Lenin and Stalin in Russia, Mao Tse-tung in China—have accepted the necessity of carrying out changes irrespective of the cost in lives, money, and materials, without heed to humanitarian considerations, and with ruthless dedication to the belief that the end justifies the means. As of 1961 Castro seemed bent on following the example set by the builders of Communist Russia and Communist China.

By contrast, other non-Western leaders, each in his own way, and within the framework of his country's traditions and resources, have sought to reconcile change with concern for the sensitivities and the welfare of human beings. This was true of Tito who, after starting out on the same path as Lenin and Stalin, has increasingly liberalized Yugoslavia's political institutions; of Nehru, who has sought to modernize India in accordance with the Hindu philosophy of reconciliation between conflicting elements by nonviolent means; of the military men —Ataturk, Nasser, Ayub Khan—who have striven to improve the lot of their peoples without resort to force; of Betancourt in Venezuela; and of Nkrumah and Sékou Touré in Africa.

The dramatic, and as yet unanswered, question is whether those non-Western countries which have avoided violence and have respected human values will succeed in the long run in carrying out the far-reaching transformations needed to lead their peoples into the promised land of modern life, or will be judged by future historians to have failed as compared with Russia and China because of their preference for moderation. When that verdict is reached it will be necessary to decide whether mankind is better served by changes adopted under high pressure and enforced by police methods or by relatively slow adjustments (rapid though they seem when compared to the experience of the West) achieved by peaceful means, with respect for the rights of the individual.

2. *Need for Strong Government.* Whatever the pace, governments which undertake change will need to command sufficient authority so that they can determine the objectives of change and plan the operations necessary to fulfill them. This means that new governments may, in the initial stages and perhaps for years to come, reject the practices made familiar by Western democracy. The degree to which they reject them, however, may differ from country to country.

The USSR and Communist China have had governments dominated by the leaders of a single political group, the Communist party, with Khrushchev as well as Stalin combining the roles of party leader and head of state. As the two Communist countries, however, have developed their economies, they have increasingly brought to the fore the men and women who direct new industries and implement new scientific ideas, not all of whom are Communists. A significant and potentially far-reaching divergence has emerged between Russia, which now ranks as second to the United States in industrial development, and China, which still seeks to approach the level of Britain in steel production. In Russia some of the principal leaders, notably Khrushchev, have displayed a pragmatic attitude toward Communist doctrine. In China adherence to "pure" communism as defined by Lenin and Stalin has become a paramount objective of the government, which assumed the role of defender of the Communist faith. The Chinese regard Russia as too soft on Western "capitalism" and "imperialism" and frown even more on Yugoslavia, which has been denounced in Peiping more vociferously than in Moscow as "heretical."

In non-Western countries which have not adopted communism, the new governments have introduced various forms of authoritarianism without attempting to impose a totalitarian system on their citizens. A number of these governments, in fact, outwardly resemble Western democracies. They have more than a single political party (for example South Korea, Turkey until 1960, Burma, Indonesia, India, Ghana), and in a few instances (Burma, Israel, Indonesia) have acquired a multiplicity of political groups reminiscent of the Weimar Republic in Germany or France before de Gaulle. They hold elections on a more or less regular basis, and have parliaments—although parliamentary life may be frequently disrupted by such varied phenomena as the transfer of governmental power by civilian rulers to the military, as U Nu did in Burma; or seizure of power from civilians by the military, as in Egypt by General Naguib, in Turkey by General Gursel, in many Latin-American countries by men like Colonel Péron and Sergeant Batista; boycott of parliament by a minority party bereft of hope that it might obtain power through the electoral process, as in Japan under former Premier Kishi; armed revolt as in Cuba with Castro; dissolution of parliament for a prolonged period, as Sukarno did in Indonesia in 1960; and many other extraparliamentary devices. Or a non-Communist government may introduce single-party rule, as in Egypt or Cuba, where Castro has denounced all political opponents as "antirevolutionary."

The non-Communist governments may also from time to time adopt some of the same practices as Communist governments. They may find political opposition irksome, and silence, jail, or exile their critics, as has been done in South Korea, Turkey, Egypt, Indonesia, the Dominican Republic. They may, as in Turkey with Menderes, censor the press, jail recalcitrant editors, close down universities whose students and professors have voiced dissent with official policies. They may confiscate the property of those whom they call "enemies of the state," and even try to assassinate them in exile.

And non-Communist governments may seem to have one feature in common with Communist regimes: their admiration, often adulation, for one leader, a "charismatic personality," who at a given moment in history embodies the nation's aspirations and who can do no wrong, even if he is subject to criticism from some quarters. In this respect there is similarity between such otherwise different men as Lenin and Nehru, U Nu and Nkrumah, Nasser and Castro. This feature, however, can hardly be regarded as peculiar to non-Western countries when we think of Winston Churchill, Franklin D. Roosevelt, Dwight D. Eisenhower, Charles de Gaulle, and Konrad Adenauer. Rather the charismatic personality may be characteristic of a period in history when human beings, overwhelmed by the complexity of life and fearful of the future, seek refuge from their problems and relief from their anxieties by pinning their hopes on a single leader.

Of all the non-Western countries, India has been most successful in adapting democratic institutions to the economic and social conditions of a nonindustrial society. Not only does it have the physical institutions of democracy, but, within the limits of its material resources, it has infused them with a living sense of the democratic philosophy which emphasizes the equality of all human beings before the law, irrespective of race, color, religion, sex, and caste. True, Mr. Nehru is impatient of criticism, and on occasion has sought to silence those who have attacked him in the press or on the platform; but the Indian government has by and large observed legal procedures even in dealing with the Communists, as in the state of Kerala, has respected the rights of opposition parties, and has protected freedom of thought and speech, in and out of Parliament.

Where the non-Communist governments differ profoundly from the Communists is in refraining from attempts to impose a single pattern of thought and conduct on their citizens, to brainwash the individual, to keep him under constant government surveillance. They do not force him to bow to government-enforced orders, subject to threats ranging from public disgrace and loss of jobs, to imprisonment, forced labor, and death. None of these governments have gone through the period of all-embracing statism characteristic of Russia before the death of Stalin and Communist China under Mao Tse-tung, or of Yugoslavia until Tito began to liberalize his Communist system in 1950.

A number of non-Communist governments, however, agree that democratic institutions of the Western model, even if in part adaptable to non-Western conditions, cannot meet their most immediate political problem, which is the creation of grass-roots institutions that would provide illiterate villagers with experience in political democracy. This need they are trying to fill with new institutions of their own devising, such as the community development blocks in India's villages and Pakistan's basic democracies—local units where voters can choose between candidates whom they know at first hand.

The distinguished American historian, Charles Beard, is said to have remarked that it did not matter what political system a country has; if there are independent courts and local self-government the country will have democracy.

This dictum could be substantiated in independent India, which lacks many of the features Westerners regard as essential for the operation of democracy, yet has succeeded in establishing and, what is more important, maintaining democratic institutions amid the turmoil of national liberation from Britain's colonial rule which was accompanied by chaos, bloodshed, and the disruption of partition. True, India adopted a constitution three years after achieving independence. It has a parliamentary democracy at the center and in the states; it holds free elections by secret ballot; it has oppostion parties which do not hesitate to challenge the ruling Congress party; it safeguards the basic freedoms of the individual. And it has independent courts which have protected citizens against the state even under the most difficult and controversial circumstances, notably in the case of Communists accused by the government of endangering law and order.

What had been hitherto missing in India's political structure—both under the British and since independence—was a local political self-governing unit which would express the will of the people at the grass-roots level and mobilize the energies and enthusiasm of India's millions of villagers for the national task of reconstruction. As the Indian government pointed out in 1958: "For centuries the Indian villager has not only been illiterate and isolated, but not even permitted to practice democracy. For many villagers, in many villages, the sense of independent citizenship in an independent country is wholly new; the responsibilities of citizenship, of local initiative, of public impulse and cooperation are as yet only dimly perceived." True, pre-British India had had, and still retains, the village council of five—the *panchayat*—which has been regarded by some historians as a prototype of democratic self-government. But the panchayat was usually the product not of democratic election but of agreement between leading villagers—the landlord, the moneylender, the principal craftsmen—as to who would rule the village and enjoy the honors and perquisites of office.

To remedy this lack, the government decided in 1958 to establish elective block development committees in organized village blocks, each composed of 100 villages, totaling 50,000 to 80,000 people. In 1959 there were 2,400 of these blocks, and by the end of the Second Five-Year Plan in 1961, the number is expected to rise to 3,500. Members of the block committees will be chosen by indirect elections: groups of five village panchayats will elect one representative, and thus each committee will have a block membership of 20. Each committee, following training to be provided by the government and a period of experience, will be made into a statutory body and equipped with both the power and the resources to function effectively.

This far-reaching program of democratic decentralization has exceptional importance, from India's point of view, as a contrast to the communes of Communist China which cover an area roughly comparable to the Indian block but are tightly controlled by the central government, itself controlled by the Communist party. The block development committees are regarded as in harmony with the Gandhian traditions of village service and responsibility. According to the Indian government, they will "test and demonstrate the critical issue of our times—whether the long illiterate villagers, long deprived of the opportunity to practice democracy, can now, with training and guidance, successfully participate in and direct their own advancement."

The significance of the block committees is all the greater because they will be called on to help administer India's community development projects through which the villagers, on their own initiative, are encouraged to start a variety of projects important for the welfare of the community—from schools to small dams, from brick kilns to veterinary and hospital services—with the government ready to give financial aid and the technical assistance of trained village-level workers.

Hitherto the community projects, which offer great promise for village self-development, have been criticized on the ground that they had become instruments of government bureaucrats rather than, as originally planned, instruments of the village people themselves. A distinguished American rural sociologist, Dr. Carl Taylor, said in an article in 1959 that "The development of the people, the development of unpaid local leaders, the maximum possible contributions of village level workers, who work with the people and the people's chosen leaders and self-created groups, are the very essence and genius of community development." It is hoped in India that the newly adopted "democratic decentralization" of the villages through the creation of block committees will help to make community development, as Dr. Taylor suggested, a "people's program instead of what it has been so far, a government program."

A somewhat similar objective has inspired the system of "basic democracies" introduced in Pakistan in 1959 by Marshal Ayub Khan. Pakistan, in contrast to India, had found it difficult to operate a Western-type democracy in a country divided into two wings—West Pakistan, with its backward agrarian economy, ruled by big landowners, and East Pakistan, more advanced agriculturally, industrially, and intellectually, with liberal-minded men among its political leaders. After Ayub Khan, in October, 1958, had deposed and sent into exile General Iskander Mirza, who had previously taken over power from the civilian government and abrogated the newly proclaimed constitution of 1956, the military regime made a study of what it described as the "failure of the Western type of democracy in Pakistan."

This study reached the conclusions that "Western democracy presupposes a high degree of national and political awareness so that people understand the value of their votes in terms of broad national policy; mass literacy needed for broader outlook and perspective; and an advanced system of mass communications for speedy and accurate dissemination of information on a wide scale." As compared with these prerequisites, the present situation in Pakistan, according to the study, revealed that a "vast majority of our population live in rural areas having inadequate communication facilities; the percentage of literacy is very low; as a result their understanding of political responsibilities in terms of broad national policies is limited; and because of their illiteracy and living in isolation it is not possible for them to judge the merits of persons with whom they have no immediate personal contact." Given these circumstances, the study concluded, "people are accustomed to look towards officials for leadership and guidance for centuries; most of the intelligentsia being in government employment, sufficient local leadership did not grow; and dependence on government help weakened the initiative of the people. Basic democracy would foster leadership."

The government decided that it faced two alternatives. It could "wait for ideal conditions and try to educate the people so as to make them aware of their self-interest, and hold elections on a national basis after they have been so educated." This, however, "would mean waiting for a generation or more before elections can be held." The alternative was to "hold elections now at the level at which people are already aware of their self-interests and are in a position to choose between the competing candidates."

Choosing the latter course, the government developed the concept of basic democracies. Under this concept, as pointed out by Louis Dupree, representative of the American Universities Field Staff in Southeast Asia, "the whole of Pakistan is to become a school, beginning at the village level, to teach the people their roles, rights, and responsibilities, both as individuals and as members of larger political units." The basic democracies have a five-tier hierarchy, or six, if the central government is included. These five stages consist of (1) union councils, or panchayats, and union and town committees (a rural union consists of several villages having a total population between 10,000 to 15,000 people, and although smaller, is somewhat comparable to the block committees of India); (2) *Tsehil* (West Pakistan) and *Thana* (East Pakistan) councils, which consist of several unions, with an average total of 144,000 people; (3) district councils; (4) divisional councils; (5) provincial development advisory councils.

The significant feature of this hierarchy of basic democracies is that the various councils at all levels, while semi-elected, have elected chairmen; the councils act as administrative units with authority over taxes, local trade, and so on; and they are responsible for devising and implementing programs in connection with officials of the Village AID (Agricultural and Industrial Development). By the selection of the personnel of these councils the basic democracies make possible the participation not only of those who have been accustomed to wield power because of their traditional status as landowners, moneylenders, and so on, but also of the poorer villagers who had previously had no opportunity to take a part in local institutions, thereby broadening the base of future nationwide democracy. In Mr. Dupree's opinion, the basic democracies system will prepare the Pakistanis for eventual fully representative government, and may serve as a new pattern of democracy for other underdeveloped countries with a similar background of traditional, nondemocratic leadership.

While Communist institutions cannot be compared with the institutions of non-Communist, even if not always democratic, countries, it may be said that even the councils of collective farms and factories in the USSR, and to a lesser extent the agrarian communes of Communist China, provide opportunities for administrative experience and for decisions about the selection of leaders at the grass-roots level which had not existed under the prerevolutionary regimes of either country. In this sense, however inadequate, such councils may prove to be the training grounds for the exercise of responsible representative, government at some future time.

The test of the efficacy of any set of political institutions in underdeveloped countries, however, will be not only the extent to which they represent the citizens but, first and foremost, their capacity to meet the economic problems of human beings who are emerging from Stone Age or premedieval or pre-Industrial Revolution conditions into the age of atomic energy. Will the new governments subject their peoples to the strains and stresses of an austere economic transformation? Or will they try to assure their immediate welfare? Or can they do both?

# 2

# Economic Austerity:
# With or Without Welfare?

ALL non-Western countries, whether rich or poor in natural resources, whether confronted or not with a population explosion, face the same basic economic problem: how to use their human and material capital most effectively to modernize their economies. Where they differ is as to the methods they should—or could—use to tackle this problem.

Out of the world-wide debate about methods three main approaches have emerged.

The first method is that of severe austerity during the initial period of economic transformation, with a minimum of concern for the immediate welfare of the people and little or no consideration for the needs of consumers.

This is the method of communism, as preached and practiced by the USSR from the death of Lenin in 1924 to the death of Stalin in 1953, and by Communist China since the establishment of the Mao Tse-tung regime in 1949. In both the USSR and in mainland China, Communist governments forced the population to labor under conditions and for objectives set forth in a series of five-year plans and to place their savings at the disposal of the state for investment in the development of land, raw materials, and industrial enterprises, all of which are state-owned.

To obtain the people's unquestioning support for this all-embracing transformation of a backward into a modern economy, the Communist leaders have imposed control over the thoughts and actions of their citizens through total direction of family life, political activities, education, the press and other media of communication, and the arts, and by officially excluding organized religion or, at best, tolerating its unofficial survival.

While this transformation was under way, satisfaction of the human desire for spiritual self-expression and material amenities has been deliberately postponed to an undetermined but anticipated future. In this respect, as Camus has pointed out, communism is a secular way of withholding rewards until an indefinite time which the individual may not witness but is encouraged to foresee for his descendants, as devout Christians think of rewards not on earth but in heaven. Paradoxical though it may seem to members of a non-Communist society, communism, by its system of setting aside today's earnings for tomorrow's fulfillment, provides a means for the kind of self-denial of present comforts to achieve future gains which is made possible by capitalism, with this basic difference: that both current self-denial and ultimate gain are determined not by the individual but by the state, which claims to represent and act for the benefit of the collectivity known as the nation.

The core of the Communist approach is the principle of state ownership of all of the nation's resources, both men and materials. In the Communist society of the USSR the individual is a member of a collective group, whether a factory or state farm where he is an employee of the state, or of a collective farm where he, along with other members, contributes his labor for a reward assigned to him out of group-earned funds in accordance with the work he has performed. In the USSR, however, the individual retains the right to cultivate for personal needs a bit of land, leased from the government which owns it, to build his own house on that land, and to sell his produce in the free market at a price not controlled by the state. Thus, after over forty years of communism, during which the state has laid the foundation for modernized agriculture and for the production of heavy as well as light industrial goods, the individual has a limited opportunity for modest private enterprise, subject to government permission. Unless another war makes a mockery of all predictions, it is expected that this limited opportunity to acquire personal possessions will gradually expand as a new class of managers of farms and factories, technicians, scientists, writers, educators, and artists takes over positions of power and influence in the state, although with no change in the basic principle of state ownership of resources.

Until recently this was not the case in Communist China, where economic transformation such as that wrought in the USSR has been under way for only a decade. There the peasant has been forced to live in military agrarian communes, retaining no personal property—no house, furnishings, small tools, rabbits, chickens, or vegetables, which are available to the Russian peasant, nor could he engage in private trade. Nor could the city worker in Communist China, like his counterpart in the USSR, obtain additional monetary rewards through higher quantity or quality of work and spend the additional funds thus earned on the purchase of consumer goods, whether clothes or a TV set, books or saucepans, for the personal use of himself and his family. Whether Communist China, for doctrinal reasons, will maintain greater austerity than the USSR even after it has raised productivity to a level comparable to that of Moscow for a population now three times larger, or will follow the example of gradual relaxation set by the Russian Communists even before the death of Stalin, but markedly accelerated under Khrushchev, is one of the most tantalizing questions of our times. If Russia's experience is any guide, communism regards austerity not as a permanent way of life but as a temporary period of belt-tightening during which citizens are expected to sacrifice personal comforts for the economic advancement of the state.

Following countrywide famines in 1960, brought about, in the views of some experts, by lack of incentives to production. Peiping indicated in 1961 that it might adopt Moscow's system of giving the peasant an opportunity to produce food on his own bit of land. The pressure of China's growing population, which at the present stage of national consolidation is regarded by its leaders as an asset in the struggle with "imperialism," may foreclose a relaxation there on the pattern set by the Russians. But should relaxation come, it may signal, as in Russia, a less militant foreign policy and an attempt to reduce tension in relations with other countries.

Outside the immediate circle of the Communist countries (which in terms of geography has so far been limited to Eastern Europe, Russia, and mainland China), Cuba, a year and a half after the Castro revolution, had been subjected to increasing state control over its economy comparable in basic respects to that exercised by communism.

Fidel Castro has established what he calls "a directed economy." This is how Tad Szulc, *The New York Times* South America correspondent, described it on June 5, 1960:

> The state's domination of the economy ranges from a virtually complete hold over agriculture, which is the backbone of Cuba's livelihood, to an increasing sway over industry and the penetration of commerce.

It is the state that determines the volume and the type of land production, directs foreign trade, operates all construction activities, and even concerns itself with such details as the retail distribution of meat, eggs and potatoes, and prescribing the end of the oyster season.

Although segments of industry and much of the internal commerce, including in both cases United States interests, are still permitted to function as private concerns, they are at the mercy of the state.

Private industry's sources of raw materials are controlled by either the system of licensing imports and providing foreign exchange or the government's power to regulate the flow of domestically produced materials.

Commerce sees its sources of supply drastically curtailed by import restrictions, and Cuba traditionally is dependent on foreign goods. At the same time the regime's policy of eliminating the middleman in dealings in agricultural products is destroying old trade patterns. The regime's philosophy is that profit margins must be reduced to bring down prices.

Special legislation makes it possible for the government to seize concerns on charges that the owners were illicitly enriched during the regime of President Fulgencio Batista or in the event of "labor conflicts." As the government now tightly controls the labor unions, it is believed that such conflicts could be induced, if needed.

The Castro government has reinforced the impression that it will seek to model its economy on that of the Communist countries by a series of actions. Among these have been its incessant attacks on the "imperialism" of the United States and on the grasping nature of American "capitalism"; its decision to invite to Cuba political leaders and technicians from both the USSR and Communist China; and its determination to expand trade with the Soviet bloc. Cuba had also alienated other Latin-American countries which had initially greeted Castro's revolution against the Batista dictatorship with sympathy but subsequently turned against it when Castro, too, began to act as a dictator. This was made clear by the unanimous decision of members of the Organization of American States on August 29, 1960, to denounce the acceptance by Cuba of aid from and intervention by the USSR and Communist China.

The Communist economic system has two main objectives on the domestic scene, as distinguished from its impact on the international scene. The first of these objectives is a state-directed effort, embracing all human activities, to overcome economic and technological backwardness through the creation of new institutions and the introduction of new methods of collective work. The second is an equally all-embracing effort to harness the energies of all individuals to the needs of the nation as defined by political leaders who are, at one and the same time, leaders of the single political party and of the government.

Many Westerners have described the Communist system as "monolithic" and have assumed that, unlike the pluralistic society of democratic nations, it is not subject to internal fissures and is invulnerable to change. This impression of the impregnable solidarity of the Communist system has been welcomed and encouraged by the Communists, who claim that their society is free of the "internal contradictions" which, in their belief, assail democracies. This impression, however, is in fact belied by the internal struggles that raged even under the iron rule of Stalin between the official view and the "deviations" of right and left which, under a less rigid system, would have found expression in opposition political parties challenging Communist orthodoxy—as it has been challenged within the Communist bloc by what Russian and Chinese critics call the "heresy" of Marshal Tito. It has been belied, too, by the significant differences between the Communist economic system of the USSR and of Communist China; and even more by the departures from orthodoxy made by Yugoslavia in the 1950's which, in turn, affected not only Poland under President Wladyslaw Gomulka, but also, and more important, Russia itself, hitherto the source of inspiration to the world's Communists.

Yugoslavia, at the other end of the spectrum from Communist China, has liberalized the economic pattern set by Moscow instead of making it more stringent. Having severed the umbilical cord which had held Yugoslav communism to that of Russia, Marshal Tito blazed new trails in three sectors of the economic front. He gradually decollectivized collective farms, replacing them with farm co-operatives which have a precedent in the experience of many Yugoslavs, particularly the Croats; he decentralized the direction of industries, entrusting increased authority to regional and local administrators; and he gave workers' councils a voice in the operation of factories, thus creating an opportunity for a form of economic democracy.

These changes were understandably distasteful to orthodox Communists in Moscow, whose right to proclaim the true faith was challenged by Marshal Tito's assertion that the Yugoslavs, not the Russians, were simon-pure Communists who based their beliefs and practices on the two prophets—Marx and Lenin—not on the interpretation of their ideas by Stalin. Yet under Khrushchev the USSR, while continuing its agricultural collective system, has modified it by the reorganization of the machine and tractor stations, once instruments of direct relations between the state and the collective farms, into agencies which sell or rent farm machinery directly to the collectives. The USSR has also decentralized its vast network of industrial enterprises, whose control and administration had previously been centered in Moscow, placing greater authority and initiative in the hands of local industrial managers, as Yugoslavia had done with its far more modest industrial complex. And Khrushchev, prodded and aided by one of his closest associates, Anastas I. Mikoyan, has vigorously encouraged increased output of consumer goods, accelerated construction of housing, and permitted greater latitude of expression in literature and in the arts.

Western students of the Soviet economy, among them Harry Schwartz of *The New York Times,* have also noted that Soviet economists increasingly tend to base their conclusions not on Marxist dogma, but on theories familiar to Western economists. For example, Professor Leonid V. Kantorovich, the inventor of linear programming, a mathematical technique by which complex economic problems can be solved in terms of the most rational answer, in his book, *Economic Calculation of the Best Use of Resources,* has argued that decisions about allocations of resources should be made not on the basis of labor time alone, as urged by Marxists, but on the basis of the most effective use of the scarcest resources. It is significant that Professor Kantorovich's ideas, although challenged by orthodox Marxists, have received wide circulation in the USSR.

These and other changes in the USSR seem to indicate that Khrushchev has been moving, if not through explicit adjustments of Communist dogma at least through pragmatic decisions on economic, as well as political and social policies, toward a position midway between what might be called the rightist deviation of Tito and the leftist deviation of Mao Tse-tung. The Soviet Premier has declared that, "In questions of ideology, we have firmly stood and will continue to stand firmly, like a rock, on the principles of Marxism-Leninism." This would appear to put him into competition with Tito, who also claims to be a direct intellectual heir of Marx and Lenin (but not Stalin, whom Khrushchev had attacked in his celebrated address to the Twentieth Congress of the Communist party in 1953).

But judging by the article which appeared in *Pravda* on June 12, 1960, commenting on the publication, forty years before, of Lenin's book, *Left-Wing Communism: An Infantile Disorder,* Khrushchev is also critical of the economic practices of Communist China. The article deprecates those countries which seek "to build socialism on the basis of imperialist handouts or attempts to skip entire historic stages," a description which would fit Yugoslavia, recipient of aid from several Western countries, notably the United States. But it also quotes Khrushchev's address to the Twenty-first Congress of the Communist party when he said, "We must not hurry and hastily introduce what has not yet ripened. That would lead to distortions and compromise our cause"—a statement which can be interpreted as a criticism of Mao Tse-tung's strenuous attempt to create agrarian communes. Khrushchev opposes "the search for a separate path to socialism for each country individually." If each country seeks its own path, "it may well result in so many 'paths' that people will get lost, as in a forest, and will not know how to reach their goal. In life there is only a single, Leninist path toward the construction of socialism and communism, a path tested by historical experience, the path of the Great October Socialist Revolution."

What is not made clear in the *Pravda* article is that the USSR itself has undergone significant economic changes as its industrialization has advanced, but without spelling out the ideological adjustments these changes have brought about. However, acceptance of the idea that the goals now reached by the USSR could have been attained by other means—some less burdensome, as in the case of Yugoslavia, others more rapid, as in the case of Communist China—might cast doubt on the efficacy of the method of development followed by Moscow.

In the Communist countries austerity has hitherto been pushed beyond the point where it may seem necessary for the country itself, in order to devote surplus production, where it is achieved, to foreign aid, with the aim, on the international scene, of thereby winning prestige, and gaining the support of the underdeveloped countries in the global struggle between communism and democracy. This drive to aid underdeveloped countries has been undertaken not only by the Soviet bloc —under the leadership of the USSR, with significant contributions by the Eastern European countries, particularly highly industrialized Czechoslovakia—but also by Communist China, which is far from having achieved the productivity level and the capacity to improve its own people's living conditions of the USSR.

Many observers believe it is through economic aid to Asia, the Middle East, Africa, and Latin America, rather than through continued arms buildup, that the Communist countries will wage the most important battles of the cold war. In this way the Communists will seek to demonstrate that their system is more effective in developing underdeveloped economies, not only through evidence of their own success at home, but also of their capacity to give aid abroad—from a steel mill for India to the construction of the High Aswan Dam for Egypt, from the building of schools in Guinea to the paving of streets for Kabul. Within the international context the subject of world-wide debate is whether the policy of austerity, based on calculated withholding of immediate satisfactions for the sake of investment in basic enterprises, will or will not eventually contribute more to the long-run welfare of people in underdeveloped areas.

At the other extreme from Communist austerity is the rejection of austerity by non-Communist countries intent on satisfying their peoples' immediate wants for improved living conditions. This approach is usually supported on the ground that the most healthy thing for an underdeveloped economy is to limit intervention by the state to a minimum, to encourage by all available means private enterprise at home and private, as distinguished from governmental, aid from abroad, and to place no curbs on consumption by the population other than those imposed by poverty. This approach has the dual attraction of avoiding governmental economic controls associated with political dictatorship, and the outward appearance, if not always the reality, of prosperity— as contrasted with the austere, often depressing living conditions of Communist lands in the early stages of economic transformation.

The nonausterity policy may not prove harmful, for a time at least, in countries which have a favorable ratio of resources to population, as in Thailand, the Philippines, and some Latin-American nations, or which over a considerable period of time receive substantial financial aid from abroad, as in the case of United States aid to Brazil. The danger is that, in the absence of over-all direction, both internal and external resources may be dissipated on "conspicuous consumption" both by individuals and by the state (for example, the building of luxury hotels in Cuba under Batista and in Venezuela under Jiménez amid general poverty) without either creating a foundation for future development or satisfying continued public demand for rising living standards. Under such circumstances the economy, although outwardly healthy and relaxed, may in fact remain stagnant, and even begin to deteriorate; may be ill-prepared for emergencies and, even more, for contests on the international scene with better-organized countries; and prove eventually unable to undertake the "take-off" into modernization. Should this be the case, present satisfaction may jeopardize the possibility of future welfare; and the existing gap between the few rich and the many poor, left unbridged, may widen dangerously as time goes on, with consequent unrest and revolution at home. This would encourage intervention by foreign countries ready to capitalize on internal maladjustments—as has happened in the Congo and in Laos.

The third approach which has been tried for the economic development of underdeveloped countries is what might be called the Indian method, because it has been applied most extensively and with the greatest determination in India since that country achieved independence in 1947. This is the "mixed economy" method: over-all development under five-year plans drawn up and directed by the state, but within a flexible framework where some sectors of the economy are assigned exclusively to the state, others exclusively to private enterprise, and still others to the state and to private enterprise acting together in partnership.

The Indian government, which describes its economic system as "socialism," has three objectives. It seeks to modernize a premedieval agriculture and to establish light and heavy industries—from fertilizer to steel, from locomotives to antibiotics; to achieve these targets through the voluntary co-operation of all citizens, without coercion such as has been used in the USSR and Communist China; and to satisfy a modicum of consumer needs—primarily food and clothing—but within limits set by the government for the allocation of natural resources, skilled man power, internal finances, and foreign aid.

To meet these three objectives, India has devised a planning system markedly different from that of Russia and China in its emphasis on the choice of priorities. In India industrialization was deliberately postponed until a minimum of food had been provided. In contrast, also, to the crash-program character of the Russian and Chinese five-year plans, which stress speed irrespective of the sacrifices, physical and spiritual, inflicted on the people, India's planning is "gradualistic," in keeping with its political policy of slow adaptation to the needs and opportunities of a modern society.

Russia and China, animated by motives of national prestige and military security, as well as by the determination to improve the lot of their people, are trying to "catch up with and outstrip the capitalist world," to use Stalin's famous slogan. By contrast, India, which is not trying to compete with the West but only hopes not to be outdone by its neighbor, China, has as its first consideration the welfare of its people, modest as this might seem when compared with Western standards, or even with the standards of some other non-Western countries which have a more favorable ratio of resources to population.

While India's economy is described as "socialist," actually, as of 1960, 90 per cent of the country's enterprises, including agriculture which is entirely in the hands of individual owners and furnished 92 per cent of the country's total income, was privately controlled, with only 8 per cent of the total coming from government-owned enterprises. Instead of imposing collectivization of peasant farms, as has been done by the Russians, or of military agrarian communes, as was done by the Chinese in 1958, the Indians encourage agricultural co-operatives, co-operation of the peasants in community development projects that embrace hundreds of villages, and voluntary contributions of labor by the peasants to various projects in their villages or in neighboring areas, such as the building of schools, dams, roads, and so on.

In spite of its efforts to increase food production under the first two plans which covered the period 1951-61, India had not succeeded by 1959 in reducing the dangerous unbalance in the ratio between food and population. According to a study made that year by a Ford Foundation team at the request of the Indian government, at the present slow but steady rate of increase the gap between food supply and demand will be 28 million tons of grain by the end of the Third Five-Year plan in 1966. The team warned that "no conceivable program of imports or rationing can meet a crisis of this magnitude," and urged India to assign top priority to agriculture and to undertake an emergency program of action to mobilize India's resources of soil, water, and manpower.

India's planners, while agreeing on the need for a greater effort in agriculture than has yet been achieved or even contemplated, believe that stepped-up industrialization is also a top priority which the government could disregard or postpone only at its peril. India's industry shows the characteristics of socialism far more clearly than does its agriculture. For while land remains in the hands of private owners, a small sector of industry, representing only about 8 per cent of the national income, as already pointed out, is controlled, directed, and operated by the government. The pattern for some government-operated enterprises had been set by the British long before independence. Transferring to India their own tradition of government ownership of basic utilities, the British built, owned, and operated the railways, as well as posts, telegraphs, and telephones, a practice also customary in other democratic countries of Europe.

When the Indians first came to power, they were inclined—like the British Laborites with whom some of their leaders had been well acquainted during their studies in Britain—to believe that nationalization would be a universal panacea for industry. They nationalized a number of enterprises, among them Indian airlines, eleven internal and two external, and more recently the life insurance companies. As time went on, however, they became disillusioned with the curative powers of nationalization, and after a series of readjustments settled for a relatively limited number of government-controlled enterprises. This list includes industries working solely for defense; the production of steel in new mills (steel had been nationalized in Britain by the Laborites after 1945 and then denationalized by the Conservatives in 1950), but with existing private mills left in the hands of their owners; and enterprises regarded as in the national interest—such as fertilizer plants—which private owners may not be interested in initiating.

What India has done with its economic development is to follow the traditional Hindu way of seeking to reconcile "this *and* that," as its philosopher Vice President Radakrishnan has put it, instead of trying to make a choice, as Russia and China have done, between "this *or* that." India has sought to reconcile state planning with private enterprise, the output of food with that of industry, speed in some segments of the economy with gradualism in others, government initiative with encouragement of private voluntary action. The basic question asked about India's mixed voluntary economy is whether it will generate the sense of urgency, the concentrated effort on the part of the population, which communism with all its ruthless disregard of human values has succeeded in generating; or whether its "deliberate speed" will prove too slow for the stark necessities of our times, when underdeveloped countries cannot afford the gradualism which proved practicable for the Western nations during the centuries of their economic modernization. Should this prove to be the case, then India, in spite of all its good intentions, will lose the momentum required to achieve the "take-off" into a modern economy.

Both India and its Western well-wishers face a dilemma. In theory, its gradualist method is obviously far more humane than that of communism in Russia and China, and over the long run could build a more solid base for the country's future development; but if India cannot demonstrate its capacity to satisfy the modest needs of its people, gradualism may prove its nemesis in comparisons which are inevitably made between its economy and that of China, and thus between democracy and communism, with the final award going to communism. Yet if India were to try the Communist pattern, not only would it incur the same criticisms which the West now makes of the method used by Moscow and Peiping but, what may ultimately prove more serious, its own population might reject this approach.

Even a brief study of non-Western areas reveals the variety of methods which have been used in the twentieth century by the underdeveloped countries to modernize their economies. Some experts have contended that the non-Western countries will have to pass through the same stages of economic development as the nations of the West did between 1500 and 1950. Basing their calculations on this assumption, they anticipate a long period before Asia and the Middle East, Africa and Latin America, can reach the technological level of the Western nations which, meanwhile, it must be assumed, will have forged ahead, with the result that, as the Swedish economist Gunnar Myrdal has pointed out in his little book, *Rich Lands, Poor Lands,* the rich will get richer and the poor will get poorer. Pessimistic predictions about the future of the non-Western countries are often based on the theory, advanced by Arnold Toynbee, that once a non-Western country has accepted one aspect of the West's experience it must accept all of it. And this, it is believed by many, is bound to take a long time.

Yet is total acceptance of Western experience necessary? In the West we automatically reach this conclusion because we tend to believe that the Western way of life is a universal norm, and that other peoples, who have not shared the historical experience of the Western nations, must sooner or later adopt this norm—or find themselves outside the pale of modern society.

But is this conclusion justified by known experience? Is it possible that there may be several norms; that communism is creating a norm different from that of Western capitalism, but that meanwhile several other norms are being developed, based on the experience of various systems, like the mixed economy of India? What we do know is that human beings have shown an astonishing capacity for maintaining their customs, traditions, ideas—even the human beings who existed in North America and Asia some thirty-five thousand years ago—and yet, after encountering new situations, have selected those aspects of the hitherto unknown which seemed desirable for their purposes while rejecting others. In describing the pre-Columbian art of the Americas, Jane P. Powell of the Brooklyn Museum, in her absorbing little pamphlet on the *Ancient Art of the Americas*, says, "There is an amazing diversity of media, of purpose, of character and style within the whole of pre-Columbian art. These infinitely creative people, while specializing in several techniques, utilized whatever material their environment provided, or was gained from trade or conquest in distant places. . . . Foreign influences were readily accepted, but were usually absorbed within the original style which was strong, persistent, and sensitive to the various currents within the society."

This is the process of selective assimilation we are witnessing in the twentieth century, as various non-Western countries devise their own economic systems out of the wide range of methods now available, combining those elements which seem most desirable for their needs. Japan is the most striking example of this selectivity, through which, beginning in the 1860's, it grafted modern science and technology onto the living traditions of its ancient civilization, drawing for its science, technology, and industrial organization, its politics, and even its arts, on such diverse sources as the United States, Britain, Germany, France, and Italy, as it once had drawn its religions and its art forms from China.

Russia and China, in spite of their violent anti-Westernism, have utilized the industrial experience of the West in the development of their primarily agrarian economies, and in this sense the Communists in both countries can be regarded as Westernizers. India, standing between West and East, has absorbed the ideas and the practices both of Britain's democracy and of its industrial system, the first to be developed in the West, yet has adapted them to its own conditions. More recently it has also blended into its economy some of the successful agricultural practices of Japan and China (particularly in rice-growing), of small-scale industries in Japan, Italy, the Scandinavian countries, and of heavy-industry techniques from Russia, Czechoslovakia, and West Germany as well as Britain and the United States (particularly in steel-making). And in North Africa President Habib Bourguiba, who has been deeply influenced by French ideas and is strongly opposed to communism, nevertheless has paid heed to the views of some of Tunisia's economists who contend that Socialist, or even Communist, organization can be useful to underdeveloped countries.

It cannot, therefore, be taken as a foregone conclusion that the non-Western countries must inevitably pass through the same stages of economic development as the nations of the West. On the contrary, by adapting to their twentieth-century requirements the twentieth-century inventions of the West, the non-Western nations may not only be able to jump over centuries, but they may actually find that in some sectors of their economy they can start with the newest models instead of having to retain existing obsolete models seen in some of the advanced countries. Japan succeeded in doing this with its textile industry, while Britain's Lancashire mills, first product of its Industrial Revolution, lagged behind.

Technology, however, is but a means to an end. The end, in this case, of creating a new society will depend not merely on new techniques, but on new relationships within ancient social orders. Will industrialization, the great modern equalizer, enhance or destroy the great civilizations of the non-Western world?

# 3

# Social Transformation
# Amid Traditions

IN CONTRAST to the experience of Western countries, where the process of psychological and social
adjustments was stretched over centuries, the non-Western peoples
must suddenly face up to startling transformations of their way of life
while they are still deeply rooted in ancient traditions that have remained unchanged through the ages.

The experience non-Westerners go through under these circumstances is comparable to that of Western man when, in the age of
Copernicus and Galileo, he was suddenly confronted with the realization that the earth, far from being fixed in a stable and immutable
world order, was in fact orbiting around the sun in the midst of a
limitless universe. As the brilliant critic Marjorie Nicolson has so well
put it, "the circle of perfection," of an ordered and preordained existence that gave man a sense of security, was broken by scientific knowledge, and above all by the possibility of glimpsing through the "optik
tube"—the telescope—the newly discovered marvels of outer space.

No wonder that the English poets of the seventeenth century
expressed both the despair and the exhilaration of their contemporaries. John Donne, whom the new discoveries filled with a pessimism
that makes him kin to all of us—Westerners and non-Westerners—in
our era of change and anxiety, cried out: "And new Philosophy calls
all in doubt," and again, "'Tis all in peaces, all cohaerence gone; All
just supply, and all relation." But for others astronomy opened doors
to intellectual adventures which fired the imagination and tested minds
and souls to the uttermost limit. Thus Thomas Traherne sang ecstat-
ically: "I felt no Dross nor Matter in my Soul, / No Brims nor Borders,
such as in a Bowl . . ./ We see: My Essence was Capacitie." And
Henry More expressed the matchless excitement of intellectual delight

225

in a period of far-reaching transformation when he wrote: "th' infinite I'll sing/ Of Time, of Space . . . I'm brent/ with eager rage, my heart for joy doth spring/ and all my spirits move with pleasant trembeling."

The non-Westerner today, like the Westerner of the seventeenth century, finds himself caught between two worlds—the world of unquestioning faith in long-accepted values and the world of new values whose acceptance threatens the foundations of ancient faiths. He wants the advantages of the new, which consist not merely of material comforts but also of spiritual emancipation from tyrannies —the tyrannies of secular rulers and of an authoritarian priesthood, both intolerant of dissent; of the joint family; of caste, or clan, or tribe; of superstition and the fears superstition breeds; of ignorance; and of poverty regarded as without earthly cure. At the same time he is repelled by some of the aspects of the new—by loss of belief in ruler and priest, in the authority and the accompanying sense of security offered by the family; by the pressures of competitiveness in a modern economy, the shoddiness of machine-made culture, the neon lights of big cities, the sense of being lost in "the lonely crowd," of not "belonging" to a settled, generally accepted social order.

Like the hero of the Japanese novel, *Some Prefer Nettles,* the non-Westerner seeks to identify himself with the new—and this means with Western ideas and practices—but he also longs to reject them and return to the old, which the hero finally does. This painful swing of the pendulum from one extreme to the other is just as noticeable among students who belong to the new generation (which might be expected to feel more attuned to change than the old) as among the mature intellectuals or the landowners, the industrialists, or the rural folk. In fact, the young are more troubled than the old because, unlike their elders, they have no memories of the past which might serve as an anchor amid the storm churned up by the impact of the West on the non-West.

The resulting mental and emotional confusion, which has, in social terms, the characteristics of schizophrenia in an individual, is apt to erupt into uncontrolled frenzy at the bidding of leaders capable of arousing mass fury. This is what happened in Japan in June, 1960, when the scheduled good-will visit of President Eisenhower coincided with the debate in the Japanese Diet concerning the new United States-Japanese security treaty, with the result, as it seemed to opposition groups, of placing the seal of American approval on the government of Premier Kishi, formerly a supporter of Japan's pre-1945 militarist policy. Such an eruption of feeling may come just as easily—or even more easily—from the educated as from the illiterate, and from those hostile to Western customs as from those who have never seen a Westerner face to face and therefore cannot advance any realistic grounds for their feelings toward the West.

This sentiment of revulsion against and rejection of the new is often described as anti-Westernism, and is believed by many Westerners to be inspired by Communist propaganda. Yet the sentiment existed in nineteenth-century Russia long before Karl Marx wrote *Das Kapital* and Lenin came to power. In its time it caused a profound rift between pro-Westerners like Alexander Herzen, who ultimately sought refuge in England, and opponents of Westernism like Dostoevski, who believed that Western ideas would destroy the faith of Holy Mother Russia. In fact it was the Communists, both in Russia and China, who far from rejecting the science and technology of the West—as an older generation steeped in traditional religion and opposed to rationalism might have done—sought to master both, and tirelessly adapted them to the conditions of their backward societies.

What non-Westerners reject, whether they are conscious of it or not, is not the contribution the West can make to their development as individuals and to the development of their societies. They reject some of the by-products of a technological civilization such as de-tribalization, the breakdown of understanding between generations, the decline of all authority (which opens the way to anarchy), the tendency to accept the cheap and the shoddy in preference to the treasured and the beautifully wrought in human relations, in the arts, in the entire way of life.

This rejection has a universal, rather than a non-West versus West character. Boris Pasternak's Doctor Zhivago rejects not so much the Soviet state or the Communist way of life as the encroachment on the individual's existence and conscience made by the collectivity in the modern mechanized state. One has the feeling that Dr. Zhivago, had he lived in the United States, would have opposed "the organization man" and "the hidden persuaders" as much as he opposed the Soviet bureaucrats, although obviously he would not have felt as hemmed in personally here as he did in the USSR. Yet Pasternak demonstrated the truism that "stone walls do not a prison make" when, under a stringent dictatorship, he persisted in being his own self and writing as he thought best, displaying a deep-seated sense of personal integrity and a freedom from subjection to the approval of others which are rare even in democratic societies but are found among other contemporary Russian and Eastern European writers.

Pasternak's capacity to retain his values under a social order whose values differed profoundly from his was inspired by a religious faith not often present amid the moral upheaval of non-Western peoples in this century. What happens to those younger individuals who have lost their faith in anything was vividly described by John D. Rockefeller IV in his article, "Students in Japan: An Intimate Glimpse," in *The New York Times* of June 5, 1960, when he wrote:

> Another reason the younger generation of Japanese must struggle to carry their own burdens is that they have neither religion nor faith. For the young, Shintoism died with the war. Buddhism survives on tourists, and Christianity affects less than one half of 1 per cent of the population.
>
> Furthermore, all prewar concepts of behavior and attitude have been discredited in the eyes of the young. They fear and distrust their government, convinced that it is trying to centralize control and remilitarize Japan with the help of the Americans (almost to a man, the voting students vote against the Kishi government).
>
> The young Japanese does not have the instinctive confidence and trust in his country that Americans have in theirs. Indeed, they have little knowledge of or interest in the prewar culture and nature of Japan, for they feel it bears no relation to them. Consequently, in times of personal trouble, there is no God to turn to, no solace in prayer, no minister to seek help from, no comfort from a national sense of well-being and even, as we have seen, no acceptable parental guidance.

The adjustment required of non-Westerners is not merely the psychological adjustment of the individual, such as was made by Pasternak who, when offered an opportunity to exchange life in Russia under communism for life in a country free from dictatorship, decided to remain in the land he loved. What non-Westerners find they must do is to go through a social adjustment, the transformation of a long-established and long-respected social order. The individual must learn not only to accept a new way of life for himself, but also to participate in the transformation of the group to which he belongs. And these two adjustments—of the individual and of his group—must take place, let us bear in mind, not in a leisurely way, but often with dramatic suddenness, in a few years, or even a few months. It is not surprising that this rapidity of change causes a state of shock, even of paralysis of the will in some, of disorientation leading to irrational outbursts in others.

To understand the state of mind of non-Westerners, we must try to imagine how we might feel if we were suddenly transported to Mars or to the moon, where everything would look to us strange and therefore frightening, unknown and therefore beyond comprehension; and where our first reaction might well be to shut our eyes and wish ourselves back among familiar sights, sounds, and smells.

The rise of a new elite of technicians and professional men and women—a new middle class—in what was still a feudal society and the conflicts that arose as a result, have been well described in a small pamphlet, "A New American Policy Toward Africa," issued in February, 1960, by The Africa League of New York, composed of a group of American scholars.

> When the European trader, administrator, Christian missionary and educator arrived in Africa, he needed people with whom he could deal, people who shared with him some common thoughts, hopes and language. To the extent that he did not find them he started to create them, educating Africans to be his subordinates in the new trades, governments and learning-places he wished to establish. These offices, shops and schools were located in cities, new or expanding ones, cities like Accra or Leopoldville, Tunis or Salisbury.
>
> The people who received a modern education became in time clerks and nurses, doctors and teachers, engineers, mechanics, chauffeurs, telephone operators, and interpreters. They were not necessarily related to the important people of pre-colonial society. Often the contrary was true; they were descendants of commoners or "captives." But the pay and prestige from their new professions made them less inclined to pay homage to their village and regional chiefs. Out of this conflict grew the struggle we see in most of modern Africa today between clerk and chief, fetish priest and doctor.

The problems of social adjustment can be illustrated by four situations: that of the intellectual confronted by a new social order; that of the young army officer who seeks political change; that of the landowner confronted by a new economic order; and that of the peasant confronted by a newly industrialized neighborhood.

The non-Western intellectual is usually first exposed to the West through education, whether received directly in Western schools in his homeland, usually run by missionaries, or at universities in Western nations, usually those which have ruled them as colonial subjects. The intellectual becomes fascinated by the ideas of the West, which for the most part differ profoundly from those of his own culture and challenge the ideas in which he has been nurtured under the guidance of religious mentors within his family, caste, or tribe. Thus not only do Western secular concepts raise questions about the political and social concepts of non-Western peoples, but Christianity, whether Protestant or Catholic, raises questions about the traditional faith, be it Hinduism or Buddhism, Confucianism or Shintoism, Islam or paganism.

This all-embracing challenge is more far-reaching if the society in which the non-Westerner lives has previously been closed to outside concepts. It is more far-reaching in Islamic lands—where men of other faiths are regarded as "infidels" and teaching has been done by rote, not through free discussion and criticism—than in a flexible society long open to ideas from many sources and willing, like India, to absorb them into its own philosophy.

Exposed to Western ideas, the non-Western intellectual begins to feel torn between the culture of the West and that of his own land. In his autobiography, Jawaharlal Nehru has brilliantly described the resulting state of mind:

I have become a queer mixture of the East and West, out of place everywhere, at home nowhere. Perhaps my thought and approach to life are more akin to what is called Western than Eastern, but India clings to me as she does to all her children, in innumerable ways; and behind me lie, somewhere in the subconscious, racial memories of a hundred generations of Brahmins. I cannot get rid of either that past inheritance or my present acquisitions. They are both part of me, and, though they help me in both the East and the West, they also create in me a feeling of spiritual loneliness not only in public activities but in life itself. I am a stranger and an alien in the West. I cannot be of it. But in my own country also, sometimes, I have an exile's feeling.

Depending on his own temperament, the non-Western intellectual may either try to become Westernized, rejecting his own culture, and thus become, to use the apt French phrase, *dépaysé,* or a man without a country; or try to cling to his own culture, rejecting that of the West, and thus fail to benefit by an important share of mankind's intellectual heritage; or try to create his own synthesis, and develop his own values as an individual or as a representative of his people. The third course is what Nasser has called the search for "identity," either personal or national.

In any of these three cases, during the period of adjustment, the intellectual feels ambivalent, without roots, belonging neither here nor there. This feeling is accompanied by a sense of guilt due to the belief that by participating, however slightly, in Western ideas, he has disconnected himself from his own people, with whom he is thus "out of touch"—and must get in touch with them again. This is a familiar theme in the life of the Russian intellectual, as reflected in the novels of Turgenev and the plays of Chekhov. Bazarov, the young doctor in Turgenev's *Fathers and Sons*, feels alienated from the old order, as represented by his father, but far from wanting to withdraw from his environment he wants to be in contact with his own people, with the peasants whom nineteenth-century liberals idealized as the true expression of the Russian soul. Like many of his contemporaries he wants to "go to the people," to serve them through his knowledge of medicine even though he may die from the effects of an infection resulting from the performance of his duties. It is interesting that in many non-Western countries, as varied as Algeria and Chile, the doctor is the prototype of the "savior" or "helper" of the poor and humble —for example, Camus' doctor-hero in *The Plague*. The same simultaneous rejection of the old order and search for fulfillment through service to the masses—in the dark villages of Russia, in the wretched slums of Calcutta—recur in the novels of non-Western countries.

An important aspect of this passionate desire for service to humanity, felt by the non-Western intellectual amid the breakdown of traditional society but not always understood in Western countries, is that communism often provides intellectuals with the sense of integration in a new order, which they ardently seek—and often fail to find in traditional non-Communist societies. The intellectual wants to be an integral part of the society in which he lives; he does not want to be left on the side lines in a period of revolution; and he is ready to accept— in fact he welcomes—the invitation of the Communists to become associated with the workers and peasants, "the people" he wants to serve. Intellectuals tend to be a minority in any society. They do not want to be isolated from their own people, they want to share their people's ethos, even if they are nihilists like Bazarov. Only after a Communist revolution has been won, and the period of ardent struggle is over, does the intellectual revert to the self-questioning which made him what he is. And then he may find it as difficult to accept the dogma of the new order as he once found it difficult to accept the authoritarianism of the old.

To achieve spiritual satisfaction, the intellectual must express his own ideas—through writing, painting, music, sculpture, wherever his talent lies. To do this effectively he must avoid intellectual exile—as Pasternak vividly realized—even if he has to be or chooses to be exiled physically. He must be able to draw on the sources of his people's inspiration. Otherwise, when he first comes in contact with the writing and the arts of the West he is tempted merely to imitate the works of artists nurtured in another tradition. The Russians may have had a point, shocking as it is in the Western view, when they excluded foreign ideas and examples until they felt strong enough to receive them without succumbing to the temptation of becoming merely imitators. The exclusion of Westerners and their ideas by Japan until 1854 may have strengthened that country to meet modern concepts and to make its own choice as to which it would accept or reject.

For the initial reaction of a non-Westerner exposed to Western models, unless he rejects them out of hand, is to extol their quality and to denigrate his own. This attitude of self-humiliation before the achievements of the West sets up new psychological tensions. The non-Western intellectual needs to express himself in his own art forms. Otherwise sooner or later he feels frustrated at the thought that he is producing mongrel works. Westerners can help non-Western colleagues by expressing respect for their achievements when this represents an honest judgment but without resorting to exaggeration, which can be a dangerous form of denigration in reverse.

Not only is the intellectual—the man or woman dedicated to the study and practice of the humanities, the sciences, and the arts in their wide range of professions—ill at ease in the rapidly changing society of non-Western lands. So is the talented individual of even limited education who finds that what he has learned gives him at an early age a special status in a still predominantly illiterate environment. He thus obtains ready access to positions of influence and power which under the more stable conditions of a long-organized nation might not be open to him until he had reached middle or even old age.

In the new nations of Africa young men who have moved directly from a precarious livelihood as leaders of anti-colonial movements, with or without a sojourn in jail (like the hero of Conton's *The African,* a thinly fictionalized account of a leader who resembles Nkrumah), often point out with pride that they are first-generation literates in their families or tribes.

In Latin America and in the Middle East, where education was long restricted to the wealthy or the aristocratic (and under Islam has offered no access to modern science and technology), youths of lower social groups who have obtained the opportunity to learn by serving in the professional armed forces tower over their uneducated and tradition-bound contemporaries. Kemal Ataturk or Nasser, Kassim or Perón or Batista, whose social origins might not have qualified them, under ordinary circumstances, to become political leaders, benefit by the wider contacts achieved through education and military service. At the same time, aware of their social disabilities in the Egypt of King Farouk, or the Iraq of King Faisal, or the Argentina of big land-owning aristocrats, many of these young military officers are pre-disposed to rebellion against the existing social order.

Like Napoleon in a comparable period of upheaval, they know they lack political legitimacy. But they make up for this lack by such talents for leadership and organization as they possess. And they have at their command two factors of power which politicians of higher social ranks might well envy them. They have an organized military following of fellow officers who, at least initially, share their background and their views and are ready to take the risks of overthrowing the regime in office; and they have control of weapons. It is not surprising, therefore, that under strikingly similar political, economic, and social conditions, countries of the Middle East and West Asia—Turkey, Egypt, Iraq, and Pakistan—and of Latin America—the Dominican Republic, Peru, Cuba, Venezuela—have in modern times been politically led by mili-tary officers, and that, in Turkey, Lieutenant General Cemal Gursel, when he seized power in May, 1960, from Premier Adnan Menderes, did so with an invocation to the spirit of his military predecessor, Kemal Ataturk.

These officer-politicians are often regarded by Westerners—accus-tomed to the idea that the armed forces are by definition reactionary in politics—as inclined to conservative views. In reality, because of their often lowly social origins, their acquaintance through education with new ideas, their ambitions both for themselves personally and for their country, the young officers are usually rebels against the *status quo*—whatever its form, secular or religious—and receptive to revolu-tionary ideas. But while the young officers may be rebels against an existing political order and supporters of economic and social reforms, as has been true of Kemal Ataturk, Nasser, and Marshal Ayub Khan, they are not found backing Communist movements. On the contrary, they regard themselves as defenders of peace and justice against Communist threats, as in the case of General Ne Win in Burma and General Nasution in Indonesia. And on the eve of General Gursel's coup in Turkey, Ismet Inonu, leader of the Republican party, addressing fourteen generals and admirals at a meeting held in his home, said in a statement which was also issued to the press: "The protection of the country's ideals of progress rests with retired military men. It is the military group which protects the health of the society."

To the intellectual and to the young officer, the landowner—whether he comes of the aristocracy or the gentry—represents the old order, or, to use the phrase of the French Revolution, the *ancien régime*. For in a changing society agriculture is on the decline as a significant factor of the country's economy, while industry, based on science and technology, is in the ascendant. With some notable exceptions (Count Leo Tolstoy was such an exception in Tsarist Russia) the landowner is accustomed to a position of superiority in a long-established social order, is proud of the traditions of his group, of his land, of his social prestige, and of the political influence he wields because of his prestige. He sees no reason for change; he opposes innovation, not only in agriculture, but in the society as a whole; he regards all those who threaten his role as radicals, upstarts, troublemakers, as crude people without tradition. He is disturbed by the demands of agricultural workers for the end of serfdom as in Russia, of slavery as in the American South. But he either accepts these demands more or less peacefully, as in England in the seventeenth century or Russia in 1861; or is forced to accept them as a result of civil war or revolution, as in the American South, France in 1789, Russia under Stalin, China under Mao Tse-tung.

What the landowner finds more difficult to face is the rise of industry, which challenges him on several fronts. First, industry is a challenge to the financial status of the landowner. Industrial wealth, accumulated through the investment of capital in manufacturing enterprises and through trade in manufactured products enters into competition with the wealth derived from land—and seems most menacing when landowners are least receptive to change and least willing to modernize agriculture. Second, industry is a challenge to the landowner's position in society. The new owners of industry compete with the landowners not only in terms of financial affluence, but also of social influence and, thereby, of political power. Even if a man like Colonel Perón had never appeared on the scene in Argentina, there would have been a struggle for power between the conservative land-owners and the "radicals" who were becoming interested in industrial development and in political liberalism. Third, industrial development brings about the rise of still another social group which menaces the position of the landowner—the factory workers (the *descamisados* or "shirtless ones" to whom Perón ardently appealed and who were the backbone of his movement), who sooner or later, by joining together in labor unions, become a new political challenge to the power of the landowners. But, fourth, and most disturbing of all for the landowner, is the feeling that the industrialist is a *nouveau riche*, a *parvenu*, who has come up from the people (and thus, in effect, from "nowhere"), often the descendant of serfs or slaves, perhaps himself a former serf or slave who may have achieved success directly at the expense of his former masters.

This latter theme is emphasized in Chekhov's *The Cherry Orchard*, which struck a deep chord not only in pre-Bolshevik Russia, but also in other countries that have since passed through Russia's experience. In this play the landowners know that the game is up, that they have no capacity to improve their land and thereby gain new wealth; that they have no money for the pleasures of travel to Paris and other luxuries to which they have become accustomed; that the sensible thing to do is to sell their land to the new industrialist, son of their former serfs who, unlike them, has adapted himself to the new eco-nomic order and will build houses where the cherry trees have always bloomed. But Chekhov's landowners are torn between two emotions. They want—and sorely need—the help of the *parvenu*, the *nouveau riche*, yet they are angry or sad, according to their nature, about the stark necessity of being indebted to him for survival, and would not dream of having any social relationship with him.

The truthfulness of this portrayal is underlined by the interest that Chekhov's work, particularly *The Cherry Orchard*, aroused in post-World War II Japan. The heroine of *The Setting Sun* by Osumi Dazai, daughter of an aristocratic landowning family reduced to pov-erty by the economic stringencies of the war and the American occu-pation, is forced to work on the soil with her hands to support her aged mother and herself. But when an elderly industrialist, friend of the family, comes to call on her and asks her hand in marriage, she turns fiercely upon him, saying, "What do you think this is? *The Cherry Orchard?*"

Chekhov was remarkably sensitive to the tensions of the social and psychological adjustment of the landowners to the rise of the new middle class. Turgenev, writing about the gentry's encounter with the young intellectual of the lower bourgeoisie (the student who is a tutor to a landowning family) showed that the intellectual might be acceptable on a country estate because he is educated; he might even become the lover of a married woman, mother of his pupil, but he is frowned upon as a possible suitor for the hand of a landowner's daughter, as in the play, *A Month in the Country*.

None of these themes are unknown to Western countries. The only difference is that themes which were familiar there in the eighteenth and nineteenth centuries, during the Industrial Revolution and the political changes it precipitated, no longer make news in France or England or the United States (although they still do in West Germany or Italy). They are, however, the stuff and substance of life in non-Western lands whose social transformation of traditional societies is at the stage where Western nations were a hundred or two hundred years ago. But comparable situations exist in areas where Westerners, through choice or accident, coexist with non-Westerners, as in Algeria or Kenya, or with Negroes in the American South (it is not surprising that Joshua Logan was able to transpose *The Cherry Orchard* into a Southern setting in his play, *The Wistaria Trees*, with only minor alterations).

In these areas the former landed aristocracy opposes changes in relations between races more than does the industrial group, which needs educated skilled labor and believes that its own prosperity depends on the prosperity of the non-whites. In Atlanta and Little Rock, in Birmingham and Montgomery, the merchants and professional leaders are on the side of reform in racial relations, not necessarily because of sentiment or philanthropy but because of self-interest, because a better-educated Negro who can earn a higher income is expected to be a better customer of businesses operated by whites.

This social and psychological adjustment takes place in every society which is passing from agrarian economy to industrialization. But the problems created by this adjustment are aggravated where the owning class is foreign in origin and the new elements who are coming to power are natives—Algerians or Kikuyus. For then not only do the new elements want to wrest financial resources and political power from foreign owners of land in a double revolution, but this revolution also assumes the proportions of civil war, as in Algeria, or defiance of the colonial ruler, as in the case of the Mau Mau uprising in Kenya.

A difficult adjustment is also faced by the rural inhabitant who has traditionally lived in the closed static society of the village, as in Turkey; the caste, as in India; the tribe, as in Africa; the clan, as in the countries of the Middle East, and is suddenly confronted with new ideas and practices brought in by industrialization. As the sociologist Daniel Lerner has well pointed out in his study of change in the Middle East, *The Passing of Traditional Society,* in the long-established social order, even if there is no caste system, occupations are set, with everyone in his place and a place for everyone. Those who deviate in any way from the established rules of society are viewed with suspicion. Lerner illustrates this point in his chapter, "The Grocer and the Chief," which describes how change came to a Turkish village, when suddenly this closed traditional society is exposed to influences from the outside. A road is built. Cars come to the village, bringing in visitors from the cities, even from foreign lands. New occupations are made possible by the use of a bus which takes villagers to work in nearby factories or by building factories in the village area. This is also the case in Kamala Markandya's beautiful novel of the transformation of an Indian village, *Nectar in a Sieve.*

The villagers obtain cash through work in factories. They can now buy goods they had never even seen before. Farming declines, as improved agricultural methods permit more production with fewer workers, and villagers, released from the land, go more and more into industries. The radio owned by Lerner's village chief—his principal status symbol—establishes communication with the outside world.

True, villagers who go to the city may find themselves crowded into slums, and still living in poverty, like the workers in Gorky's somber play *The Lower Depths.* But men begin to fix their "eye on higher places." The skilled man becomes more important than the traditional leader; the grocer, who brings in modern goods is more important than the chief. Similarly, the labor union leader—Sékou Touré in Guinea, Tom Mboya in Kenya—is more important than the chief of the African tribe. But the traditional man need not disappear, unless he bodily resists change. In a nondictatorial society he can, if he is willing to accept change, incorporate the new into what he knows of the old.

Thus, whatever the confrontation—between the intellectual and a changing society; between the young officer and the old political order; between the landowner and the new economic order; between the rural inhabitant and the new industrial system—those who are not filled with despair at the sight of new horizons, but can experience a sense of "happy trembeling," may hope to effect the creative confluence between tradition and change which has marked the adaptation, and hence the survival, of all now existing civilizations, and to do so without the terror and the bloody convulsions of the French, Russian, and Chinese revolutions.

Western observers, impatient to see non-Western peoples develop at one and the same time the political institutions, economic practices, and social conditions, as well as the modern art, literature, and music familiar to the nations of the Atlantic community, are not always aware of the span of time required for the vast and painful changes involved in the process of adapting ancient lands to twentieth-century conditions. Impatient Westerners might heed the advice of John Adams who, writing to his wife about the charms of Paris as seen in terms of the needs of the young American republic, said: "It is not indeed the fine arts which our country requires; the useful, the mechanic arts are those which we have occasion for in a young country . . . I must study politics and war, that my sons may have the liberty to study mathematics and philosophy. My sons ought to study mathematics and philosophy, geography, natural history and naval architecture, in order to give their children a right to study painting, poetry, music, architecture, statuary, tapestry and porcelain."

# 4

# Nonalignment
# or Alignment?

CONCERNED as the world is with the political, economic, and social transformations which are taking place in the emerging nations, the crucial question in a period when two ideological blocs, one led by the United States, the other by the USSR, confront each other, is the position each new nation, as it emerges, will take in this historic confrontation.

Will it become aligned with one of the two blocs, and if so, with the United States or the USSR? Or will it choose to remain nonaligned, under the standard of "positive neutralism" first raised by India, which has since made a powerful appeal to many new nations of Asia, the Middle East, and Africa, and might even find followers in Latin America, notably Brazil under President Janio Quadros. If most of the non-Western, non-Communist nations opt for "positive neutralism," will this create around the globe dangerous vacuums of military power—and will this then invite intervention by the Communists—if not military, because of their own fear of unleashing nuclear war, but by economic and technical aid followed by political penetration? And would such penetration force the anti-Communist bloc to take countermeasures which, although preferably economic and political in character, could, under some circumstances, through no one's reasoned choice, lead to an armed clash?

The answers to these questions are of immediate importance. For it is estimated that in 1961, out of the total of over one hundred nations which will be members of the UN, fifty will be nations which have achieved independence since World War II in Asia, the Middle East, and Africa; and their number could be further increased if one or more countries of Latin America should join their voting ranks, dissociating themselves from support hitherto usually given to the

United States. Moreover, except for Germany (whether it is admitted to the UN as a single united nation or as two segments, West Germany and East Germany, which would cancel each other out), new members in the future will come from the non-Western sector of the world, primarily Africa, but also Asia, if Communist China is eventually admitted, and some decision is made about the now divided countries, Vietnam and Korea. Thus the role of the emerging nations, each of which has one vote, just like the great powers of the Communist and anti-Communist blocs, will become increasingly significant for both the West and the USSR.

Hitherto the Western nations, and particularly the United States, which has had least experience with colonialism, had feared that the new non-Western members of the UN would automatically adopt an anti-Western position because of their past hostility toward colonial rule, and thereby align themselves with the USSR and its Eastern European satellites in the Soviet bloc. To avert this eventuality, regarded as disastrous for the West, some Western spokesmen, among them the late Lord Cherwell, scientific adviser to Sir Winston Churchill, had urged the adoption of a "weighted" vote in the UN, instead of the present "one nation, one vote" system, on the theory that this would give the great powers superior strength in determining the decisions of the UN which might otherwise be made to their disadvantage by small nations not only hostile but also inexperienced in world affairs. A weighted vote might be regarded by the new nations as a violation in the international forum of the democracy which the West is urging them to accept in their internal affairs, and as just another way for the white peoples to impose inequality on nonwhites—and therefore summarily rejected. But even if such voting could be introduced, no Western expert has as yet discovered a formula of weighting which would redound to the benefit of the United States, Britain, and France without at the same time enhancing the influence of other great powers—today, the USSR as well as neutralist India; tomorrow, mainland China.

By a striking paradox, the West, but particularly the United States, which unlike some of its Western allies has seen the world as divided into two main camps—the camp of democracy and the camp of communism, with no mutations of the two systems in between—appears to be in agreement with the Communists on a fundamental point, implicitly if not explicitly. This point is that when the non-Western peoples who have until now been "standing outside history," to use Lenin's phrase, achieve both independence from the colonial rule of the West and a start toward industrialization, which they, like the Russians, regard as the hallmark and the chief weapon of the West, they will inevitably enter on their new life in an anti-Western state of mind and thus, if not actually eager to align themselves with the Soviet bloc, at least predisposed toward friendly relations with it.

Thus the United States—which has understandably developed far less historical perspective than the old nations of Western Europe, who have learned through long experience that nothing in the life of men, and therefore of nations, is inevitable or eternal—has worked on one basic assumption. This assumption is that during the cold war the object of its foreign policy—and thus of the policy of the anti-Communist bloc whose leadership it had accepted, not without reluctance—should be to prevent all contacts between the emerging nations and the Communist powers, both Russia and China. It has consequently sought to prevent not only military contacts through acceptance of Soviet-bloc arms, but also economic, for fear that economic aid, even though it might seem beneficial to the recipients, would be tantamount to the thrust of the camel's nose into the tent, and ultimately bring the entire Communist animal among unsuspecting peoples of Asia, the Middle East, Africa, and even Latin America.

The Communists, for their part, were long convinced that the peoples living under colonial rule would, by definition, be opposed to the West, not only to the Western nations which had actually conquered them and still retained domination, but, more recently, also to the United States, because of the military and economic alliance forged by this country with Europe's colonial powers in the 1949 North Atlantic Treaty Organization (Britain, France, Belgium, The Netherlands, and Portugal). In fact Lenin, who initially had expected that, in accordance with the prediction Karl Marx made in mid-nineteenth century on the basis of his knowledge of Britain and Germany, the Communist revolution would be staged around the globe by the "proletarians" of all countries (who in *The Communist Manifesto* were urged to unite for this purpose), changed his view after World War I and at the Second Congress of the Communist International in 1920 suggested a new slogan: "Proletarians of all countries, and oppressed nations, unite." Lenin justified this slogan by saying, "Of course, from the point of view of the *Communist Manifesto,* this is wrong. But the

*Communist Manifesto* was written under completely different conditions; and from the point of view of the present political situation, this is correct." As Professor Alfred E. Meyer of Columbia University has pointed out in his study, *Leninism*, by 1920, "in Lenin's opinion the class struggle had merged with the struggle between nations."

In the post-World War I years, when in accordance with Marxist theory the proletarian revolutions the war had been expected to precipitate in the highly industrialized nations of Europe failed to materialize, the Communists, instead of insisting on united action by "proletarians" who had not risen up against capitalism (as Marx predicted they would do), urged the formation in Western Europe of "popular fronts" embracing all political groups except fascists. In this, however, they achieved significant success only in France. Then the Nazi invasion of Western Europe led to the creation of resistance movements that included all anti-Nazi elements, among them Communists, who were well organized and many of whom displayed great heroism against the then common enemy. This opened the way for the inclusion after World War II of Communists in some of the postwar governments, notably in France and Italy.

Although the Communist parties of these two countries, whose economic and social conditions continued to fan discontent among workers and intellectuals, retained a strong hold on voters, they were gradually excluded from governments which adopted a middle-of-the-road or even right-of-center position. As time went on, some of the harsh features of capitalism (which, Marx had believed, would inspire proletarian revolutions, bring about the overthrow of "exploiting elements" by violence, and lead to the downfall of "imperialism," which he regarded as the inevitable result of competition between capitalist countries for raw materials and markets) were eliminated. This change was brought about by the expansion of universal suffrage, the consequent increase in the political influence of the "proletariat," the improvement of technology, the resulting increase in productivity, and the rapidly growing acceptance, by authoritarian as well as democratic governments, of the need for greater concern about human welfare. After World War II the tide of Communist ideology (which in 1919 had rolled only as far as Hungary, and this for the brief span of the Bela Kun regime), engulfed Eastern Europe, from Poland to Albania. This was an area where democracy had never been a vital force except for Czechoslovakia, created as an independent state only in 1919. But

Communist political power did not push westward into Europe, where democratic institutions, even if not always firmly rooted, as in Germany and Austria, had at least been long known to highly industrialized peoples.

The geographic limit thus set to communism is often attributed to the military barrier established with the creation of NATO. Significant as was the psychological impact of this barrier, the USSR, if determined to conquer Western Europe, might well have gambled on this course at a time when its land forces, which had not been demobilized like those of the Western powers, were far superior to those at the disposal of NATO. It is always dangerous to make hypotheses, particularly about highly controversial matters, but future historians may come to the conclusion that the spread of communism in Europe was held in check not by the West's armaments but by far-reaching changes in the ideas and practices of Western European countries, whose economic systems could no longer be described as "capitalism" in Marx's sense of the term, for they had adopted various forms of mixed economy and had introduced various degrees of socialization and "welfare statism."

From the 1940's on it was in the non-Western countries, still on the threshold of industrialization or in the throes of its early and harshest stages, not in the technically developed nations of the West, that communism, so it seemed, might hope to find the most fruitful field for proselytizing. There it might reap the greatest ideological and power rewards, both in terms of "proletarian" revolution against capitalism and of onslaught on "imperialism," represented not only by Western colonial administrations but also, in Marx's original terms, by "exploiters" who, to boot, were not only merchants and bankers, but also white men treating nonwhites in ways that could only arouse resentment and fan revolt. Lenin noted this combination of circumstances that seemed made to order for a series of successful Communist revolutions which might not merely alter the political landscape of Asia, the Middle East, and Africa, but also have profound repercussions in Europe. He summed up his thought by the celebrated phrase: "The road to Paris leads through Peking." He also saw some important similarities between the 1917 situation of Russia which, although obviously not ruled by a Western power, had in his opinion a "colonial" relationship to the advanced Western nations because of its as yet undeveloped, primarily agrarian, and raw-material extractive economy. He believed that Russia's example would inspire other undeveloped countries, which would thus come to accept the leadership of the Communists. In his view, Western Europe had undergone an economic and social development that was *sui generis* and could not be adapted to that of the backward non-Western countries, for which Russia, not Europe or the United States would serve as model and guide.

After Lenin's death in 1924, Stalin, having rejected the concept of "permanent revolution" advocated by his rival Trotsky, concentrated on the goal he considered of first priority—that of "building socialism in one country"—and used international communism increasingly as an instrument of national policy for the USSR. He maintained this course during and after World War II, with growing emphasis on the primacy of the interests of the USSR as leader of world communism. Thus he disregarded the national aspirations of other Communist countries in a way which caused Marshal Tito, as already pointed out, to declare that the Russian dictator was pursuing a policy of "imperialism" which, to Tito's dismay and disillusionment, bore a striking similarity to what he, a devout Communist, had once regarded as an exclusively Western policy. Stalin, moreover, continued to assert, in accordance with Marxist theory, that war between communism and "imperialism" is "inevitable," thereby precluding the possibility of accommodation with non-Communist countries, except for strictly limited purposes dictated by Communist tactics.

Since Stalin's death his successor, Nikita S. Khrushchev, has increasingly stressed that the world situation has undergone far-reaching changes; that the advent of nuclear weapons, which would destroy Communist as well as non-Communist societies, has made it necessary to avoid war; that "peaceful coexistence" between Communist and non-Communist countries is not only possible but highly desirable; and that Lenin had approved of this concept. Khrushchev's arguments against war and in favor of peaceful coexistence, far from being publicly abandoned after the U-2 incident of May, 1960, which ushered in a revival of the cold war, were elaborated and presented with increasing frequency in Communist journals and public addresses by the premier and his associates in the USSR, as well as at the Bucharest conference of Soviet-bloc countries in June, 1960. It became more and more evident that these arguments were addressed not only to the Western nations, and to the emerging countries of the non-Western areas, all of whom fear war, which would destroy their burgeoning hopes of independence and economic development. They were addressed first and foremost to Communist China, which had made it clear that it does not regard war, however destructive, as a calamity, had made moves which could not be reconciled with peaceful coexistence, particularly against India and Nepal, and had indicated that it regarded the USSR as condoning "imperialism" when Moscow voted for the UN Security Council's resolution in favor of international action in the Congo.

In an extensive critique of "dogmatists" and "sectarians" published in August, 1960, *Kommunist,* the theoretical and political organ of the USSR Communist party, while making no reference to Communist China, stated that "in existing conditions, the manifestations of a limited nationalism, the attempts to oppose ill-understood national interests to the international obligation of strengthening the camp of socialism as a whole, are more dangerous than ever." The "dogmatists," according to the *Kommunist* article, are trying to apply old formulas dating back dozens of years to totally different current conditions by asserting that war will be ended only after the liquidation of the "exploiting" classes in all the countries of the world and by failing to admit the possibilities in the present epoch of a transition in many countries from the capitalist system to the socialist system without war. "Imperialism," said *Kommunist,* "has not only ceased to be a general system, but also the dominant force in the world. In our days it is not imperialism, but socialism [*i.e.,* communism] which has become the dominant factor in international relations, for it is socialism which determines social evolution."

With regard to the controversial question as to whether war is or is not necessary to bring about the end of capitalism, *Kommunist* declared: "Certainly, capitalism would perish more rapidly as a system in a world war than under conditions of peaceful coexistence. But it would happen that the degree of destruction provoked by the war would make the march of society toward communism considerably longer." According to *Kommunist,* "the revolution is without any doubt the result of the internal evolution of each country, but it is not necessarily an event isolated from the evolution of the world as a whole." Most significant of all, *Kommunist* declared that while the transition to "socialism" is not to be made solely by the parliamentary road of votes, but also by "vast action" outside parliament (presumably propaganda of all kinds), it asserted that "peaceful" parliamentary methods alone represent "revolutionary Marxism/Leninism." On the basis of this conclusion, Communists in underdeveloped countries were urged to co-operate with all other political groups in what appeared to be a new effort, this time in the non-Western areas, to build "popular fronts."

The continuing exposition by the USSR of the double-barreled thesis that war, under existing nuclear arms conditions, would destroy Communist as well as anti-Communist and non-Communist countries, and that what remains of "capitalism" and "imperialism" can be removed in the future without resort to armaments, by "peaceful" struggle within and outside parliaments, seemed designed to achieve three aims. The first was to present the Soviet bloc in the role of nonaggressor, as compared with the Western bloc, and especially the United States, accused of "aggressive" aims. The second was to reassure the neutralist nations which live in acute fear of being dragged into a nuclear struggle between the two blocs. The third was to allay in Communist countries' anxiety about the possibility of war, and therefore about the uselessness of continuing peaceful construction. Professor Yuri Frantsev, deputy editor in chief of *Pravda,* who before 1957 edited the principal Soviet philosophical journal, *Questions of Philosophy,* in a full-page *Pravda* article on August 7, 1960, quoted Mr. Khrushchev's view that war is no longer "fatalistically inevitable." Developing this view, he contended, "One cannot fail to see that a war in modern conditions would result in considerable damage to productive forces, and that humanity would suffer enormous destruction that would reduce the new society to ruins." (The term "new society" describes the Communist systems of Russia, China, and Eastern Europe.) If war were regarded as inevitable, he pointed out, there was no point in "fighting for peace." This in turn would only have a demoralizing effect on people in Communist countries. They might ask, "Why create things if the fruits of our labors will be destroyed by war?"

The statement issued on December 6, 1960, by the conference of representatives of 81 Communist parties held in Moscow for nearly a month—an exceptionally long and turgidly written document—bears the marks of what non-Communist observers on the scene had described as a hard-fought struggle to arrive at an agreement between the views of two groups within the Communist bloc. These are the views of the USSR, represented by Premier Nikita S. Khrushchev, and supported by all the Eastern European countries with the exception of Albania;

and those of Communist China, presented at the conference by its president, Liu Shao-chi, supported by the Communists of Albania, as well as of North Korea, Indonesia, and some of the Latin American countries, notably Cuba.

Advance discussion of the new Communist manifesto in the Western press had raised the question whether, in effect, we were witnessing a three-ply, and not only a two-ply, division within the Communist bloc. This division was thought to be between what we might term the left wing, led by Peiping; the right wing, led by Yugoslavia; and the center, led by Mr. Khrushchev, whose statements since the issuance of the Declaration and Peace Manifesto of 1957 had often attacked both the "dogmatism" of the Chinese Communists and the "revisionism" of the Yugoslavs.

The new Moscow document obviously had as its main objective the restoration of unity between the USSR and Communist China. Actually it read as if it were a compilation of two completely separate statements brought together within a common framework for purposes of expediency, not as an expression of genuine agreement about basic convictions. The result was a sort of point-counterpoint, with each Russian view balanced off by a Chinese view. But such efforts as Mr. Khrushchev and President Liu Shao-chi made to reconcile their respective policies for public consumption were not extended to Marshal Tito, who has been treated by both Russian and Chinese Communists as a "heretic" since Yugoslavia left the Cominform in 1948, and in recent years has been the target of particularly violent attacks from Peiping.

Whatever differences of opinion Moscow and Peiping have had in the past and may hold in the future, they appeared to agree on their estimate of the present state of affairs in "the capitalist system" against which "the socialist system," continues its historic struggle. The manifesto declared: "Our time, whose main content is the normalization from capitalism to socialism initiated by the great October revolution, is a time of struggle between the two social systems, a time of socialistic revolutions and nationalistic liberalistic revolutions, a time of the breakdown of imperialism, of the abolition of the colonial system, a time of transition of more peoples to the socialistic position, of the triumph of socialism and communism on a world-wide scale. It is the principal characteristic of our time that the world socialist system is becoming the decisive factor in the development of society. . . . Today it is the world socialist system and the forces fighting against imperialism, for a socialist transformation of society, that determine the main content, main trend and main features of the historical development of society. Whatever efforts imperialism makes, it cannot stop the advance of history. A reliable basis has been provided for further decisive victories for socialism. The complete triumph of socialism is inevitable."

The "inevitability" of the decline of "the capitalist system" is attributed to the decline of material production in the "capitalist" sector, to the resulting prospect of economic upheavals, to the existence of a "distorted militarized economy" in the "imperialist" United States, and to the breakup of Western colonialism, for which the Communists take full credit. All of these developments are contrasted with trends in the "socialist" sector, which are depicted in rosy colors, as "an earnest of victory in the struggle for peace, democracy, national liberation, socialism and human progress."

It is this predicted "inevitability" of the weakening of "the capitalist system" which led Mr. Khrushchev, as early as 1956, to reach the conclusion that war between the two systems was no longer inevitable, since the triumph of socialism would be achieved by means other than war which, according to his views, would destroy not only capitalism, but also communism. It is on this point—whether war is or is not necessary to bring about the final triumph of communism—that Moscow and Peiping have been engaged in a prolonged and often bitter dispute.

The gap between the two positions is bridged, but not closed, by the manifesto's prediction that in the "near future" Communist forces will gain new successes and capitalism will be further weakened. "In these conditions," the manifesto declares, "a real possibility will have arisen to exclude world war from the life of society even before socialism achieves complete victory on earth, with capitalism still existing in a part of the world." This statement seems to imply that, should the "near future" not bring about the circumstances on which Mr. Khrushchev has hitherto based his policy, the issue of the inevitability of war might be reopened—and that at that time Peiping, and not Moscow, might be in a position to determine the final decision. Yet the manifesto echoed Mr. Khrushchev's oft-stated view that modern warfare would bring unheard-of destruction and death to hundreds of millions of people.

At the same time, Peiping was given satisfaction by the statement's acceptance of two points it had advanced—that the possibility of a new world war may have been underestimated by Mr. Khrushchev (such underestimation is now proclaimed to be a doctrinal error), and that a third world war would not mean the end of civilization, but only of capitalism. Mr. Khrushchev, however, could derive satisfaction from the fact that the statement endorsed his call for peaceful coexistence and the principle of negotiation with the West. This point, which had been at the core of the Moscow-Peiping controversy, presumably gave the Soviet Premier an opportunity to reopen negotiations with the United States and other Western countries, which were cut off by Moscow following the U-2 incident in May, 1960. But how such negotiations could profitably be conducted in the future was then put in doubt by Moscow's acceptance of the thesis, advanced by Peiping, that the "imperialist" United States is the chief enemy of "the socialist system" and cannot be regarded as peace-loving—a thesis propounded by Mr. Khrushchev in late 1959 and early 1960.

Moreover, the statement made clear that "peaceful coexistence" does not mean a real truce with capitalism, but rather provides "favorable opportunities . . . for the development of the class struggle in the capitalist countries and the national liberation movement of the peoples of the colonial and dependent countries." This seemed to give Peiping a free hand to promote militant movements in areas where critical events are in the making, and where the Chinese have already shown a lively interest, notably Algeria and Cuba, not to speak of neighboring Asian countries. At the same time, however, the statement set forth the view of Mr. Khrushchev that Communists must seek joint action with Social Democratic parties and unions, and that the "bourgeoisie" in underdeveloped countries and colonial states may play a "progressive" role in the struggle against "imperialism" and "feudalism"—an approach followed by Moscow, for example, with respect to India.

The juxtaposition of seemingly divergent Russian and Chinese versions of future policies to be followed by world communism may not resolve the controversy between Moscow and Peiping, but it could give Mr. Khrushchev, for the short run at least, greater authority in pursuing a flexible policy toward the West than he had been able to enjoy as long as he had to fend off repeated ideological attacks by Communist

China. Whether or not he can in fact achieve such flexibility will depend on which of the two great Communist powers will henceforth have the upper hand.

The doubt, for the time being at least, was resolved in favor of Mr. Khrushchev, for the statement declares that the Communist party of the Soviet Union is "the universally recognized vanguard of the world Communist movement" and strongly condemned "dogmatism and sectarianism," hitherto attributed by Moscow to Peiping, adding that these heresies "can also become the main danger at some stage of development of individual parties." Moreover, the statement asserted that "The interests of the Communist movement require solidarity in adherence by every Communist party to the estimates and conclusions concerning the common tasks . . . jointly reached by the fraternal parties at their meetings." This represented the strongest demand for party solidarity made since the days of the Communist International, which was dissolved during World War II. Yet this point, too, like all the other main points of the statement, was counterbalanced—and conceivably contradicted—by the declaration that the Communist parties are "equal and independent," which seemed to bar the primacy of the USSR and to give Communist China at least a coequal role in the leadership of world communism, to which it has long aspired.

This aspiration to coequality, however, was in turn seemingly challenged by the fact that the USSR is, for the time being, industrially more advanced than Communist China, and that Peiping remains heavily dependent on Soviet production in its efforts to achieve industrialization—a fact stressed by Liu Shao-chi in a speech he made in Leningrad following the end of the Moscow conference.

But, whatever unresolved questions remain between Moscow and Peiping with regard both to world policy and to relations between Communist parties—and the manifesto seemed to indicate that they are legion—no doubt was left as to the official attitude of the two great powers toward Communist Yugoslavia. The manifesto declared that the Yugoslav Communists have betrayed Marxism-Leninism and that they "carry on subversive work against the Socialist camp and the world Communist movement."

This uncompromising statement should, presumably, end all hopes in Belgrade for a reconciliation with the USSR and its Eastern European satellites. Yet the harsh words of the manifesto, apparently inserted at the insistence of Peiping, in turn contradicted the noticeable easing of relations between Yugoslavia and its Communist neighbors (with the one exception of Albania, which supports Communist China), that has taken place since the cordial conversations held by Mr. Khrushchev and Marshal Tito in New York during the United Nations General Assembly. For its part, Yugoslavia has not hesitated to accept from the West new financial aid designed to facilitate the trade and monetary reforms it plans to carry out during 1961—and this aid, paradoxical as it may seem, includes credits from West Germany, which broke off relations with Belgrade in 1957 as retaliation for Yugoslavia's recognition of the government of East Germany.

The Communist manifesto confronted the United States with a re-iteration of Moscow's belief that the alleged weaknesses of the West, taken together with the alleged strengthening of the Communist na-tions, will soon spell the victory of communism without resort to war. This belief, temporarily at least, has been bolstered by Peiping's acceptance of a statement which contains this view as a possible alter-native to its own conviction that the possibility of war continues to exist, and should not be feared. Whichever view prevails—that of Khrushchev or of the Chinese Communists—we cannot count on main-tenance of the *status quo* in any area of the world, and must be pre-pared for a non-war struggle as strongly and imaginatively as for a war struggle.

Today we have at least three major choices:

1. A major military attack on the Communist sector, in the hope of crushing any idea it may have of developing further its political and economic, as well as military strength. This alternative is difficult for the United States to accept, for the same reasons that the Russians find it difficult—because of the mutuality of destruction now made possible by nuclear war.

2. Aloofness from the Communist sector, withholding either attack or negotiation, for a given period during which we would rally the moral and material resources of the non-Communist countries for eventual all-out peaceful competition with the Communist sector. The difficulty of this alternative is that it is impossible for us, as well as for the Russians, to make time stand still. Decisions of all kinds must be taken now, and not in some far tomorrow, and are called for by the needs and actions of our allies and of uncommitted countries, as well

as by those of the Communist sector. Nor can we be certain how many of the non-Communist, but also nonaligned, countries would support us during a period of aloofness.

3. Renewal and continuance of negotiations with the Communist nations not only about nuclear tests and conventional armaments, but a wide range of nonmilitary topics of concern to both the Communist and the Western blocs. Mr. Khrushchev promptly indicated that he would seek such negotiations with President John F. Kennedy, and so determined an opponent of bilateral talks between the United States and the USSR as Chancellor Konrad Adenauer made it known that he would consider such talks as desirable.

Mr. Khrushchev's position in the matter has been strengthened by Peiping's acceptance of his view about the noninevitability of war. At the same time, Peiping's doubts concerning the ultimate wisdom of this doctrine limits the time he can have for negotiations before he is again pressed for a change of policy by the Chinese Communists, and by militant elements in other areas of the world who support Peiping, and who offer a challenge to Mr. Khrushchev's position as Communist leader which he does not face within the USSR. It does not seem practicable, however, to expect that negotiations with Moscow alone might now bring useful results. Henceforth the United States may find it necessary to accept the inclusion of Peiping in any projected negotiations, irrespective of whether or not it recognizes the government of mainland China or acquiesces in its admission to the United Nations. If we are willing to undertake such talks, we would be in a stronger position to enlist the support of the nonaligned nations, as suggested by the second alternative, in the nonmilitary contest with the Communist sector. In such a contest we would have the backing of at least one Communist country, Yugoslavia, which in spite of its harsh experience with the Soviet bloc, has neither abandoned its own convictions nor found it necessary to resort to war.

Thus, in the uncommitted areas of Asia, the Middle East, and Africa, where changes in conditions and consequently in men and institutions proceed at a dizzying pace, both Communist and anti-Communist blocs seek to reassure the emerging nations that they need not fear war—the West by offering military and political aid against Communist encroachments, and the East by proclaiming that war is no longer necessary to bring about the downfall of a fast-declining "imperialism." By assuming that the continuing struggle between Western democracy and communism will be conducted in the future not by force of arms but by nonmilitary methods, both blocs put increasing emphasis on economic aid, technical assistance, and propaganda for their philosophy and their way of life. Under these circumstances, the test of strength becomes not the efficacy and up-to-dateness of armaments (which in the absence of agreement on disarmament and uncertainty about a nuclear test ban continue to be produced in a spiraling arms race), but the appeal which one or the other of the two ideological systems is making today, or can be expected to make tomorrow, to the as yet unaligned new nations of the world; and perhaps also to those already aligned, but susceptible to changing their minds.

Which side will be strongest in this test that has all the elements of a suspense story, as governments rise and fall with kaleidoscopic speed, from Laos to the Congo, from Cuba to Korea? Even more important: Will either side win? Or will new ideas, or new combinations of ideas as yet unborn, bring about the creation of systems which cannot be classified as either democracy or communism?

Prophecy is perilous. But as of 1961 it seems that the anti-Communist bloc and the Communist bloc, taking fundamentally different concepts of the world as their point of departure, have both made the same error. Both have assumed that the choice must be reached in terms of "either-or"—either democracy on the Western pattern, and this means the pattern of a few countries on both shores of the Atlantic Ocean, or communism, and this means today the pattern achieved by the USSR and followed with some variations by its Eastern European satellites, but not that of Communist China. In the past, paradoxically, the United States has often appeared to express an anti-Marxist dogmatism almost as unbending as the dogmatism of Marx, now in process of "revisionism" in Moscow, and to expect equally clear-cut adherence to its beliefs by potential converts.

Reality, however, does not lend itself to the strait jacket of intransigent ideologies, and again and again throws into confusion the most carefully elaborated diagnoses. In trying to measure the ideas and policies of other countries by their own yardstick, both the United States and the USSR have committed errors of judgment. The United States has tended to assume that the political concepts of democracy would make an appeal to underdeveloped countries sufficiently powerful to overcome any temptation they might have to adopt some or all of the economic and social methods developed in Russia and/or Communist China, and that they would align themselves unquestioningly on the side of the anti-Communist bloc. The USSR, for its part, has assumed that the urge to carry out far-reaching economic and social changes would cause underdeveloped countries to reject the political methods of democracy. These are regarded by the Communists not only as obsolete, but as actually not adapted for the needs of Asia, the Middle East, Africa, and Latin America, which are expected by Moscow to copy, in whole or initially at least in part, the economic and social methods of Russia (but not of Communist China), and to place themselves on the side of the Communist bloc.

What neither the United States nor the USSR seems to have taken into serious consideration is that the newly emerging peoples would want to think not in terms of this or that set of existing institutions, or of the aspirations of this or that existing bloc, but in terms of their own particular interests and aspirations, and would insist on making a free choice unguided by either the West or the East. The fact is, as Dr. Cornelis de Kiewiet, a Boer, a distinguished historian of South Africa and president of the University of Rochester has pointed out, that not just two forces—democracy and communism—operate on the world stage in the second half of the twentieth century, but three: the third being nationalism.

This third force, which in each new country is shaped by different circumstances—geography, history, economic resources, social development—gives each a different national identity, to use the phrase made famous by Nasser. The result is that while all the emerging nations have many basic features in common, each has differences which must be taken into consideration in the making of policy by the great powers, whether those of the democratic West or the Communist East. There can be no standard approach to these nations. Each requires individual study and individual treatment. Each may represent an interesting, perhaps disturbing, mutation of features which both blocs had regarded as established beyond question. A policy which assumes that the new nations will sign a blank indorsement of either democracy or communism without studying the fine print and introducing their own caveats and innovations is doomed to failure.

In two major respects the reaction of the non-Western nations is predictable. First, all of them desire, chiefly, equality with the great powers which either have ruled them in the past or would like to dominate them in the future. By equality the Asians, Middle Easterners, Africans, and Latin Americans do not mean that they want to kill, expel, or repress all foreigners, white or nonwhite, who may be living in their midst. On the contrary, under conditions they consider to be equal, they usually welcome foreign co-operation, and often first of all that of their former colonial rulers, as India has done in Asia, and Ghana and Nigeria have done in Africa. What they want is independence from "colonial" rule, and thus freedom to choose what their relations with other countries will be, and with whom and on what terms they will deal in politics and economics.

They also want equality in terms of economic development. This means that they want to acquire not only the tools of science and technology which have made possible the great advance of the Western nations in past centuries, and that of the USSR, and more recently of Communist China, in our time, but also the technical capacity to carry out their future economic development with increasing participation by their own people—a capacity to be achieved through education, both in science and in administration. And they want to have an equal status in the world community, so that they can vote individually or through their own blocs, such as the existing Asian-Arab-African bloc, on problems which affect their existence, even if the individual countries differ among themselves on specific issues, as Tunisia, Ethiopia, Ghana, and other African countries, for example, differed on important points about the Congo during the 1960 debates in the UN Security Council.

This passionate desire for equality leads to the second foreseeable aspect of the future policies of non-Western countries. They can be expected to resent and oppose any action by the great powers, whether Communist or anti-Communist, which seems to threaten their freedom of decision and action, or to interfere with their plans for economic development and social transformation. Thus Egypt resented the 1956 decision of the United States and Britain, followed by that of the World Bank, to withhold financial aid for the construction of the High Aswan Dam, and sought and obtained such aid from the USSR. Thus Cuba, when the United States, in response to Castro's anti-American statements and actions, ended the Cuban sugar quota, sold some of its sugar to the Communist countries. Thus Yugoslavia, when it came to the conclusion that the USSR was "imperialist" and did not respect its "national socialism," turned to the United States and other Western countries first for economic and, subsequently, for military aid. Thus Egypt, refused arms by the United States because of fear that they might be used against Israel, bought arms from the Soviet bloc in return for cotton which it could not sell in the American market. Thus Morocco insisted on the termination of United States bases on its territory; Egypt demanded that Britain leave the Suez Canal zone and nationalized the canal; and Panama has been threatening to demand control of the Panama Canal. And when ideological differences between the USSR and Communist China reached a high pitch during the summer of 1960, some Russian technicians were withdrawn from China at Peiping's demand.

This insistence on freedom of choice in world affairs is variously called "non-alignment," "neutralism," or even "positive neutralism."

It seems only yesterday that the late John Foster Dulles, in a commencement address at Iowa University in 1956, said, with India in mind, "Neutralism is immoral." But even then President Eisenhower, that same summer, had declared that he understood the position of India and other neutralist countries. In his opinion, this position was like that of the United States in the early days of the Republic when this country was determined to remain free of military and political commitments. Yet Mr. Dulles continued to argue that "those who are not with us are against us."

Only four years later, so rapidly does the wheel of history turn, the new Secretary of State, Dean Rusk, when questioned by the Senate Foreign Relations Committee in January 1961 about his views on neutralism, calmly replied:

"Well, I do not believe that we ourselves should be unduly concerned about what might be called the genuine neutralism because if a new nation is internally vigorous, viable, strong, progressive, its orientation in foreign policy is not so important as its health and strength, its orientation as a neutral . . .

"I do not believe we ought to ask commitments of a sort that would make it difficult for them to lead their own peoples in development, or difficult for them to draw together in regional associations of their own, as the opportunity might arise, or difficult for them to take their proper place in such an organization as the United Nations." And Mr. Rusk went on to say that we can work together with other countries on common practical problems in many fields, "without having political pledges which may in many cases be beyond the competence of the governments concerned to make good on."

What Dean Rusk's remarks mean, in effect, is that neutralism, instead of being regarded as equivalent to a nation's bankruptcy, now has a future. We now see it as a positive, not a negative, factor in world affairs.

But before discussing the impact of neutralism on the international community, and the results it may bring, we must ask ourselves what are the reasons for neutralism. Is it the result of whim on the part of a given statesman—a Nehru, a Sukarno, a Nkrumah? Or is it the outgrowth of deep-seated conditions in a country which chooses to be neutralist? And in spite of Mr. Rusk's reassurances, does neutralism represent an immoral attitude on the part of a nation?

What we know of neutralist countries—and in neutralist ranks we find a Communist country, Yugoslavia, as well as non-Communist nations which had been expected to join our side—shows that neutralism is a natural consequence of two important aspects of underdeveloped countries. The first of these is a passionate, sometimes from our point of view obsessive preoccupation with the need to make up for lost time economically and socially—a preoccupation which obscures all other concerns. They are unwilling to be diverted from economic endeavors by preparations for war; and they fear that such preparations would dissipate their meager resources. This need has now been recognized in the United States. On October 14, 1960, President Eisenhower said to representatives of 15 African nations visiting Washington: "We do not urge—indeed we do not desire—that you should belong to one camp or the other. You cannot afford to waste your money which is needed to build the hospitals, the schools, the roads that your people need— you cannot afford to put that money into costly armaments."

The second, which is inextricably linked to the first, is an equally passionate desire to stay out of war, which in the view of newly independent countries would destroy hopes of achieving an improvement in living conditions—the goal they had sought to win by achieving political independence. And the danger of such a war, in the opinion of the neutralists, is greatly enhanced by alignment of nations into two blocs, each equipped with the latest models in nuclear weapons.

To avert this danger, and to assure their own development, an increasing number of countries, among them the newly emerging nations of Africa, have followed the example of India in choosing nonalignment—the phrase by which the Indians describe their position, and which is more accurate than neutralism. What has been the impact of this rapid expansion of the nonaligned sector in the world community?

First, nonalignment has created a common denominator among otherwise widely diverse nations—from Communist Yugoslavia to India, protagonist of democracy in Asia, to Muslim Egypt—and in Africa even Nigeria, which had been expected to support the Western bloc, seems to prefer the path of neutralism. And it would not be surprising, as the controversy between the United States and Cuba mounts, that some of the Latin American countries—notably Brazil—may decide to become nonaligned.

Second, the neutralist countries, finding that they have common objectives, tend to work together in the United Nations, where they have grouped themselves in a loosely organized Afro-Asian-Arab bloc. The views of this bloc are often shared by some of the Latin-American countries, whose political, economic, and social conditions are far more similar to those of Africa, Asia, and the Middle East than to those of Western Europe and the United States.

This does not mean, as many Westerners had feared, that the Afro-Asian-Arab bloc, with the support of some Latin-American countries, always acts as a monolithic group. Far from it. There are some significant divergences within this bloc—as there are in great-power blocs of the West and of the Communist world. To take only one example: Tunisia, as well as some of the former French territories in West Africa—notably Tchad, the Ivory Coast, Senegal—have been more lenient toward France about Algeria than Morocco, Ghana, Guinea, and Egypt. As of now, neither the Western bloc nor the Soviet bloc can count on continuous, unalterable support by any one of the neutralist countries, or by any group of these countries. Both great-power blocs must win such support by their own efforts. The neutralist countries, most of which are small and weak, now have a leverage on the great powers which they could not have obtained if each had acted alone.

This leads to two other important impacts of neutralism. For, third, the neutralist countries benefit greatly by the strategic position they occupy in the world community. Instead of being dependent on only one great power, or power bloc, for aid and trade, the neutralist countries are in the favorable position of being in a buyer's market; they can seek aid from both sides, with a good chance of getting something from both. If this looks to some disgruntled Westerners like a sort of international bazaar-bidding operation, it might help us to bear in mind that in an earlier period of history this kind of operation was regarded here as shrewd Yankee trading.

But more important for the world's future, the neutralist nations are in effect a growing buffer area between the two great contestants—the United States and the West, on the one hand, the Soviet bloc on the other, with Communist China waiting in the wings. Some Western experts—as well as Polish—have argued that a neutralized zone in Central Europe, as proposed in the Rapacki plan, would be an effective way of preventing a nuclear clash on that continent. Others believe that Laos should have been encouraged to remain neutral, instead of joining the West. In a sense the neutralist countries together form a de-nuclearized bloc, which without resort to arms—except, on occasion, small weapons—keep an uneasy balance between the great powers which are still engaged in an arms race. In this sense neutralism could prove a benefit to the great powers, by assuring them, at a time of crisis, a pause long enough to permit reflection and attempts to explore possible conciliation.

Significant as these benefits may prove, some of us may still ask whether neutralism does not remain in essence an immoral attitude. For, it can be argued, a moral person, or a moral nation, must make choices, must take sides, must stand up and be counted. Otherwise, it is said, there is a danger of complete surrender of responsibility, which can lead to acceptance of totalitarianism.

This is a persuasive argument. It sets up a high ideal of personal, and national, conduct. But if we are honest with ourselves, we shall have to admit that most of us as individuals fail to live up to this ideal. To give but one example, most of us know, in our hearts and minds, that we should do everything in our power to oppose segregation and promote integration. Yet how many of us actually practice what we are often ready to preach? Usually we salve our consciences by invoking the need for "gradualism."

The kind of perfect moral decision which we expect—but seldom get—from individuals, is even harder to achieve in the case of nations, which are composed of diverse elements and diverse views, and unless ruled by totalitarian governments, seldom speak with a single voice. The United States itself, while urging India to take a strong stand on Hungary or Tibet, had in the past been reticent about taking a stand on Algeria, or South Africa, or dictatorial governments in Latin America. Yet there, too, human lives were being lost, and liberties were being trampled. And other peoples have not yet forgotten what to them was our neutralism in the Spanish Civil War, whose outcome cast a dark shadow on the image of democracy.

Thus we not only stand to benefit by neutralism in a world of continuing tension. We also may come to see in neutralism a way of thought from which we are ourselves not free. This should make us more tolerant of the nonaligned nations. But if we genuinely find neutralism repugnant, then this should inspire us to stand up and be counted ourselves on the revolutionary issues of our times.

Nothing is gained by demanding that a nation should be "with us" unless the decision we ask it to make is based on its own convictions. Neutralists true to themselves are more valuable than untrustworthy allies. Polonius' advice to Laertes is as sound in relations between nations as between individuals:

> "This above all: to thine own self be true,
> And it must follow, as the night the day,
> Thou canst not then be false to any man."

Neither the Western countries, nor the USSR, all of whom have insisted firmly on their national sovereignty and have in various ways sought to impose their demands on weaker peoples—and this not in ages lost in the mists of time, but right in the middle of the twentieth century—can in good faith demand that the emerging peoples should make the big jump from nationalism to a consciousness of the international community which the advanced nations themselves have not yet had the courage or imagination to make. The most that can be hoped for is that the emergence of more and still more nations will result, not in the creation of political vacuums which tempt intervention by the great powers, or of economic chaos and civil strife, but in increasing efforts to knit the legitimate interests of these new nations with those of the advanced older countries which once held "dominion over palm and pine."

Today the existence of these new nations, and the very fact that the great powers, opposing each other, feel the need to seek their sympathy and support, creates a new balance of forces which could have constructive results offsetting the risks of world-wide destruction threatened by the bipolar balance of power between the two great blocs of the West and the East, which has existed since the end of World

War II. Nonalignment, as Mr. Nehru, who first urged this policy, had predicted, has increasingly served to prevent clashes between the two blocs by maintaining uncommitted buffer areas between them. As the London *Economist* said on August 27, 1960:

> Even the superpowers are today increasingly inhibited in their policies by the upsurge of the underdogs. The United States defers to Latin American opinion in the matter of the Dominican republic or Cuba. The Soviet Union's leaders may talk rocketry, but it hesitates to bite. The result is, admittedly, a power vacuum in areas that no great power can dominate; a vacuum into which the United Nations is likely to be sucked in every time of trouble.

The essential thing to do now is to work out, and keep developing, methods by which the United Nations, representing the world community and not the interests of this or that bloc, can take constructive action in these power vacuums with the consent of the majority of its members. The value of such action has already been demonstrated, on a small scale by the intervention of UN forces between Egypt and Israel in Sinai and in a far larger setting in the Congo. In general, the new nations, far from acting in a foolhardy and irresponsible manner, as former colonial powers had predicted they would do, have co-operated loyally with the UN, where they feel that they have a far better opportunity to obtain disinterested advice and aid than if they had to deal singly, or in groups, with either the Communist or the anti-Communist bloc. As Modibo Keita, president of the Sudan, has said, "The small have no place in the corral of the large."

The UN, under the leadership of Secretary General Dag Hammarskjold, has, to quote the *New Statesman* of August 13, 1960, shown in the Congo that if given the opportunity, it could "provide something which no colonial power, no matter how high-minded, has succeeded in creating: a genuinely disinterested paternalism. The underdeveloped areas are universally and desperately in need of help from the advanced countries, not only in money and machines but, even more important, in doctors, engineers, scientists, and teachers. Until now, they have been forced to turn either to the West—whose technicians were tainted with the stigma of colonialism—or to Russia—whose help can only be obtained at an unknown political price. Now the UN offers a third and acceptable choice." For Mr. Hammarskjold, as the *New Statesman* puts it, is "The Missionary without a Dogma."

When Tennyson wrote eloquently in the nineteenth century about "the Parliament of Man, the Federation of the world," his vision seemed to be but the dream of a poet. Today it is becoming the goal of practical statesmen in emerging nations, such as Julius Nyerere of Tanganyika, who has said, "I have said before that we would like to light a candle and put it on top of Kilimanjaro which will shine beyond our borders, giving hope where there was despair, love where there was hate, and dignity where there was humiliation."

# Selected Bibliography

## GENERAL WORKS

Almond, Gabriel A. and Coleman, James S., editors. *The Politics of the Developing Areas*. Princeton, Princeton University Press, 1960.

Black, Eugene R., *The Diplomacy of Economic Development*. Cambridge, Harvard University Press, 1960.

Bronowski, J. and Mazlish, Bruce. *The Western Intellectual Tradition: From Leonardo to Hegel*. New York, Harper, 1960.

Emerson, Rupert. *From Empire to Nation: The Rise to Self-Assertion of Asian and African Peoples*. Cambridge, Harvard University Press, 1960.

Heilbroner, Richard L. *The Future as History*. New York, Harper, 1960.

Myrdal, Gunnar. *Beyond the Welfare State*. New Haven, Yale University Press, 1960.

Pannikar, K. M. *The Afro-Asian States and Their Problems*. London, Allen and Unwin, 1959.

Rostow, W. W. *The Stages of Economic Growth: A Non-Communist Manifesto*. Cambridge (England) University Press, 1960.

Ward, Barbara. *The Interplay of East and West: Points of Conflict and Cooperation*. New York, Norton, 1957.


## RUSSIA AND YUGOSLAVIA

Armstrong, Hamilton Fish. *Tito and Goliath*. New York, Macmillan, 1951.

Deutscher, Isaac. *The Great Contest: Russia and the West*. New York, Oxford University Press, 1960.

Djilas, Milovan. *The New Class*. New York, Praeger, 1957.

Fischer, George. *Russian Liberalism*. Cambridge, Harvard University Press, 1958.

Maclean, Fitzroy. *The Heretic: The Life and Times of Josip Broz-Tito*. New York, Harper, 1957.

Meyer, A. L. *Marxism*. Cambridge, Harvard University Press, 1954.

———. *Leninism*. Cambridge, Harvard University Press, 1958.

Salisbury, Harrison. *An American in Russia*. New York, Harper, 1955.

West, Rebecca. *Black Lamb and Grey Falcon*. New York, Viking Press, 1941.

Whitney, Thomas P. "Has Russia Changed?" *Headline Series,* Foreign Policy Association—World Affairs Center, No. 141, May-June, 1960.

## MIDDLE EAST

Ben-Gurion. *Rebirth and Destiny of Israel.* New York, Philosophical Library, 1954.
————. "Israel's First Decade and the Future." *The New York Times Magazine,* April 20, 1958.
Bisbee, Eleanor. *The New Turks: Pioneers of the Republic, 1920-1950.* Philadelphia, U. of Pennsylvania, 1951.
Crossman, R. H. S. *A Nation Reborn.* New York, Athanaeum, 1960.
Finnie, D. H. *Desert Enterprise.* Cambridge, Harvard University Press, 1958.
Issawi, Charles. *Egypt at Midcentury.* London, New York, Oxford University Press, 1954.
Kimche, Jan and David. *A Clash of Destinies: The Arab-Jewish War and the Founding of the State of Israel.* New York, Praeger, 1960.
King, Seth S. "A New Battle for Israel's Happy Warrior," *The New York Times Magazine,* July 19, 1959.
Lacouture, J. and S. *Egypt in Transition.* London, Methuen, 1958.
Little, Tom. *Egypt.* London, E. Benn, 1958.
Litvinoff, Barnet. *Ben-Gurion of Israel.* New York, Praeger, 1954.
Nasser, Gamal Abdel. *The Philosophy of the Revolution.* Buffalo, New York, Economica Books. Introduction by John Badeau.
St. John, Robert. *Ben-Gurion: The Biography of an Extraordinary Man.* Garden City, New York, Doubleday, 1959.
Thomas, Lewis and Frye, Richard L. *The United States and Turkey and Iran.* Cambridge, Harvard University Press, 1952.
Wheelock, Keith. *Nasser's New Egypt.* New York, Praeger, 1960.


## ASIA

Barnett, A. Doak. *Communist China and Asia.* New York, Harper for Council on Foreign Relations, 1960.
Brecher, Michael. *Nehru: A Political Biography.* London, New York, Oxford U. Press, 1959.
Creel, H. G. *Chinese Thought: From Confucius to Mao Tse-tung.* New York, The New American Library (Mentor), 1953.
Dean, Vera Micheles. *New Patterns of Democracy in India.* Cambridge, Mass., Harvard U. Press, 1959.
Fischer, Louis. *The Story of Indonesia.* New York, Harper, 1960.
Hanna, William. *Bung Karno's Indonesia.* New York, American Universities Field Service, 1960.
Harrison, Selig. *India: The Most Dangerous Decades.* Princeton, N. J., Princeton U. Press, 1960.
Kuo, Ping-Chia. *China: New Age and New Outlook.* London, Penguin Books, 1960.
Nehru, Jawaharlal. *The Discovery of India.* New York, The John Day Co., 1946.
————. *Toward Freedom.* Boston, Beacon Press, 1958.
North, Robert C. *Moscow and Chinese Communists.* Stanford, Stanford U. Press, 1953.
Padover, Saul, editor. *Nehru on World History.* New York, Day, 1960.

Palmier, Leslie H. "Sukarno, The Nationalist," *Pacific Affairs*, June, 1957.
Payne, Robert. *Mao Tse-tung: Ruler of Red China*. New York, Schuman, 1950.
Riencourt, Amaury de. *The Soul of China*. London, Jonathan Cape, 1959.
Symonds, Richard. *The Making of Pakistan*. London, Faber, 1950.
Tinker, Hugh. "Nu, The Serene Statesman," *Pacific Affairs*, June, 1957.


## AFRICA

"A New American Policy Toward Africa," The Africa League, 360 Riverside Drive, New York City.
Conton, William. *The African*. Boston, Little, Brown & Co., 1960.
Huxley, Elspeth. *The Flame Trees of Thika*. New York, Morrow, 1959.
Nkrumah, Kwame. *Ghana: The Autobiography of Kwame Nkrumah*. New York, Nelson, 1957.
Nyerere, Julius K. "We Cannot Afford to Fail," *Africa Special Report*, December, 1959.
Phillips, John. *Kwame Nkrumah and the Future of Africa*. New York, Praeger, 1961.
Ritner, Peter. *The Death of Africa*. New York, Macmillan, 1960.
Thompson, Virginia and Adloff, Richard. *French West Africa*. Stanford, Stanford U. Press, 1959.


## LATIN AMERICA

Betancourt, Romulo. *Venezuela: Politica y Petróleo*. Mexico-Buenos Aires, Fondo de Cultura Economica, 1956.
Buell, Raymond L. *Problems of the New Cuba*. New York, Foreign Policy Association, 1935.
Dubois, Jules. *Fidel Castro: Rebel-Liberator or Dictator?* Indianapolis, Bobbs-Merrill, 1959.
Lieuwen, Edwin. *Arms and Politics in Latin America*. New York, Harper for Council on Foreign Relations, 1960.
Nelson, Lowry. *Rural Cuba*. Minneapolis, University of Minnesota, 1950.
Matthews, Herbert. *New York Times* articles on Castro revolution.
Powell, Jane P. *Ancient Art of the Americas*. Brooklyn, New York, The Brooklyn Muscum Press, 1959.

# INDEX

Abbas, Ferhat, 148
'Abduh, Sheikh Muhammad (quoted), 63
Adenauer, Konrad, 73, 205, 252
Adjei, Ako, 155, 156
Africa, 10, 12, 17, 18, 23, 24, 37, 40, 124 ff., 168, 239, 240, 241, 243
  contrast between, and Asia, 68, 69
  Europe's contribution to the development of, 128
"Africa, A New American Policy Toward," 229
"Africa for the Africans," policy of, 142, 163, 164, 166
Africa League of New York, The, 229
*African Afterthoughts*, 128
African Agricultural Syndicate of the Ivory Coast, 150
African Association, Tanganyika, 165
African government, white settlers under authority of, in Tanganyika, 166
*African Interpreter*, 155
Africans, understanding the, 127
Afro-Asian Convention, 70
*Afro-Asian States and Their Problems, The*, 199
"Agrarian Movement in Hunan," Mao's report on, 112
Agrarian Reform, National Institute of (INRA), Cuba, 184
Agrarian Reform Law, The (Egypt), 64
Ahmadu, Sir Alhaji, 135
aid to Latin America, United States, 189
Albania, 21, 23
Alexander, King, 31
Algeria, 69, 70, 124, 125, 126, 135, 148, 231, 237, 249
  Bourguiba supports demand of, for independence, 147
  Tito backs policy of independence for, 39
Allenby, Lord, 54
*All Men Are Brothers*, 107
alphabet reform in Turkey, 51–52

American Revolution, 10, 67
American States, Organization of (OAS), 186, 214
Anatolia, western, 48, 50
Angarista, General Isaías Medina, 188
Ankara, 50
anticlericalism in Latin America, 170
anticolonialism
  of Lenin, 91
  of Nkrumah, 156–157
Anti-Fascist People's Freedom League (AFPFL), 82, 83, 85
anti-Yankeeism in Latin America, 168, 169, 174
anti-Westernism, 115, 116, 227
apartheid, 125, 144
Appiah, Joe, 156
Arab League, 149
Arab Refugee Administration, UN, 44
Arabs
  clash between Jews and, 40–44, 46, 55
  number of, in Palestine, 56
Arab states, 58, 60, 61, 63
Arden-Clarke, Sir Charles, 157, 158
Argentina, 233
Armenians, expulsion of, by Turks, 49
Asia, 10, 12, 17, 18, 23, 24, 37, 40, 66 ff., 168, 239, 240, 241, 243
Asian nations, territorial integrity of, 69
assimilation, selective, 223
Atatürk, Kemal, 13, 42, 46 ff., 203, 233
atomic bombs, 14
  *See also* nuclear weapons
atomic energy, 72
Attlee, Clement, 83
Aung San, 82
austerity, economic, 211 ff.
Austria-Hungary, 31, 41, 60
  *See also* Hungary
authoritarian government, 11, 71, 124, 133, 134, 135, 168
authoritarianism, 91, 144, 197 ff.

1 KHRUSHCHEV ..............USS[R]
2 TITO ....................Yugoslavi[a]
3 KEMAL ATATURK........Turke[y]
4 BEN GURION ..............Israe[l]
5 NASSER ......................Egyp[t]
6 U NU ..........................Burm[a]
7 NEHRU ........................Indi[a]
8 AYUB KHAN ............Pakista[n]
9 SUKARNO ............Indonesi[a]
10 MAO TSE-TUNG ........Chin[a]
11 MAGSAYSAY .....Philippine[s]
12 BOURGUIBA ..............Tunisi[a]
13 HOUPHOUET-BOIGNY
                              Ivory Coas[t]
14 NKRUMAH ................Ghan[a]
15 TOM MBOYA ............Keny[a]
16 NYERERE ..........Tanganyik[a]
17 CASTRO ......................Cub[a]
18 BETANCOURT ......Venezuel[a]